A VOYAGE TO ARABIA FELIX
Jean de La Roque

1715 saw the first, anonymous, publication of *Voyage de l'Arabie Heureuse* by Jean de La Roque. Such was the interest aroused by this book that English translations appeared in 1726, 1732 and 1742. This new edition (a facsimile of the second and best English edition of 1732) is the first to appear in the last 260 years.

The book describes two voyages made by merchants from the French port of Saint-Malo in 1708–1710 and 1711–1713. Their destination was Mocha on the Red Sea coast of Yemen and their objective was to purchase coffee, for which there was a growing demand throughout Europe. At this time Yemen was independent and enjoying economic importance as the main supplier of coffee. The first voyage exemplifies the usual hazards of ocean travel, and the intense economic competition between the European powers which often resulted in battle. Difficulties did not end on reaching the destination. In Mocha they had to establish relations with both local and Indian traders. During the second voyage to Mocha the French captain was asked to provide a doctor for the 'King' [sic] of Yemen in his capital Muab, in the Yemen highlands. One of the ship's surgeons, M. Barbier, was escorted to Muab and attended to the Imam. Barbier describes geographical details and notes on the social customs of the day.

Jean de La Roque compiled his book from letters and meetings with those who had taken a leading part. He was particularly interested in the natural and social history of coffee, and his two chapters on these subjects are of fundamental interest to all concerned with the history of coffee. The English editor of the book added an account of Sir Henry Middleton's forced journey to San'a in 1612. This provides a contrasting picture of local etiquette to that acquired one hundred years later by the French during their voluntary visit.

The French merchants' voyages heralded a new era in the exploration of Arabia and Niebuhr used this information in his exploration of Yemen. The market for Yemeni coffee persisted for some years and, therefore, added to this new edition of La Roque is a description of the trade in Mocha and Bayt al-Faqih by a French trader at the end of the eighteenth century: a translation of *New Travels in Arabia Felix; or, Notes on trade in the Red Sea and some remarks on the customs, habits, laws, armies, public revenues and population of Yemen in Arabia Felix, compiled there, in 1788*, by M. Cloupet of the Île-de-France.

The expert on Yemen Carl Phillips has provided new introductions and bibliographies on both texts to indicate their significance and place them in context.

A

VOYAGE

TO

ARABIA FELIX

(1708–10)

And

A JOURNEY FROM MOCHA TO MUAB (1711–13)

And

A NARRATIVE CONCERNING COFFEE

And

AN HISTORICAL TREATISE CONCERNING COFFEE

Jean de La Roque

And

AN ACCOUNT OF THE CAPTIVITY
OF SIR HENRY MIDDLETON
at Mocha by the Turks in 1612

Together with

NEW TRAVELS IN ARABIA FELIX (1788)

M. Cloupet

With introductions and
bibliographies by Carl Phillips

THE OLEANDER PRESS

The Oleander Press
16 Orchard Street
Cambridge CB1 1JT
England

The Oleander Press
1133 Broadway, Suite 706
New York, N.Y. 10010
U.S.A.

The Oleander Press acknowledges the kind assistance
rendered by Darren Lomas of the British Library.

British Library Cataloguing in Publication Data

La Roque, Jean de
  A voyage to Arabia Felix. - (Arabia past and present)
  1. La Roque, Jean de - Journeys - Yemen 2. Cloupet - Journeys
  - Yemen 3. Yemen - Description and travel 4. Yemen - Social
  life and customs - 18th century
  I. Title II. Cloupet
  915.3'3043

  ISBN 0-906672-50-3

"Arabia Past and Present" series

Typeset in Great Britain and printed and bound in India

CONTENTS

A Voyage to Arabia Felix *Jean de La Roque*

New Travels in Arabia Felix *M Cloupet*

LIST OF ILLUSTRATIONS

INTRODUCTION
Carl Phillips

Jean de la Roque (1661–1743) was born in Marseilles, the son of a merchant who in 1644 had travelled to Constantinople and the Levant. Amongst the goods that his father brought back from the Orient was coffee, a commodity for which the European demand was rapidly increasing. Perhaps due to his father's activities he studied oriental languages and developed a curiosity for the Levant and Arabia and their trade with Europe.

La Roque made several journeys to the Levant and perhaps as a consequence of this edited Laurent d'Arvieux's *Travels in Palestine*. D'Arvieux had lived in Sidon from 1653 to 1665. Later he settled in Constantinople and in 1679 was appointed consul at Aleppo. In 1686 d'Arvieux returned to Marseilles and lived there until his death. La Roque might well have met him in Marseilles. In the same volume, alongside d'Arvieux's *Travels*, La Roque included his own translation of Abu'l-Feda's *Description of Arabia* dating from the fourteenth century. The *Travels in Palestine*, which contains a general description of Arabia, was first published in Paris in 1717. However, this was preceded in 1715 by the first publication of *Voyage de l'Arabie Heureuse*. La Roque was prompted to compile and edit the contents that form part of this book after reading an article in *Le Mercure de Trévoux*, a paper produced north of Lyon for which La Roque served as a correspondent. As he states in his preface, the story was of a voyage to Mocha, and he was interested to know more about Arabia, a part of the East which he had not himself been able to visit.

The first voyage to Yemen

La Roque entered into correspondence with, and eventually met, Godefroy de la Merveille who had taken part in the first voyage to Arabia in 1708–10. The voyage was organized by merchants from the Breton port of Saint-Malo. Their destination was Mocha on the Red Sea coast of Yemen and their objective was to purchase coffee directly from its country of production, with de la Merveille acting as director of the company of traders (subrécargue). At this time Yemen had a monopoly on the export of coffee, the plants of which had been imported from neighbouring Ethiopia some time earlier. The drinking of coffee had spread throughout the Ottoman Empire in the sixteenth century. In 1635 the Ottoman retreat from Yemen allowed Indian merchants to increase participation in the trade at the southern end of the Red Sea. In the latter part of the seventeenth century, when the European demand for coffee had increased, Red Sea trade was still dominated by the Ottomans in the northern and central parts, and by the Indians in the south. Merchants from Cairo and Surat were the main conveyors of goods from this region and consequently most coffee reached Europe through ports like Marseilles, having been shipped via the Egyptian marketplace. The objective of the merchants from Saint-Malo was to purchase the coffee directly and therefore at greater profit to themselves.

As a result of this two ships, the 'Diligent' and the 'Curieux', departed from Brest harbour in January 1708 on the first French voyage to Yemen.

The description of the first voyage is both concise and poignant. It must be remembered that, in addition to the usual hazards of ocean travel, this was a time when intense economic competition between European powers often resulted in battle and the taking of prizes, something in which the Malouins took an active and notorious part. Both ships had been fitted for battle and before reaching Cádiz had already taken two English prizes. Later in the voyage, following a five~hour battle in the seas near Ascension Island, they took a Dutch vessel named the 'Great Conqueror' (Grand-Vainqueur). However, the voyage also had its casualties and the lack of provisions clearly made life very arduous. By the time they had rounded the Cape of Good Hope, the crews were already suffering from scurvy.

Nearing their destination, the ships called at the island of Socotra and then the port of Aden where, despite their refusal

The Leaues of the Coffee tree, as big as Nature.
Drawn from the Original.

to remove their shoes, they gained access to an Arab interior which is described in some detail along with a description of the town. Finally, one year after their departure from France, they arrived at their destination and a treaty was signed by the ships' captains and the Governor of Mocha.

Their trials and tribulations did not end on reaching Mocha, where it was also necessary to establish relations with local merchants and the Banian traders. The latter, who originated from Gujarat, were generally considered to be idolatrous and tolerated by the Arabs only because of their role in trade. But the

French found not only the Banians enigmatic, but also the local inhabitants of Mocha, and the privations suffered by local women.

The coffee was grown not in the coastal area around Mocha, but in the hill country further to the east. The main town where the harvested coffee was then brought for sale was Bayt al-Faqih, a two-day journey north-east of Mocha. The French merchants were able to acquire a house in Bayt al-Faqih to conduct their dealings, before returning to rejoin the crews in Mocha for the return voyage.

The two ships departed in August 1709, just over six months after they had arrived, and one and half years since their departure from France. The return voyage was to take them a further nine months and occurred not without incident. West of the Maldives, a second Dutch ship, on its way to Surat, was intercepted and taken as a prize, its cargo including a quantity of silver and gold. But, by the time the ships approached the shores of Brittany some of the crew had turned mutinous. One of the main protagonists of the discontent appears to have been Guillaume Sérot who, shortly after his arrival back on land, was gaoled for stealing a gold bar.

La Roque's account of the first voyage to Yemen provides a telling account of maritime trade at the beginning of the eighteenth century and the political geography of the Indian Ocean. The descriptions of Aden, Mocha and Bayt al-Faqih add further details about life and commerce in Yemen. However, La Roque's account remains silent about the underlying cause of the discontent on board one of the French ships and the events culminating in the arrest and imprisonment of Guillaume Sérot. Details about these events have emerged only in recent years and provide further insight in to the background of the first voyage to Yemen; its objectives, its success, and above all, its failings.

It transpires that the 'Curieux' had been an English frigate, taken in battle by the acclaimed corsair Duguay-Trouin, during a battle off The Lizard in October 1707. Its original name had been the 'Ruby' and Beauvais Le Fer sought from

Lempereur de la Lève, director of the Saint-Malo navy, permission to buy the 'Ruby'. His request was forwarded to Pontchartrain, the Naval Minister, and King Louis XIV accepted the request.

It was usual for ships taken in battle to be renamed and the 'Ruby' was no exception. Its new name, the 'Curieux', is most significant. In modern accounts of the exploration of Arabia it is usual for the information gained from the voyages sponsored by the merchants of Saint-Malo to be seen as incidental to their main commercial goal. The dawn of scientific exploration in the Red Sea is usually credited to Carsten Niebuhr and the Danish Expedition which visited Yemen half a century later than the voyages described by La Roque. However the first French voyage was not devoid of a scientific objective since it appears that Louis XIV had stipulated that a M. Gobert, the King's Engineer, should join the 'Curieux', equipped with all the instruments necessary for mapping the land and islands, the wind patterns and observed magnetic variations, and the manners, customs and religions of the people in the countries they visited. Unfortunately there is no trace of any such records having been kept, their absence explained by the death of Gobert during the outward voyage on 3 August 1708. However, this was not the only misfortune to befall the voyage and, although the loss of scientific information is lamentable, other events made an even greater impact on the well-being of the enterprise.

The 'Diligent' was the smaller of the two French ships. It weighed 400 tons, carried 130 men and was equipped with 50 cannon. Its captain was Julian Lebrun de Champloret. The 'Curieux' weighed 600 tons, carried 232 men and was similarly equipped with 50 cannon. The captain of the 'Curieux' was Philip Walsh, a Catholic born in Dublin in 1666 who, having fled Ireland and the English Protestants, arrived in Saint-Malo in 1685.

At an early stage in the voyage an altercation took place between Guillaume Sérot and Philip Walsh. In Cádiz, Sérot and some of his companions got drunk and when they came back on board ship, Sérot struck a blow at the captain. This action was clearly a bad omen for the rest of the voyage and especially the return from Mocha. Before reaching their destination, Philip Walsh died of a fever on 11 September 1708. He was succeeded by Le Chevalier des Cognets, Charles, brother of de la Lande, the second-in-command on board the 'Diligent'. However, during the several months spent in Mocha, Le Chevalier Charles de Cognets died. At this point Godefroy Merveille assumed responsibility for the 'Curieux' but, on departing from Arabia, command passed to the 5th Lieutenant, Guillaume Sérot. This was undoubtedly a catastrophe for the entire expedition and explains the mutinous state of the crew during much of the return voyage.

The 'Curieux' returned alone to the port of Saint-Malo on 8 May 1710. In the meantime the captain of the 'Diligent' had become ill and his ship returned to Saint-Malo on 9 July under the command of Jacques Hayes. Furthermore, during the undoubtedly disorganised return to port, 'The Great Conqueror' which had been captured from the Dutch during the outward voyage, was taken once again, this time by the English, shortly before reaching Saint-Malo.

The first voyage to Yemen and the intention of acquiring directly a cargo of coffee was in many ways a success. One can understand therefore the desire on the part of La Roque to portray the positive achievements of his fellow countrymen. The descriptions of the places they visited and the procedures undertaken to meet their objective are also informative. However, what La Roque clearly omits are some of the negative aspects of the voyage. It had been estimated that it would take about one year whereas in actual fact it took nearer two and a half years to complete. In different places foreign vessels were taken in battle and this enhanced the economic benefits of the voyage. However, a hefty toll was also paid and in total more than 100 men from the two crews died in the course of the voyages and the time spent in Arabia. Due perhaps to the unfortunate death of Philip Walsh, the crew of the 'Curieux' had become ever more unruly and many stole and pillaged what they could. Consequently, in addition to Guillaume Sérot, several more members of the crew were imprisoned on their return to France. The loss to the English of the Dutch ship, 'The Great Conqueror' is not without irony, and, as if this were not bad enough, it was deemed that the coffee brought back from Mocha was not of good quality and was more expensive than that being offered for sale by the Dutch. Nevertheless none of this deterred the merchants of Saint-Malo from embarking on a second similar venture the following year.

The second voyage and the visit to the Imam of Yemen

Two ships, the 'Peace' and the 'Diligent', set sail for Mocha, departing from Saint-Malo in January 1711 under the command of de la Lande and Thomas Colin de Briselaine. They reached their destination early in December the same year. On arrival at Mocha they were informed that the 'King of Yemen' [sic] was ill and requested a French doctor to attend to what appears to have been an abscess. The ruler of Yemen at this time was the Imam al-Mahdi Muhammad bin Ahmad (1687–1718) who resided at al-Mawahib (Muab), a short distance north-east of Dhamar, in the southern Yemeni highlands.

The captains of the French ships quickly realised that economic advantage might be gained if a doctor were sent to tend the Imam's illness. Consequently Major de la Grelaudière of the French garrison in Pondicherry, a "man of spirit and conduct", was provided with a retinue of men which included M. Barbier, an experienced surgeon, though not the chief one, from on board the 'Diligent'. Carrying a number of gifts that included pieces of cloth and a pair of pistols, they set out from Mocha on 14 February 1712, followed by a train of many camels and other beasts of burden.

Their first halting place was Mawza' (Mosa) and in the following two days they made their journey through the mountains towards the city of Ta'izz (Tage), where, as might be expected, their attention was drawn to the many fine mosques.

Travelling north from Ta'izz to al-Manzil (Manzuel), via Jiblah (Gabala), they saw for the first time cultivated coffee trees. From al-Manzil they undertook to reach Dhamar (Damar) by way of Yarim (Yrama). Dhamar lay only a short distance away from the palace of the Imam at al-Mawahib.

The journey from Mocha had taken eight days and they remained in al-Mawahib for a further three weeks, sufficient time in which to restore the Imam's health. During their stay, the two Frenchmen were able to observe some of the local customs. In particular they witnessed the pageantry that accompanied the Imam's attendance at Friday prayers. Though they made relatively few observations relating to the surroundings of al-Mawahib and other places they passed through, what they did record is of value as the first information of its kind collected by Europeans travelling free from duress. Furthermore, on the return journey to Mocha they were able collect specific information about coffee trees.

At the same time as Major de la Grelaudière and M. Barbier had travelled in the southern highlands, Desnoyers, chief surgeon of the 'Diligent', had resided at Bayt al-Faqih. While there he studied everything he could relating to coffee. The information from both sources provided a valuable contribution to the two chapters on the history of coffee which La Roque includes in his book.

The 'Peace' and the 'Diligent' departed from Mocha on 10 July 1712 and arrived back in Saint-Malo on 11 June 1713. The cargo on this occasion earned them a profit of 133.75 %.

The publication of *Voyage de l'Arabie Heureuse*

Barely two years after the second voyage had been completed, the first edition of *Voyage de l'Arabie Heureuse* was published in Paris. At this time La Roque had yet to publish his translation of Abu'l-Feda's *Description of Arabia* but no doubt thought the information obtained from the voyages to Mocha and the journey to al-Mawahib would be of broad appeal. Combined with the growing interest in coffee, the original publication must have attracted a wide audience, as reflected in the number of French, Italian, German and English editions published shortly thereafter. The translator of the second English edition was clearly of the opinion that the book deserved translation for the information it provides about Arabia, and, perhaps with the benefit of hindsight, suggests that La Roque's translation of Abu'l-Feda's *Description of Arabia* would have been a more suitable accompaniment to this volume rather than to d'Arvieux's *Travels in Palestine*. The important point highlighted here is just how little was known about the geography of Arabia and in particular the inland parts of the country at the beginning of the eighteenth century. Knowledge of Arabia, and in particular Yemen, was vastly improved before the end of the century, both as a result of continued trade and exploration. However, the situation in the early part of the century prompted La Roque's English translator to make one omission and one addition.

Although the map originally accompanying *Voyage de l'Arabie Heureuse* was included in the first English translation of 1726, the translator of the second edition chose to omit it, deeming it as not sufficiently accurate to warrant inclusion. Despite its obvious shortcomings, today the map has its own intrinsic value. In a recent commentary about *Voyage de l'Arabie Heureuse* it is stated that "one of the most important aspects of the book is the map of southern Arabia. Completed in 1715 by Guillaume de Lisle, who was to be appointed Geographer Royal to Louis XV in 1718, and who has been described as 'the father of modern geography', it was probably the best available map of the area before Niebuhr" (The Arcadian Group 1994: 116). For this reason and for the sake of completeness the map has been reinstated here in this new edition.

The addition comprises the account of the captivity of Sir Henry Middleton and his forced journey to San'a. La Roque had said it was unfortunate that Major de la Grelaudière and M. Barbier were unable to travel north of al-Mawahib as far as San'a. Therefore the English translator considered it pertinent to publicise further the journey of Sir Henry Middleton.

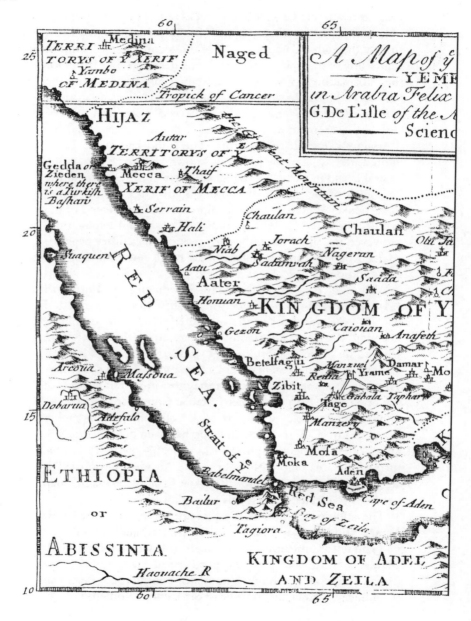

A Map of ÿ YEME in Arabia Felix G.De L'Isle of the Scienc

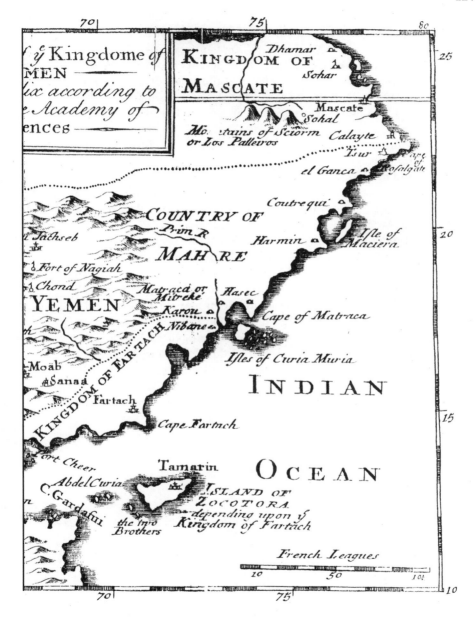

Middleton and several of his men were taken to Dhamar along the same route as that followed by Major de la Grelaudière and M. Barbier. Kept in captivity in San'a, Middleton provides only a few details about the town. However, following their release, some more details are provided along the route back to Mocha. After leaving San'a they passed through Sayyan (Siam) and Zarajah (Surage). From there they travelled to Dhamar (Damare) and then to Yarim (Ermin) and al-Makhadir (Mohader). Betwen al-Makhadir and Ta'izz (Tayes), Middleton refers to the presence of coffee houses, and in Ta'izz he remarks on the amount of indigo which was grown. From Ta'izz they made their way back to the Tihama by way of Yafrus (Eufras) and Mawza' (Mowssie, Moasa) and finally Mocha.

Middleton's captivity in Mocha and his forced journey to San'a had been brought about by the duplicitous actions of the Governor of Mocha, Rajab Agha. It appears that the English translator was unaware that, one year earlier in 1609, Rajab Agha had been the Governor of Aden and through a similar action had caused the Englishman John Jourdain to undergo a journey from Aden to San'a. The translator of La Roque, who chose to include the account of Middleton's journey to San'a to show that an Englishman had been one of the first Europeans to visit the city at such an early date, would no doubt have been dismayed to learn that a Frenchman was one of Jourdain's group of coerced travellers.

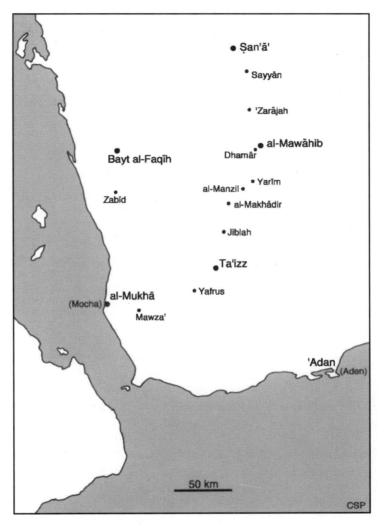

Map of South-West Yemen

ACKNOWLEDGMENTS

I should like to thank the library staff in Saint-Malo who provided copies of articles not readily available elsewhere. In particular I thank the librarian Jean-Pierre Brown, who has done so much to raise our awareness of links between Saint-Malo and Yemen, for answering my enquiries. Without his research, many details of the first voyage to Mocha in 1709 would remain concealed.

BIBLIOGRAPHY

The following books, consulted in writing the introduction, are intended also as a guide to further reading. References have been provided for all the French and English editions of La Roque's *Voyage de l'Arabie Heureuse*, and likewise for those of d'Arvieux's *Travels*.

Arcadian Group. 1994. *Europe and the Arab World*. The Arcadian Group/Oxford University Press, Oxford.

Arvieux, Laurent d'. 1717. *Voyage fait par ordre du roy Louis XIV dans la Palestine, vers le Grand Emir, chef des princes arabes du desert ... Où il est traité des mœurs & des coûtumes de cette nation. Avec la description générale de l'Arabie, faite par le Sultan Ismael Abulfeda, traduite en françois ... avec des notes. Par Monsieur D. L. R. (de La Roque)*. Cailleau, Paris.

Arvieux, Laurent d'. 1718. *The Chevalier d'Arvieux's Travels in Arabia the Desert; written by himself, and publish'd by Mr. De la Roque ... to which is added, a general description of Arabia, by Sultan Ishmaël Abulfeda ... Done into English by an eminent hand*. B. Barker, London. [A translation of Arvieux 1717.]

Arvieux, Laurent d'. 1735. *Mémoires, cont. ses voyages &c ; mis en ordre, avec des réfléxions par J. B. Labat.*

Bertier, M. 2000. *Petite anthologie du café*. Editions Equinoxe.

Brown, J-P. 1994. Cap sur Mokha. La première expédition des Malouins au Yémen. *Annales de la Société d'Histoire et* d'*Archéologie de Saint-Malo* : 147–165. [This article is also published in Brown 1995a : 1–25.]

Brown, J-P. 1995a. *Cap sur Mokha.* [Catalogue of an exhibition, Saint-Malo.]

Brown, J-P. 1995b. Cap sur Moka. *Qantara* 17 : 53–55.

Desmet-Grégoire, H. 1995. Les origines du café et son extension dans l'aire mediterranéenne. *In* Brown 1995a : 33–35.

Foucqueron, G. 1999. *Saint-Malo: 2000 ans d'histoire.* Editions Foucqueron, Saint-Malo.

Haudrère, P. 1995. Le Yémen et la France au XVIIIème siècle. *In* Thorval, Y., C. Ardelamir and A. Nied (*eds.*), *Le Yémen et la Mer Rouge.* L'Harmattan, Paris : 21–28.

Hogarth, D. G. 1904. *The Penetration of Arabia.* Lawrence and Bullen, London.

Jourdain, John. 1905. *Journal, 1608–17.* Ed. Sir William Foster. Hakluyt Society, Cambridge.

Kerr, Robert (*ed.*). 1824. Sixth Voyage of the English East India Company, in 1610, under the command of Sir Henry Middleton. *A General History and Collection of Voyages and Travels.* Vol. 8 : 361–405. Blackwood, Edinburgh. [This provides a fuller account of the circumstances surrounding the captivity of Sir Henry Middleton.]

Labrousse, H. 1964. Les expéditions maritimes françaises du XVIIIème siècle, en Mer Rouge et au Yémen. *In Océan Indien et Méditerranée. Travaux du Sixième Colloque International d'Histoire Maritime et du Deuxième Congrès de l'Association Historique, Internationale de l'Océan Indien.* Paris : 391–411.

La Roque, J. de. 1715. *Voyage de l'Arabie Heureuse.* Charles Huguier, Paris.

La Roque, J. de. 1716. *Voyage de l'Arabie Heureuse.* André Cailleau, Paris.

La Roque, J. de. 1716. *Voyage de l'Arabie Heureuse.* Steenhouwer en Uytwert, Amsterdam.

La Roque, J. de. 1726. *A Voyage to Arabia the Happy.* G. Strahan and R. Williamson, London.

La Roque, J. de. 1732. *A Voyage to Arabia Fœlix ... Translated*

xxii

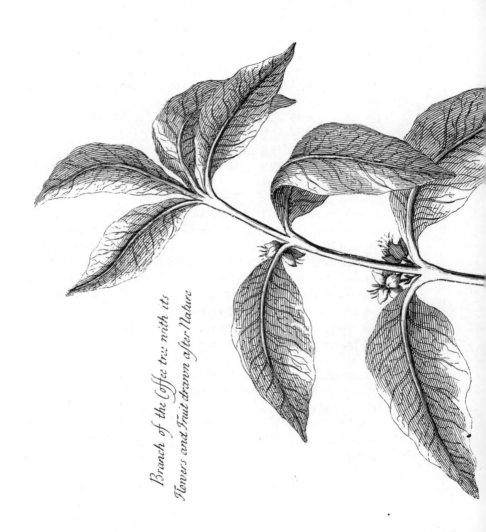

Branch of the Coffee tre: with its
flowers and fruit drawn after Nature

xxiii

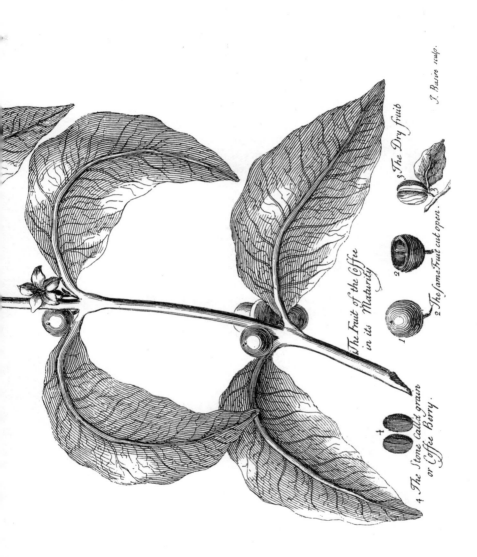

The Fruit of the Coffe in its Maturity

3, The Dry fruit

J. Bayre sculp.

2 The same Fruit cut open.

4 The Stone called grain or Coffee Berry.

from the French. To which is added, an Account of the Captivity of Sir Henry Middleton at Mokha, by the Turks, in ... 1612, etc. E. Symon, London.

La Roque, J. de. 1742. *A Voyage to Arabia Fœlix, etc.* James Hodges, London.

Le Nail, B. 1998. *Explorateurs et Grands Voyageurs Bretons.* Editions Jean-Paul Gisserot, Paris.

Lochon, C. 1995. Le rôle du café dans les relations franco-yéménites. *In* Thorval, Y., C. Ardelamir and A. Nied (*eds.*), *Le Yémen et la Mer Rouge.* L'Harmattan, Paris : 29–34.

Petout, P. 1995. Moka et la naissance d'un nouveau quartier à Saint-Malo au début du XVIIIème siècle. *In* Brown 1995a : 27–31.

Pirenne, J. 1958. *A la découverte de l'Arabie.* Amiot-Dumont, Paris.

Tuchscherer, M. 1995. Le commerce en Mer Rouge aux alentours de 1700. *In* Thorval, Y., C. Ardelamir and A. Nied (*eds.*), *Le Yémen et la Mer Rouge.* L'Harmattan, Paris : 35–58.

Tuchscherer, M. 2001. *Le commerce du café avant l'ère des plantations coloniales: espaces, réseaux, sociétés (XVème–XIXème s.).* Institut Français d'Archéologie Orientale, Cairo.

A

VOYAGE

TO

ARABIA Fœlix

Through the

EASTERN OCEAN and the *Streights*
of the RED-SEA, being the Firſt made
by the *French* in the Years 1708, 1709,
and 1710.

Together with

A Particular Account of a Journey from
MOCHA to MUAB, or MOWAHIB, the Court
of the King of YAMAN, in their Second Expedition, in the Years 1711, 1712, and 1713.

Alſo a Narrative

Concerning the Tree and Fruit of COFFEE.
Collected from the Obſervations of thoſe who made
the laſt Voyage; and an Hiſtorical Treatiſe of the
Original and Progreſs of COFFEE, both in *Aſia*
and *Europe*.

———————————————

Tranſlated from the FRENCH.

———————————————

To which is added,

An Account of the CAPTIVITY of Sir
HENRY MIDDLETON at *Mokba*, by the
TURKS, in the Year 1612; and his Journey from
thence to *Zenan*, or *Sanaa*, the Capital of the Kingdom of *Yaman*, with ſome Additions, particularly
relating to that Country and the *Red-Sea*.

———————————————

LONDON:

Printed for E. SYMON, over-againſt the
Royal-Exchange, in *Cornhill*, 1732.

THE

FRENCH EDITOR's

PREFACE.

THERE appear'd three or four Years ago, in the new Mercury, printed at *Trevoux*, a small Account of a Voyage to *Mokha*, which excited the Curiosity of every body very much, and especially mine. Because having run over one Part of the *East*, without entring into *Arabia*, I was desirous to be better acquainted with that Country than I was; and for that Reason, the Tract I have mention'd, which was too brief, did not satisfy me. This made me covet a Correspondence with the Captain of the Fleet, who was also the chief Director in that Expedition, which I brought about by means of a Friend, who procur'd me many Letters and Memoirs from him relating thereto. Afterwards, that Gentleman coming to *Paris*

A   *ris*

The French *Editor's Preface.*

ris about Affairs of Trade, which detain'd him there fix Months, I took that Opportunity to procure from him all the further Light and Information I could upon the Subject. In fhort, that Matter appearing to me ftill more curious and agreeable, I fet myfelf to compofe out of the whole a complete Relation of the Voyage to *Arabia Fœlix,* without departing in the leaft from that Character of Truth which fo vifibly appears in the Memoirs (written without Art and purely for the Satisfaction of a Friend) and which makes the principal Merit of this Sort of Writings.

With Regard to the Treaty of Commerce, and the Letters of the Potentates of the Country, which are inferted, the Director had Tranflations of them, made upon the Place by Perfons not well vers'd in our Language; but, not caring to depend upon them, I procur'd from him the Originals, which have been tranflated in the Manner I have given them here, by M. *Petis de la Croix,* Secretary and Interpreter to the King, and *Arabick* Profeffor in the Royal College, whofe profound Capacity is acknowledg'd, as his Lofs

is

The French *Editor's Preface.*

* is regretted by every body. I believe
the Curious and the Learned themselves
will, in some measure, be oblig'd to me
for having produc'd these Pieces, and in
particular † M. *Ockley*, a celebrated *Arabick* Professor at *Cambridge*, who in a
Work, which he publish'd some time ago,
invites Merchants and other Persons who
have such Letters to communicate them
to him, because he is of Opinion that
this Sort of Letters, which represent the
Genius and Manner of Expression of the
Orientals, are very proper to let us into
the Sense of many Places of Scripture.

I wish I cou'd have plac'd a good Map
of all *Arabia Fœlix* before this Relation,
but I consider it is rash to attempt any
such Thing. 'Tis easy indeed, in pursu-
ance of such a Design, to bring together
what Notices we have relating to *Arabia* in general, but that would be to multiply Errors instead of correcting them :
For Travellers have not yet penetrated so

A 2 far

* M. *de la Croix* dy'd the 4th of *December,* 1713.
† Mr. *Ockley* is also dead since. The Work here re-
ferred to is a little Treatise of South West *Barbary,*
printed at *Cambridge* in 1713, wherein are inserted the
Letters of the King of *Mo rocco.*

The French *Editor's Preface.*

far into that large Country, as is neceffary for the forming an exact Defcription
of the inland Parts of it. Setting afide the
Sea Coafts of *Arabia Fœlix*, lying along
the Ocean and the *Red-Sea*, which are
tolerably well defcrib'd, all the reft is con-
fus'd and imperfect in the *European* Geographers.

But to fupply in fome meafure that De-
fect, and keep to the principal Subject of
my Account, which properly relates to
the Kingdom of *Taman*, the fineft and
moft famous Part of *Arabia Fœlix*,
the Reader will find here a Map of that
Kingdom, drawn by M. *de Lifle* of the
Royal Academy of Sciences, with all the
Care and Exactnefs he was able; after
having not only confulted the original
Memoirs of our Travellers, and conferr'd
with the *French* Deputy himfelf, who
was fent to the King of *Taman*'s Court,
but alfo examin'd what the moft famous
Arab Geographers, and among others the
* *Sharif al Idrifi* and *Abu'lfeda* have written of that Country ; fo that, 'till we are
pro-

---

* 'Tis the Author which is improperly call'd the
Nubian Geographer, or the *Arab* of *Nubia*, who wrote
this Work in *Sicily* by Order of King *Roger* in the 12th
Century.

The French *Editor's Preface.*

provided with more ample Difcoveries,
he may value himfelf upon having prefented the World with a Performance
which ought equally to pleafe for its Novelty, and the Exactnefs with which he
has endeavour'd to execute it.

And now I mention *Abu'lfeda,* a
Geographer of great Reputation among
the *Arabs,* I muft acquaint the Reader,
that fome time ago I made an entire
Verfion of his Defcription of *Arabia,*
which had never before been publifh'd
in our Language. This Tranflation which
may ferve well enough to give one a
Knowledge of all *Arabia,* will make part
of a Work * I am engaged in at prefent,
which has no fmall Relation to this Subject, and will foon follow it, if I find
that the Publick judges favourably of this
Performance, and efteems it worthy of
their Curiofity.

* The Work meant here is the Voyage to *Paleftine,*
publifhed at *Paris* in *French.*

A 3   THE

THE

Tranſlator's *Preface.*

THIS Voyage to *Arabia Fœ-lix* deſerv'd to be tranſlated, not only on account of the Curioſity of it, being almoſt the only one of the Kind, into the Country of a People not leſs renoun'd, than the *Greeks* and *Romans,* for Conqueſts and Learning ; but alſo becauſe the Voyage to *Paleſtine,* which contains M. *d'Arvieux's* admirable Account of the *Arabs* of the Deſart, together with *Abu'lfeda's* Deſcription of *Arabia,* and which, as M. *de la Roque* intimates in his Preface, bears a great Affinity to this, is already in *Engliſh.*

I ſhould think that Deſcription of *Arabia* more properly belong'd to this Work,

than

The Tranflator's *Preface.*

than to that to which it is annex'd, as
having a greater Affinity with *Taman*,
which is Part of it, than with *Paleftine* ; and
I cannot fee why the Editor fhould only
give us one Latitude and Longitude of
every Place in the Tables, inftead of two
or three which *Abu'lfeda* exhibits from
feveral Authors. For tho' I grant him,
that Variety of different Computations,
efpecially where there is no Direction for
knowing the true, may confound one ; yet,
if he is not fure thofe which he has fingled
out are the right, is there not as much
Danger ftill of being mifled? Befides, as
there may be fome who are able to examine thofe Tables by proper Methods,
and difcover the right Numbers from the
wrong, M. *la Roque* fhould not methinks
have deprived them of an Opportunity of
doing it, by publifhing them imperfect

One would think this Author, I mean
Abu'lfeda, was fated never to appear in
any Language but his own ; for, tho' his
Geography has been often promis'd the
Publick, and actually tranflated four feveral Times, one Accident or other has ftill
hinder'd it from coming to light. *Graves*

A 4   tells

The Translator's *Preface.*

(*a*) tells us, *Erpenius* lamented that an entire *Abu'lfeda* was not publish'd, and promis'd to do it himself, but was prevented by Death, recommending the Undertaking to *Schickard.* And (*b*) *Ockley* says, *Schickard* translated him, but the Version is lost. Then (*c*) *Graves* himself undertook that Author, but the Copy was (*d*) destroy'd by those who ransack'd his House, when he was imprison'd by the *Long-Parliamnet* for sending Money to King *Charles* II. Next *Thevenot* made a Translation (*e*) of it, which we are told (*f*) after his Death pass'd into strange Hands. Lastly, Dr. *Hyde* perform'd the Work, but he tells us, (*g*) he was prevented publishing it by the Death of Doctor *Fell*, Bishop of *Oxford*; and in all likelihood it follow'd the Fate of the rest; for we have heard no more of it since: So that all we have at present of *Abu'lfeda's* are the Latitudes and Longitudes of some Places of *Ramusios's*

(*a*) Prefato *Abulf.* Descr. of *Arabia.* (*b*) Pref. to *Henley's Arab.* Gram. (*c*) Ibid. (*d*) *Renandot's* ancient Relat. Pref. p. **13.** (*e*) Biblioth. *Theven.* five Catalogus, *&c.* p. **191.** (*f*) *Renaudot*, ibid p. 9. (*g*) Pref. ad Itin. Mundi.

The Tranſlator*'s* *Preface.*

muſios's *Italian* Collection of Voyages;
the Character of *al Hind* and *al Sind* in the
French one of *Thevenot* ; and thoſe of
Chowarazm, Mawaralnakr and *Arabia,*
publiſhed in *Latin* by *Graves,* with the
French Verſion of the laſt, from a more
correct Manuſcript, by *la Roque.* But I
hope the Tranſlation, which Mr. *Gagnier*
has promis'd us in his Preface to *Abu'lfeda's*
Life of *Mohamed,* publiſh'd by him in
Arabick and *Latin,* will meet with better Luck, and make amends for ſo many
that have already miſcarry'd.

I ſhall give my Thoughts at large concerning the Geography of *Abu'lfeda* on
another Occaſion ; in the mean Time,
with regard to a good Map of *Arabia,*
which many before M. *la Roque* have
earneſtly deſir'd to ſee, I muſt obſerve,
that very little Aſſiſtance is to be expected
from that Author ; for, beſides mentioning
ſo few Towns, not above 40 or 50 at
moſt, he has given us different Latitudes
and Longitudes of the ſame Place, without taking notice what Authority they
are grounded on, or laying down any Rule
for diſtinguiſhing the true from the falſe,
which was abſolutely neceſſary where ſuch
Diſ-

The Tranſlator's *Preface.*

Diſagreement is found among his Authors, not of two or three Minutes, but often of ſo many Degrees; as in the Longitude of *Medina, Tadmor, Dafar, Aden, Sanaa,* &c. and in the Latitude of *Tabuc, Dafar, Nagran, Aden,* and even *Medina.* Then he gives the Diſtances of very few Places, and keeps up no Connection; ſo that one cannot be any way certain in laying down the Situations from him. Nor indeed are any of the oriental Geographers, that we know of, much fitter for the Purpoſe, excepting *Ibu Hawkal,* and his Copiers, *al Idriſi* (of which we have an Abridgment under the Name of the *Nubian* Geographer) *Ibu Chordabah,* &c. cited by *Abu'lfeda,* and ſuch as have wrote like them in the Way of *Antoninus*'s Itinerary, moſtly under the Title of *Maſalik wa Mamalik,* that is, Roads and Kingdoms; the Tranſlation of which, preferably to all others, ought to be undertaken by thoſe who would make Geography truely oblig'd to them; for it is from Books written in that Form only, that it can at preſent expect any conſiderable Aſſiſtance

I am

The Tranſlator's *Preface.*

I am of Mr. *Ockley's* Mind *, that a
Map of *Arabia* delineated as it ſhould be,
that is, with its proper Diviſions and Sub-
diviſions, its Town ſituated according to
their true Longitude, Latitude, and Diſtances, and the ſeveral *Arab* Tribes diſpos'd
in their proper Limits, is a Thing rather
to be wiſh'd for than executed. I queſtion
if any thing like it had ever been attempted
by the Natives themſelves ; and if no better Helps are to be found in their Authors,
than what have come to hand, it is what
we can never pretend to ; for the Accounts,
which are given us by † *Pocock*, and ||
Abraham Ecchellenſis, fix the Seats of
but a few of the *Arab* Tribes ; and *A-
buʾlfeda*, and ſuch other Authors as we yet
have, will increaſe the Number but a very
little. We have no Obſervations of the
Latitude and Longitude of the Towns of
Arabia (two or three excepted) but what
are found in *Abuʾlfeda's* Tables, which,
as I have obſerv'd, are ſo contradictory and
incorrect, that they afford as little Helps as
his Deſcription of the Country: And as
for that Abridgment of *al Idriſi*, call'd the
Nubian Geographer, (which contains the
beſt

* Pref. to his Hiſtory of the *Saracens.* † Spec. Hiſt.
Arab. || Chronicon Orient.

The Tranflator's *Preface.*

beſt Materials we have towards ſuch an Undertaking) beſides its being incorrect enough, and having other Deficiencies, it does not extend to one ſixth of the whole of *Arabia*; deſcribing only the Roads along the Sea-Coaſts, thoſe of the Pilgrims from *E-gypt, Syria,* and *Irak,* and ſome thro' the weſtern Part of *Yaman* and *Hajaz.*

To theſe few *Aſiatick,* we have ſtill fewer *European* Materials to add; *Arabia* being the leaſt frequented by Travellers of any Part of *Aſia*; nay, we have only four actual Travels, that I know of, purpoſely into *Arabia.* The firſt is of *Vertoman* or *Barthema,* who went in company with the Carawan of Pilgrims from *Damaſcus* to *Mecca,* and from thence to *Aden* and *Sanaa*; the ſecond is that of *Pitt* with the Carawan of *African* and *Egyptian* Pilgrims to *Mecca*; and the other two are thoſe of the *French* Deputies, and Sir *Henry Middleton* from *Mokha* to *Sanaa,* which you have an Account of in this Book. What elſe we have relating to *Arabia,* conſiſts of ſuch Memoirs as have been communicated to Travellers, who were not upon the Places themſelves, or of Journeys that have been made thro' the

Skirts

The Translator's *Preface.*

Skirts of the Country, in the Way to o-
ther Parts. Of the firft Sort are the Journals of the Roads the Pilgrims take from
Cairo and *Baffora* to *Mecca*, which *Thevenot* gives us in his Travels; and of the
fecond Sort are *Texeira's, de la Valle's*, and
Tavernier's Journeys from *Aleppo*, thro'
the great and little Defart to *Bagdad* and
Baffora, with fome others of lefs Note.
Among thefe alfo may be reckon'd the feveral Travels from *Cairo*, *Jerufalem*, *Gaza*,
and other Places to Mount *Sinai*; and thofe
of the *Englifh* Merchants from *Aleppo* to
Tadmor.

We are not better fupply'd with Materials for defcribing the Sea-Coafts, the *Red-
Sea* and *Perfian* Gulf, being little frequented
by *European* Ships, efpecially on the *Arabian* Sides. Don *John de Caftro's* Voyage
along the wefte'n Side of the *Red Sea* to
Sues, and that of *Soliman* Bafha from *Sues*
along the eaftern Coaft of it, join'd to the
little Account we have of it in *Thevenot*,
Ovington, *Daniel*, and another late *Englifh* Traveller, quoted by * *de Lifle*, are
almoft the only Accounts we have of that
Sea, which are yet more than what we
have

* Memoirs de l'Academie. pour l'an 17-——

The Tranflator's *Preface.*

have of the *Perfian* Gulf, excepting that we
have better Charts of it, among which is
to be reckon'd that which *Kempfer* has
publifh'd in his *Amœnitates Exoticœ.* The
Coaft between thofe two Seas is oftener
vifited, as lying more in the Way of Shipping, but not much better defcrib'd in our
Charts.

However, from thofe Materials, few as
they are, put together with Care, and the
whole adjufted by Help of fome Obfervations which we have, with regard chiefly
to the Latitude for fixing the Bounds of
this large Peninfula, a Map of *Arabia* might
be drawn, which would afford a great deal
of Satifaction to the Curious. Nor will
I allow, with M. *la Roque*, that this
cannot be done without increafing the
Confufion which reigns in the Maps; except indeed the Work unfortunately falls
into the Hands of our common Map-
Makers, who, underftanding little or nothing of the Matter, will only confider how
to fill up Spaces with the Names they find.

As to the Map of *Taman* prefixt to the
Voyage, it is faid indeed, that in drawing
it, M. *de Lifle*, befides *Abu'lfeda* and
al Idrifi, had recourfe to the moft famous
Arabian

The Translator's *Preface.*

Arabian Geographers; but, upon Examination, I cannot find any thing more in it, than what might be had from those two, and some other Helps before-mention'd. And I perceive, by his placing *Sanaa* half a Degree more to the South, than perhaps it should be, that he was unacquainted, as well as the Editor, with the Voyage of Sir *Henry Middleton.*

This Ignorance of Sir *Henry*'s Voyage has run the Editor into a Mistake, and made him flatter himself, that the *French* were the first *Europeans* who penetrated so far into *Arabia Fœlix*, and been at the Court of the King of *Yaman*; whereas Sir *Henry* had been further up the Country before them, and seen *Zenan* or *Sanaa* the capital City, which the Editor with so much Regret owns his Countrymen had not seen. It was as well with a Design to do Justice to our own Nation, by setting that Matter right, as to give the Publick some fuller Information on the Subject, that I thought fit to add the Travels of that famous *Englishman* to these of the *French* Deputies.

The short Notes which I have also added, either for Explanation or Connection, wherever they appear'd to be necessary, will,

The Tranflator's *Preface.*

will, I hope, further contribute to the Reader's Satisfaction. And I have done my beft to fettle the proper Names, and Terms (generally corrupted) according to their true Orthography. This Relation will ferve to give great Light into the Hiftory of a Country, we have hitherto had very little Knowledge of; but I need dwell no longer upon a Subject, the very mention of which is fufficient to excite the Curiofity of every body.

A

The APPROBATION

Of M. Burette, *King's Chancellour, Lecturer, and Professour, Regent Doctor in the Faculty of Physick at Paris, Member of the Royal Academy of Inscriptions and Medals, and Royal Censor of Books.*

I HAVE read, by order of M. the Chancellour, this *Voyage to ARABIA FŒLIX, through the Eastern Ocean,* &c. and I believe the Publick will receive it with so much the more Pleasure, as they will find in it Discoveries equally curious and faithful, with Relation to a Country very little known to our Geographers and Travellers.

Paris, June 22, 1715.

Sign'd   Burette.

THE Sieur *Renaudot* another Member of the same Academy, p. 24. of his Preface to, *Anciens Relations des Indies, & de la China de deux Voyageurs Mohametans,* translated from the *Arabick,* has these Words : ' I have lately seen a-
' mong others a *Voyage to* Arabia Fœ-
' lix, in which there are many curious
' Observations, relating to the present
' Time.'

A

VOYAGE

TO

ARABIA FŒLIX.

LETTER I.

A Relation of the Voyage from their Departure out of France, *till their Arrival in the first Port of* Arabia Fœlix

 Intend, Sir, to satisfy your Curiosity, touching the Voyage which I made to *Arabia Fœlix,* in quality of Captain of a Vessel, and Director of a Company of Merchants of St. *Malo :* who were the first *Europeans* that

Design of the Voyage.

A   resolv'd

resolv'd to set on foot directly, and without the Intervention of other Nations, a
Trade into that Country, and particularly
that of Coffee ; which the *French* had always before bought of the *Turks* in the
Levant, and sometimes of the *English* and
Dutch. I wish that my Relation, besides
the Recommendation which the Novelty of
it brings with it, may please you by its Ex-
actness, and the Truth of the Facts which
are related in it.

Depar-
ture from
Brest.
The *Curious* and the *Diligent*, (two Vessels fitted out both for Privateering and for
Commerce, and mounted with 50 Guns
each, on the first of which I embark'd) set
sail from *Brest* the 6th of *January*, 1708,
N. S. shaping their Course for *Cadiz*. We
took two *English* Prizes in the Way ; one
of which was the *Lisbon* Packet-Boat, bound
for that Place, and the other a Ship laden
with Salt-Fish, coming from *Lisbon*. The
first was ransom'd for 750 *l*. Sterling, because it wanted its Masts ; and the other for
15000 Livers, to avoid the Trouble of carrying her to *Cadiz*.

Cadiz.
We arriv'd at that Port the first of *March*,
and, having supply'd ourselves with Piastres,
Wine and Aqua Vitæ, we set sail for *Arabia*

bia the 30th of the fame Month. We pafs'd between the Pike of the *Canaries* and *Gomera*, and from thence came to the Ifles of *Cape Verd.*

The 22d of *April* we took in Wood and Water at the Ifle of St. *Vincent*, where we found excellent Fifh, and kill'd fome *Spanifh* Goats: The Sea all about abounded with *Tortoifes*, but that was not the Seafon for them. We left this Ifle the 25th of *April*, and pafs'd the Line the 15th of *May.* Ifle St. *Vincent.*

The 2d of *June*, after we had pafs'd the Ifland of *Afcention*, we difcover'd a Veffel, which in a little time we came up with. We fought it fingly for 5 hours together, and were damag'd by it very much, when Night parted us; but next Morning we came up with her again, and, after difcharging fome Shot, fhe ftruck. Ifle of *Afcenfion.*

This Veffel was of *Middleburg*; it was call'd the *Great Conquerer*, and was going to the Cape of *Good Hope* to take in her Provifion, in order to proceed to *Batavia:* She had 205 Men on board her, and 36 Guns; her Cargo was very rich, confifting among other Things of feveral Chefts of Silver, and fome Ingots of Gold. Take a Prize.

The

The 7th of *July* we difcover'd the Cape of *Good Hope* by a great Quantity of Birds, which are met with there abouts, of different Kinds, both as to their Plumage and Sizes, the leaft being as big as Pidgeons, and the largeft like Swans. The Sea alfo in this Place was ftored with thofe Plants, which are called *Gouemon* *, or *Alga Marine*, which are as thick as ones Arm, among which one fees abundance of Bafe.

The 8th, finding ourfelves fix Leagues from the Cape, I gave Directions for lying by, and fet up the Council-Flag ; which oblig'd Mr. *Champloret*, Commander of the *Diligent* to come aboard us with his Officers, to confider what was to be done with our Prifoners.

Moft were of opinion to fet them afhore, in order to fave Provifions, which might fail us in fo long a Voyage. But I reprefented to them the Danger there wou'd be of their giving notice, both of our Seizure and Defigns, to the *Dutch* Governour at the Cape, where there is a good Port and a

---

* In Latin *Fucus* or *Alga*. Mr. *Reaumur* has given a very curious Defcription of it, in the Hiftory of the Academy of Sciences, in the Year 1711.

Fortrefs,

Fortreſs: Which wou'd infallibly happen, if we landed the Priſoners, and engage that Governour to diſpatch an Advice-Ship to the General of *Batavia*, who might there-upon ſend ſome large Ships to the Mouth of the *Red Sea*, to ſhut up the Paſſage againſt us; an Inconvenience which might occaſion the Deſtruction of our Ships by the Worms: The ſame thing having hap-pened to ſome *French* Veſſels at the Mouth of the *Ganges.*

My Advice was approv'd of, and we ſha-ped our Courſe for the Cape of *Needles* *, to the great Concern of the *Dutch* Cap-tain, who was aboard our Ship, and of his Officers: Who cou'd not help letting us un-derſtand ſeveral ways, that the Apprehenſion which I had was well enough grounded.

Cape of *Needles.*

After doubling that Cape, we paſs'd along the Bank of the ſame Name, and ſounded, finding 56 Fathom, and the bottom ſtony; the Sea ſwell'd very much tho' it was pretty fair Weather. We continued our Courſe, inclining a little too much to the Weſt,

---

* The Cape of *Needles* is ſo call'd, becauſe thereabouts the Needle of the Compaſs becomes as it were immove-able and invariable, directed due North.

being carry'd by the Currents, by which means it happen'd, that two Days after we perceiv'd Fires in the Night, which made us judge ourſelves to be near the Coaſt of the *Caffres*, which is properly the Eaſtern *Ethiopia*; we tack'd about immediately in order to keep off it, and entred the Canal of *Mozambik*.

Mozam-bik.

Shoals of Juiva.

Some Days after, on the 7th of *Auguſt*, we perceiv'd the Shoals of *Juiva*; I got up to the Top-Maſt to examine them; theſe Shelves bear a great Reſemblance to thoſe they call the *Minquets*, which are a Continuation of Rocks above Water, more than two Leagues in length, between the Iſle of *Jerſey* and St. *Malo*.

Next Day we took into Conſideration the Condition of our Men, who were much afflicted with the Scurvey, and we reſolv'd contrary to our former Deſign, which was to go to *Anjuan*, to refreſh ourſelves at *Maſſali*, a convenient Port of the Iſle of St. *Laurence*, or *Madagaſcar*, being ſo perſwaded by an *Engliſh* Officer, imbark'd on board the *Diligent*, who had been at *Madagaſcar*, and who offer'd to conduct us ſafely into that Port.

Wo

We fteer'd that Way off hand, and, hav-Steer for St. Laurence or Madagafcar.
ing crofs'd the long Bank of *Madagafcar,*
we found the Sea calm, and a kind of Spawn
or Fat of Fifh on the Surface of the Water,
which our old Seamen call'd *Sperma Cœti.*
The third Day we faw Land, and, having
hoifted all our Sails, we entred in a little
time one of the fineft Bays imaginable,
where there is a River, not doubting but it
was that of *Maffali.*

We anchor'd at the Mouth of it in eightFine Bay in that Ifle.
or nine fathom Water upon a good Bottom;
we faw at the fame time a Pirogue, or
fmall Bark of the Country, under Sail, going out turning the Point which is on the
North Side. There were in it thirty Blacks.
We immediately fent one of our Boats to
get Intelligence from them : But, having
doubled this Point, they found tiiat the
Blacks, being frighten'd, had already landed,
and carry'd their Pirogue on their Shoulders
into the Woods, which are very thick all
along that Coaft.

All our Men were able to do, was to
learn, by our *Arab* Interpreter, from fome
other *Blacks* whom they met, and gave to
drink of the Aqua Vitæ, that a King of
the Country refided not above eighteen or

A 4 twenty

twenty Leagues from thence; and that
there was a Port in that Place, where we
fhould find every thing according to our
Defire; after which they alfo took to the
Woods. For our parts, after we had caus'd
much Fifh to be caught, which are
very excellent in that Bay, judging well
that it was not that which we fought after,
and that our *Englifhman* had been miftaken,
we fet fail the 11th in the Morning, fteering our Courfe for the Bay of *Maffali*,
which was the very fame which the *Blacks*
had directed us to.

We fail'd along the Coaft at three quarters
of a League diftance; and faw fome Dwellings of *Arabs* who trade with thofe of *Ma-
fcat*, (where there is a Port of the fame Name,
near the Gulf of *Perfia*) and who build
Ships which they freight with Slaves and
other Merchandizes of *Madagafcar*. Two
fmall Veffels of thofe *Arabs*, having perceiv'd us, they were fo feiz'd with fear,
that one of them put off to Sea, and the
other ran to hide itfelf.

Port of
Maffali. Next Day, being the 12th, we anchor'd in
the Port of *Maffali*, Mr. *ae Champloret*,
who went in firft, fent our *Englifh* Officer
to demand of the King of the Country, whofe
Refidence

Refidence was but 6 Leagues from the Port, Refrefhments for our Men, and Permiffion to let them go on fhore; that Prince granted both Requefts, which oblig'd me to go and thank him.

Two Blacks, who were reliev'd in their Turns by two others, carry'd me in a *Hamack*, a Machine made of ftrong Callicoe, gather'd at both ends, and hung upon a long Pole; and which the Blacks, the one before and the other behind, carry'd on their Shoulder, The Captain vifits the King.

I convers'd with the King, by the Affiftance of fome *Englifh* fettled in that Country, who underftand the Language, and I was very well receiv'd by him. He gave me his hand, which is a Mark of extraordinary Favour, the greateft Men of his Kingdom never approaching him but to kifs his Thigh. I fhall not here give you a Defcription of the Palace and Court of this Prince, where every thing appear'd to us plain and rude enough, excepting the Gold *Crown*, which he had upon his Head, and which ending in a point at top was adorn'd with Pearls, (being pretty like thofe which Painters commonly reprefent the *Magi* with) and two fair Diamonds, which he wore upon his Fingers. We made him Is kindly receiv'd

him some Presents. That which he esteem'd
most was the *Aqua Vitæ*, which he drank;
and he smoked with our Pipes: He was also
very well pleas'd with a Pair of our Pidgeons,
two *Indian* Hens, one large and young
English Dog, which he ask'd of us, and a
Danish Dog, as being so many Rarities in his
Country.

Ball.

Neither will I speak of a very fantastical
sort of Ball, with which he entertain'd us;
and of the Collation which he eat with his
Family, and the Grandees of his Court in our
Presence, which consisted in nothing but
Pieces of Beef broil'd upon the Coals, eaten
without Bread, and without having the Skin
taken off.

King's
Person.

For the rest this Prince is tall and of a
good Aspect, tho' almost black; very corpu-
lent, and about forty Years of age.

Habit.

His Royal Seat is a great Ebony Chair,
adorn'd and inlaid with Ivory. He had on
one Shoulder a very clear Silk Gawse put on
like a Scarf, and on the other a Silver *Chain*
hung the same way, and curiously work'd,
whereat hung a little Silver *Fish*. A little
Silver *Box* or *Coffer* was fasten'd to the same
Chain, fill'd, as they told us, with Characters and Magick Figures, esteem'd to be sovereign

reign Prefervatives againſt all ſorts of Accidents. The reſt of his Habit was a kind of
Pettycoat, made of a napped Silk, adorn'd
with Pearls and Coral, having his Legs and
Feet bare, with Sandals near his Seat.

During the Audience which this Prince His
gave me, ſeated upon Mats and placed fa- Wives.
cing him, I ſaw two of his Wives paſs by,
who were very fat, which they ſay he likes;
for care is taken to fatten them when they
fall away. They are about eighteen in Number.

We order'd our Seamen to encamp in *French*
Tents and Baracks in a convenient Place, *keep a*
encloſ'd by a good Hedge, with Centries *Guard.*
plac'd every Evening after beating the Tap
tow. This Precaution was neceſſary, eſpecially ſince the King had ſent us two hundred
Women, with all ſorts of Refreſhments and
Commodities of the Country; which alſo
form'd a kind of Camp about a quarter of a
Mile from ours: They came to viſit our Men
in the Day-time with a good deal of Familiarity. Moreover the ſick *Dutchmen* were no
ſooner recover'd, than they began to think of
making their Eſcapes; above eighty actually
made off, and there went a Report alſo, that
they intended to join the Natives in order to
ſur-

furprife us, and feize our Ships; which made us keep upon our Guard, as well on Board as at Land.

Commo-
dities ex-
cellent.

Generally fpeaking there is no where to be found better Commodities, than thofe of all forts which the Country produces, tho' it be very hot, and has the Inconvenience of very bad Water. According to the Trea- ty which we have made with the King, he gave us an Ox, weighing a thoufand or twelve hundred Pounds, for a Fufee, and threefcore Pound weight of Rice for one Meafure of Powder, containing twenty eight Ounces. I dont mention the Game, the Fifh, and the Sea and Land Tortoifes which are perfectly good, and found there in great plenty. As we were upon the point of departing, the Women I fpoke of, bethought themfelves of bringing us Crocodiles Eggs, which are much like thofe of Geefe, having the Shell very white and a little rough. The *Englifh* told us that one muft break them to diftin- guifh them, and that the eating of thofe Eggs is attended with the fatal Quality of difturbing the Mind. They are fill'd with nothing but the White, with a fmall Bar of Blood in the middle.

Croco-
diles
Eggs.

Noxious
Quality.

The Sick being almoft all recover'd, and
our

our Provifion laid in, we left the Port of *Maffali*, the 23d of *September*, fteering our Courfe for *Anjuan*, where we were to take in Water. The Governour of *Moili*, as we pafs'd by the Ifland of that Name, fent us Fruits, and invited us on Shore, fhewing great Marks of Efteem for the *French*; promifing withal, to furnifh us with whatever we had occafion for at reafonable Rates: But as the Water there alfo has no good Name, we went forward towards *Anjuan*, which is but eight or nine Leagues further: We found the Currents fo contrary, that we were 5 whole Days in that fhort Paffage.

Moili or *Mælli*, an Ifle about thirty Leagues round.

We caft Anchor at *Anjuan* the 5th of *October*; there came immediately feveral Boats on board our Ships with a great Quantity of Cocos, which the *Arabs* call Nardgil, of Bananas or *Indian* Figs, of Oranges and Citrons, and alfo much Fifh, which they offer'd us to fell. I went to fee the Governour, who lives in a little Town not far off, where there is a Mofque, the Inhabitants of which fpeak *Arabic*. He treated me with the Liquor of Cocoes, and fmok'd of our Tobacco; but he wou'd not drink any of the Wine, which I had brought along with me,

Anjuan.

me, offering in other respects all that was in his Power for the Service of our Seamen.

King of *Anjuan* visits the *French*.

The King of *Anjuan* came eight Leagues purposely to see us; we regal'd him in our Vessels the best we cou'd; he eat little of any thing but Fowl, which were also by his order kill'd and dress'd by his People; and drank no Wine. He wou'd fain have bought some Powder of us; but, as he wanted it to make use of in the War with his Neighbour, the Prince of *Moili*, with whom we had no reason to be dissatisfy'd, we excus'd our-selves from furnishing him with it, having only accommodated him with some Fusees. We found there a very holy *Arab*, nam'd *Abd-alla*, who spoke *French* and *English*, and who serv'd as Interpreter. We committed a fault in not bringing him along with us, for he wou'd have been of great service to us, during our Stay in *Arabia*.

Leave *Anjuan*.

Before we quitted *Anjuan*, it was necessary to take proper Measures to reach the Isle of *Zocotora*, notwithstanding the *Musson* *

* *Musson* is a sort of Trade-Winds, which are accustom'd to blow during certain Seasons. *Musson* comes from *Mussen*, an *Arabick* Word, which signifies a fixt Time. Dr. *Edmund Halley* has written the History of Trade Winds, &c. See the Philosophical Transactions, *Sept.* 1686.

was

was already begun : Which our *Pilots* deemed impoffible, becaufe the Seafon was fo far advanc'd. They advis'd us rather to look out for a Place proper to winter in, that is to fay, to pafs the fix Months which the *Muffon* is accuftom'd to blow from the North. But I follow'd the Opinion of the Commanders of certain fmall Veffels of the Country call'd *Jons*, which are built without Nails, or any Piece of Iron, that during all the current Month one might very well fail to *Zocotora*, which confirm'd me in my firft Notion, contrary to the Journals and Inftructions which we had taken. So that after we had laid in as much Water as we had occafion for, and having left all the *Dutch* behind, who were not inclin'd to lift themfelves among our Seamen, we departed from *Anjuan*, to the great concern of the Inhabitants of the Country.

The 3d Day after we had left that Port, we loft the *Brigantine* which we had got made at *Breft*, embark'd in Pieces and fitted up at *Maffali*; fix Men loft their Lives in her out of nine, which were on board her.

Brigantine caft away.

The Day following, between the fourth and fifth Degree of North Latitude, we faw

Land

Land in the Morning four Leagues from us; it was a sandy Coast. Having spoken to Mr. *Champloret* to make up to that Land, the Inhabitants whereof had made Signs to us with Smoke, knowing besides, that on this Coast there was Gold, Elephants Teeth, and Amber Greese, we agree'd to go and anchor there in ten fathom Water; to send two Shallops arm'd with Samples of our Merchandizes, and that I should land my self in our Boat well arm'd, to see if we could treat with these People.

We shap'd our Course for sometime on that Design, but my Comrade tack'd about of a sudden, and steer'd a contrary Course by the Advice of his Pilot, who was not well enough acquainted with that Coast. We were oblig'd to follow him, and we had at first pretty good Weather, but afterwards there arose some contrary Winds. At length we discover'd the *Two Brothers*, which are two little Isles between five and six Leagues from that of *Zocotora*. We pass'd between them, which we cou'd not avoid, because of the strong Currents which set too much to the South.

Isle of Zocotora.

The next Day being the 28th of *Novemb.* we doubled a Point of *Zocotora*, on the other

other fide, of which our Charts mark the Anchorage, which is good all along the S. E. Coaft of that Ifle. Our two other Ships, the *Diligent* and the *Holland* Priz , could not get up fo far, and anchor'd where they were. They fent on Shore next Day to get Intelligence, which we alfo did on our Part; both their Men and ours faw fome *Blacks*, but fo Savage and fearful, that they cou'd not come near them, flying into the Mountains with an exceeding fwiftnefs.

That made me refolve to arm a Boat with Provifions for four Days, to make the Tour of the Ifle, in order to find out the princi-pal Town; but when I was come to the Place where our two Ships had ftay'd, I found the Winds and the Tides contrary, which oblig'd me to pafs the Night on Board the *Diligent*, and the Morning put-ting me out of conceit with that Undertak-ing, they made ready to go join my Ship, in order to anchor all together beyond the Point I mentioned before, in a very fair and fecure Bay.

The Day following, we armed each of us a Boat to fend to a Village on the Coaft, which is marked in our Charts. Our Men gave us an Account that they were very

Sen-Boat to Shore.

B　　　　　well

well received, and that they had treated them with very good Fifh.

Neverthelefs we landed the fame Day, being inform'd, that beyond a Shallow Road, which was all of Sand, and in a Nook, there was Wood; and that one might alfo find Water there; but before we reach'd it, *In danger of being loft.* there happen'd to us an Accident when we were about half a League from Land, by which we had like all to have perifh'd, through the Fault of the Sailors, who had made faft the Hatches, deceived by the Weather which then was fair. We were furpriz'd by a Hurricane, which overturn'd our Boat and fill'd it with Water; fo that it funk, and we were already up to our Middles: The Matter foon became more ferious, when at length by another Flurry of Wind, the Boat turn'd over and over, and we were oblig'd to fave our Lives, fome by Swimming, and others upon the Oars, the Seats, and other Pieces of the Boat: By good luck our great Shallop, appointed to fetch Water, having feen this Accident, crouded Sail, and took us all up; fhe alfo recovered the Boat which had been funk.

As foon as we had recover'd from this Alarm, we fet about fifhing, and taking Meafures

fures for executing our firft Project, which was to go to the principal Town to fee the Governour of the Ifland. To this purpofe, I caus'd the great Shallop to be arm'd and furnifh'd with whatever might be neceffary for this Voyage.

We arriv'd in a little time at the Village where our Men had been fo kindly receiv'd, which is 7 Leagues diftant from the Place where our Ships were at Anchor, and about a Gun-fhot from the Sea. 'Tis inhabited by *Arabs*, who have one Moskee there. I met at firft the *Sheik* * or *Syndic* of the Village, who made me a long Salute after the manner of the Country, and who, inviting me to follow him, brought me into his Houfe, where we fat upon Mats; and where, by means of an *Arab* who underftood *Portuguefe*, I acquainted him that I was defirous to fee the Governour, and the Town where he dwelt. The *Sheikh* approv'd my Defign, and made me the Offer of a Camel, and Men to conduct me, it being a Day and a half's Journey diftant.

Arrive at a Village.

---

* *Sheik*, or rather *Sheikh* fignifies properly in *Arabic* an old Man. They give this Name in the Eaft to the Heads of religious and fecular Communities: They give it alfo to remarkable Doctors, and to Princes themfelves, as a Title of Honour.

I did

I did not look upon this to be the beft
Method, I therefore refolved to make ufe
of my own Boat, being able to make the
Paffage by Sea next Morning. I then order'd a Tent to be fitted up, to pafs the
Night upon Quilts, which I had caus'd to
be brought into the Boat; and having return'd Thanks to our *Sheikh*, we retir'd accompany'd by fome *Arabs*, who ftaid to
fee us fup, and who wou'd neither eat nor
Drink, thanking us at the fame time very
civilly. We were ferv'd with very excellent Fifh, altho' it was drefs'd only with
falt Water, Onions and fweet Herbs. The
Arabs return'd very difcreetly, when they
faw it was time for us to repofe ourfelves.

Civility of the Arabs.

I had intreated the *Sheikh* to let me have
a Pilot of the Place, propofing to leave
one of my Officers in Pledge. The Pilot
arriving in the Morning before Day, we
embark'd; and the Officer went to the
Village, where he diverted himfelf all Day
in fhooting and killing a little Game, which
the *Arabs* never ceas'd wondring at.

We found ourfelves about Noon, before the capital Town, to the North of
the Ifland. I immediately fent a Man on
Shore, and the People of the Country
made

Tamarin the chief Town of Sakotrah.

made Signs to us to remove to a fhallow
Road above it. 'Tis probable the Governour had been inform'd by the People of
the Place where I had lain, that I came to
fee him; for he fent an Officer to the Bank-
fide where I landed, with twenty Soldiers
who receiv'd me, and conducted me a little
way to a fine *Arbor,* cover'd over with
Palm-trees, where I found the Governour
feated upon a large fcarlet Carpet edg'd with
Fringe, and leaning upon Cufhions.

After he had lift his Hand to his Turban, The Cap-
he prefented it to me, and made me fit tain's Reception
upon his Carpet, where he only was; his from the
little Court being feated upon fine Mats. Governour.
After a little Converfation, not well underftood on either fide, he rofe up, and of
a fudden all the Soldiers who were in Arms
under the Palms, began to march in two
Files, the Governour and I being in the
middle, to conduct us with Ceremony to
his Houfe. The Soldiers danc'd very plea-
fantly, and made the Whirl, throwing up
their Sabres into the Air with one Hand,
and catching them with the other; while
three Women, a little deeper than tawny,
march'd at the Head of the Train, fending
forth at Intervals Cries of Joy, which to

us appear'd very doleful; not to mention two little Drums, which accompany'd thefe ftrange Voices.

Entertain-
ment.

Being arriv'd at the Governours, he made me enter into an Appartment which was very bare, and without any other Furniture than Mats, where we fet down, and by means of a very aged *Arab* Officer, we talk'd about the occafion of our Voyage. The Governour wou'd have been glad that our Ships had come to anchor at his Town, offering us all the Service in his Power. I prefented him with three Fufees, and three Meafures of Powder; and prefently after there came one and fpread a Table-cloth on the Mats, at the lower end of the Hall; upon which they ferv'd up two large *Por-cellain* Difhes, fill'd with Kid and Mutton, and two other Difhes with Rice, all drefs'd after the Fafhion of the Country, which we found to be pretty good. The Gover-nour excus'd himfelf from eating, becaufe it was in his Ramadan or Lent; and we drank Wine which I brought along with me, for they had nothing but Water for us, which indeed is excellent throughout that Ifland.

The

The Repaſt being over, the Governour inform'd me that this Iſle depends on the Kingdom of *Fartaſh*, in the Happy *Arabia*; adding, that the King wou'd be very well pleas'd to ſee us, if we ſhou'd put in to any of his Ports. He offer'd me alſo a Letter for that Prince, which I accepted, and which was written off hand. He ſhew'd me alſo ſeveral Certificates of *Engliſh*, *Dutch* and *Portugal* Captains, and among the reſt of a *Frenchman* nam'd *Lebahi*, Captain of the Ship call'd the *George*, full of Praiſes for his Juſtice, and the Aſſiſtance which he had receiv'd from him, deſiring me to give him the like, which I cou'd not refuſe.

Sokotrah depends on Fartaſh in Arabia.

In ſhort, after the Governour had made me repeated Offers of Service, I took leave of him; he wou'd needs ſee me as far as without the Court of his Houſe, and gave me Soldiers who accompany'd me till they ſaw me imbark. They gave me to underſtand, that the Governour had made me a Preſent of Cows and He-Goats. I ſaw the Cows tied to Palm-trees; but when the *Arabs* went to bring them away, thoſe Animals were furious, and they had a great deal to do to maſter them. I wou'd not

The Captain returns to the Village.

B 4 ſuffer

suffer them to be ship'd, for fear of some greater Inconvenience. They made great Acclamations at our departure, and the Inhabitants shew'd many Marks of Esteem for us. Our Seamen had also been regal'd by the Fishermen who came aboard our Boat, and wou'd take no Money, contenting themselves with eating their own Bread, and drinking some of our *Aqua Vitæ*.

We return'd to lie at the Village which we left in the Morning; and after many Thanks made to the *Sheikh* for his Pilot, whom I rewarded for his Trouble, we return'd to our Ships, which continu'd to lay in Water, Wood and other necessary Provisions.

Second Visit to Governour.

I was so pleas'd with that Governour, that I cou'd not refrain making him a second Visit some few Days after, to carry him the Scarlet which he desir'd, and to bring back some Aloes with which all that Country abounds. I therefore embark'd in the same Boat, and arriv'd next Day about six in the Morning at the Port of the chief Town.

I found fifteen or sixteen Soldiers on the Shore, who conducted me to the Governour's House, where I was very handsomly receiv'd ;

we

we difcours'd much about Trade and buy.
ing Aloes, which he pretended were the
beft of all *Arabia.* They keep this Commodity in Goat-skins, which they lay up Aloes
in Vaults under Ground, covering them how pre-
with Afhes to preferve them from the ex- ferved.
ceffive Heats of the Country; and they
make choice always of that which is new-
eft and moft firm. The Governour caus'd
all that I had bought to be carry'd as far as
my Boat, and I paid him at the rate of eight
Piaftres the Quintal, weighing ninety-five
Pounds, in Piaftres of *Mexico,* which are
moft efteem'd; thofe of *Peru* not being fo
current in many Places, fince the *Portugal*
Jews, as 'tis alledg'd, have cheated the
Arab Merchants with them.

The Governour's Houfe was at the fame Other
time crouded with Merchants, fome of whom Commo-
brought Incens and Civit, others Dragons- dities.
blood and Aloes, which our Men bought
of, according to the Money which they had
about them. Our Scarlet Cloth did not
pleafe the Governour, who lik'd a Stronger
and a deeper Dye; therefore we were oblig'd to carry it back, which I was not forry
for foon after.

For

For after we had view'd the Town, which is call'd *Tamarin,* and is handfome enough, the Houfes being tarrafs'd, on which almoft all the Women were mounted to fee us, and having taken leave of the Governour, we fet fail with a brisk Gale, which encreas'd foon after; infomuch, that the Sea run very high, and the Waves began to enter our Boat, whereupon we refolv'd to make ufe of our piece of Scarlet Cloth, which we put round the fides to hinder the Waves from coming in; which fucceeded very well, and we got happily on Board our Ship about 11 a Clock at Night.

Mean time the Seafon for our Departure drew near, and we did not doubt but to purfue our Voyage very well; I took a good deal of Care to inform myfelf about the Trade of *Arabia,* from the Captains of the *Tons,* which were in the Port of *Tamarin.* They all affur'd me that I wou'd be very well pleas'd with the *Arabs* of the Coffee-Country: That there were many of them at *Aden* as well as at *Moka,* and that we wou'd be well receiv'd by all of them; but that the Port of *Aden* was propereft for us to Trade, and fupply ourfelves with

Pro-

Provifions at; the Water there being in-
comparably better than at *Moka.*

Thereupon it was debated whether we
fhou'd go directly to *Aden,* or elfe to the
Coaft of *Abyffinia* to take in Water, before we enter'd the red Sea, within which
Moka lies; I was for taking the firft Courfe
becaufe we might be able to 'make the
Paffage from *Aden,* tho' it was one hundred and fifty Leagues, in two Days time,
with the Wind which then reign'd; but
Mr. *Champloret,* flatter'd with the hopes of
finding Amber-greafe in *Abyffinia,* was
refolv'd to pafs over to that Side.

We departed then from our Bay of *Zo-* Leave *Sa-kotrah.*
cotora the 10th of *December* 1708, fteering our Courfe accordingly: Next Morning
we faw the two Ifles nam'd *Abdalcuria,*
and we pafs'd them at five Leagues diftance;
and the Day following, the Cape *Gardafui.*
We failed along the Coaft about a League Coaft of *Abyffinia.*
from Land; which is a Plain of more than
twenty-five Leagues in Length, inclos'd
with Mountains. We faw Blacks from time
to time, which walk d along the flat Shore.

The third Day we found a Village, and
a fort of Entrance or Mouth of a River.
Mr. *Champloret* fent thither his Boat arm'd,

car-

carrying *Englisb* Colours; but as soon as our Men approach'd the Village, there issued out a good number of *Blacks*, arm'd with Zagayes, and several Women who threw Stones at them, which oblig'd them to retire.

Next Morning I embark'd my self in my Boat, well mann'd, carrying with me an *Englisb* Master of a Fly-boat, who came aboard our Ship at *Madagascar*; and a *Black* whom we had taken at *Anjuan*, believing he understood *Arabic*. We coasted always along the Shore, and our Ships follow'd our Example a little more at a di: stance; when about ten a Clock in the Morning, being beside a great flat Strand, we perceiv'd Smoke at the Foot of a Mountain; we expected to have met with People there; but found it was a Cave where they had kept Cattle, and that they had put Fire to the Dung.

Chace a
Pirogue
of *Blacks*

A Moment after, observing a Pirogue of Fishermen stop at one end of that Strand, we sent thither our *Black* to get Intelligence; while we waited for his Return, I amus'd my self with causing the Shells which lay upon the Shore to be gather'd, and examining those in which the Pearls grew;

grew; but we faw the *Pirogue* fet fail of a
fudden and fly. I embark'd immediately,
and we follow'd it, crouding all the Sail
we cou'd; Our Boat plung'd and run her
fore-part under Water fhe went fo fwift,
which obliged me to take in the Mizen
Sail. A while after, the *Pirogue*, taking Advantage of our flackening our Courfe, doubled a Point and got into a Nook, where
the *Blacks* forfook it, carrying off the Matt-
fail and Oars. We found in her a large-Net
full of Fifh, and fome Impliments belonging to their Bufinefs.

I caus'd all our People to land except the
Mafter and four Men to guard her; and
putting my felf at the Head of the Troop,
I began to afcend a little Hill of Marble
and Jafper, pretty fteep, over which the
Blacks had efcap'd. We beheld from thence
a great Plain, diftant from the Mountains
above two Leagues; at the fame time I
perceiv'd fome Foot-paths: Our *Englifhman*,
follow'd by two Soldiers well arm'd, took
that to the Right; for my part I follow'd
the Track that led ftrait forwards, becaufe
I thought I faw before me at about half a
Mile diftance, a kind of fmall rifing Ground,
which I judg'd might have been the Retreat
of

Land on
the Coaft
of *Abyffi-
nia.*

of the *Negros*. I had with me three Men
arm'd with Fusees, and a fourth who carry'd a white Flag at the end of a Half-Pike.
The white Flag is a Sign of Peace, and a
Token that one has fomething to demand
throughout the *Indies*.

follow the
Blacks.

We were not over a Fufee-fhot from the
Hillock, when I faw a *Negro* put out his
Head; at the fame time I order'd a Shot to
be made, which oblig'd him and his Comrades, feven in number, to difcover themfelves by rifing upright. I advanc'd fudden-
ly with my Colours flying, making a Sign
to them to come towards me; but I had
the trouble of mounting that height, where
I found the *Negros* ftanding in a Rank five
or fix Paces from each other.

He who headed them, held a very fair
Sabre in his right Hand, which he refted
upon his left Arm; and he who was in the
Rear, had fuch an other; the reft were un-
arm'd, and had only a fingle piece of Callicoe made like an Apron to cover them.
Our *Black* of *Anjuan*, whom we had fent
towards the *Pirogue*, was with them, a little diftant from the others. I went up to
the Chief of the Troop and faluted him;

first

firſt ſaying, * *Marhaba*, a Term of Civility
much in uſe in *Africa* and *Arabia* ; he anſwer'd me the ſame way ; but for any more,
having ſpoken to him in *Portugueſe*, *Spa-
niſh*, *Engliſh* and *French*, it was impoſſible
to make him underſtand us.

Mean while the *Engliſhman* and all our
arm'd Men being arriv'd at the ſame Place,
the *Negroes* began to be terrify'd, and fled
very ſwift to the Plain, retiring under Trees
which were not far from us. Then our
Black, giving us an Account of his Voyage,
told us, that, being arriv'd at the *Pirogue*,
they immediately got on board and fled,
carrying him with them by force ; that he
had not been able to make them underſtand
him, and that for his Part he knew nothing
of their *Abyſſin* Language. At length he
ſhew'd us a ſmall Cave under that *Hillock*,
into which the *Blacks* had laid up their Fiſh ;
we there found in reality near one thouſand
Sardins, three *Tunnys*, their Nets, wooden
Diſhes, and other Pieces of Houſhold Stuff.
I took half of the *Sardins*, and the *Tunnys*,

The Blacks fly.

---

* *Marhaba*, an *Arabic* Word which ſignifies welcome to you, from the Root *Rahhaba*, to open and
make eaſy the Road.

and

and left them in one of the Difhes a *Pi-aftre* and a half.

I made the Trial once more, by fending to that black Troop one of our Men who fpoke *Portuguefe* well, but he cou'd get nothing out of them; fo that we were ob-lig'd to return to our Boat, where we found that the Sailors had prepar'd the Fifh of the *Pirogue* with very fine Salt, which they found in the Hollows of the Rocks, where the Sea enters dafhing againft them. We wanted only Wood to drefs them, which eight Men arm'd went in fearch of.

One of them ta-ken.

They furpriz'd a *B'ack* on the Road arm'd with a Zagaya, and a Leathern Buckler, who feem'd at firft amaz'd to fee white Men. They brought me to a fort of Cave by the Water Side, where we were fhelter'd from the fcorching of the Sun. We gave one ano-ther our Hands at Meeting, faluting with the Word *Marhaba*, which was all our Converfation. I gave him fome *Spanifh* Wine, which he lik'd. I obferv'd that he was very eafy, and was no longer under Sur-prize, drinking and eating with us very

Very fo-ciable.

chearfully. He wip'd his Hands, and im-tated all our Fafhions at Table; he fmoak-ed in fhort feveral Pipes of our *Virginia* Tobacco,

Tobacco, and for the laſt Regale, drank a large Glaſs of Aqua Vitæ, making a Motion towards me with it, before he put it to his Hand.

We ask'd him by Signs, ſhewing him Money, about the Proviſions of the Country, and eſpecially Oxen and Sheep, letting him ſee the Figure of thoſe Animals in a Print. He apprehended all thoſe Matters very well, and gave us to underſtand by other Signs very intelligible, and even religious enough, that by next Morning, when the Sun wou'd be of ſuch a Height, he wou'd cauſe every thing that we wanted to be brought to a Place of the Mountain, where his Dwelling was, which he wou'd ſhew us. This done, he made a Sign that he had occaſion to ſleep, and, taking his Shield and his Lance, he retir'd.

Nevertheleſs, I was not without' ſome Uneaſineſs about our Situation, becauſe of the great Wind which blew, and had ſo diſpers'd our Veſſels, that we had much ado to bring them together next Day. We had ſcarce any Proviſions in the Boat, and it was more than three Days ſail to croſs over from that barren Shore, where we were, to that of *Arabia,* which lies oppoſite. Where-

C

fore about eight in the Evening, the Wind being laid, I caus'd all my Men to embark, and we put to Sea, making the Seamen row. An Hour before Day, we difcover'd the Fire of our Ship, which had waited all Night for us, and we got on Board her in a fhort time.

Continue their Courfe.

We continued our Courfe along the Coaft of *Abyffinia*, fearching continually for a convenient Place to take in Water and Provifions ; and 2 Days after, having difcover'd a fort of Bay, which promis'd us fomething, we try'd to enter it, but the Wind and the Tide wou'd not allow us to come within two Leagues of it. Continuing the fame Courfe, we at laft difcover'd a great flat Shore, five or fix Leagues long, and one broad ; and, after founding it, we caft Anchor in 18 fathom Water, three Quarters of a League from Land.

Land again.

I put my felf foon after into the Ship's Boat arm'd, and landed, accompany'd much the fame as in our firft Adventure. This Place was very agreeable, and prefented to our View a fine Plain, which we enter'd forthwith. We found towards the middle of it fome Pathes, with the Prints of Camels Feet on them. We follow'd the Tract, and,

after

after we had pafs'd a little Grove, we perceiv'd fome *Blacks* paffing along the Sea
Shore, about five or fix in Number, who
went towards our Boat.

I never imagin'd that the 12 Seamen, Sailors
who were left to guard the Boat, (and which quit the
had anchor'd upon its Grapple, about a Stone's arm'd.
Boat un-
throw from the Shore, becaufe of the
Rocks) wou'd all have quitted her impru-
dently to land, without taking the Arms
with them at leaft, which had been left
for their Defenfe. The *Blacks*, each of them
arm'd with three or four Zagays, foon
came up to them; they gave one another
their Hands in Token of Friendfhip, and
our Men, fhewing them Money, endeavour'd
to make them underftand, that our Ships
wanted Provifions. Then the *Blacks*, turning to the Side where they lay at Anchor,
faw the *Englifh* Flag which we carry'd, and
making fome Sign of Indignation (either
that the Flag difpleafed them, on account of
fome Injury receiv'd from the *Englifh*, or
that fuch large Ships made them afraid) They
pretended to retire Our poor Sailors, inftead
of letting them go off, were fimple enough
to follow them, continuing their Demands,
and removing ftill further from the Sea-fide.

Six of 'em
flain
by the
Blacks.

At length, when they were all at a certain Diftance, one of the *Blacks* lanc'd a
Zagaya directly into the Breaſt of a Sailor, crying *Uf.* Every *Black* preſent did the ſame
to him, who was neareſt him; ſo that in
an inſtant, there were five Men ſlain. The
reſt, having fled towards the Boat, receiv'd
ſeveral Strokes of the Zagayas; one of which
dy'd ſix Days after. The firſt who entred the
Boat took a Fuſee and ſhot, tho' out of
reach, at the *Blacks,* who were buſy robbing thoſe they had ſlain; which was enough
to put them to flight.

The News of this Accident which was
carry'd to our Ships, made them very un-
eaſy upon my Account; they caus'd one
hundred and fifty Men with the Officers
to embark immediately in the Shallops, to
go in ſearch of me. I had advanced above
a League and half in the Plain, and found
my ſelf pretty near the Mountains, without having ſeen any thing but a Woman
and a young Lad, who led an Aſs loaden
with Ruſhes, and fled away very ſwiftly. I

Swiftneſs
of a *Black*
Boy.

order'd them to run after them, and I run
my ſelf, to try to catch the Boy, who ſcam-
per'd up the Mountain, and threw Stones at us
whenever we drew near him. The Report

of

of a Piftol, which I fhot off only to make him afraid, and to fee his Pace, made him difappear in a Moment, running as fwift as a Doe.

I refolv'd to get together my Troop, and return after making a fmall repaft. Advancing in the Plain, we difcover'd a Body of Men marching towards us; we took them at firft for arm'd *Blacks,* and began to put ourfelves in a Pofture of Defence. When we perceiv'd that they were our own Men, we foon join'd them, and learn'd from them the Accident which happen'd on the Shore.

They made me pafs by the Place where thofe unhappy Creatures ftill lay ftretch'd upon the Strand, and where I caus'd them to be bury'd in Prefence of the Chaplains, who were landed for that purpofe. Before we embark'd, our Men propos'd to me, to let them go in fearch of the *Blacks,* to kill as many of them as they could, burn their Houfes, and revenge the Death of the Sailors; but I thought it more prudent for us to retire, than run more Risks in a ftrange Country.

I receiv'd from my Ship many Compliments upon the Dangers which they fuppos'd I had run: There came alfo Officers

C 3   from

from both the other Veſſels, and every one declar'd that he wou'd remember *Abyſſi-nia* long enough.

We ſet ſail next Morning at Day-break; we ſteer'd along the ſame ſide twelve or fifteen Leagues further, and at Noon, after taking the Height of the Sun, we directed our Courſe for the Cape of *Aden.* We diſco-ver'd that Cape the ſecond Day, which ap-pear'd to us at a diſtance, like ſeveral Iſlands together, becauſe of the different Creſts of Mountains which form it: And the third Day we enter'd happily, and caſt Anchor in the Road of *Aden*, the beſt in all the *Happy Arabia*; as the Town of that Name, is alſo the moſt famous, and beſt known of the ſame Country.

Arrival at *Aden.*

LETTER II.

*A Description of the Town, Port and Fortifications of A-*den. *What pass'd there relating to the* French.

S C A R C E, Sir, had we cast Anchor in the Road of *Aden*, with a *French* Flag, when the Covernour sent two Boats laden with Provisions, paying us his Compliments by an Officer. We did not land that Day, because we were above a League from the Town; and that besides, we did not judge it convenient to risk ourselves under the Command of a Citadel, in a Country which was yet unknown to us.

Complement from the Governour.

But early next Morning we sent to compliment the Governour; and in the mean time we saluted him with 7 Guns from

Return'd by the Captain.

each

each Ship, which he return'd us by thofe
of the Citadel, which commanded that part
of the Road near the Town. He fent back
prefently to make us new Compliments,
and invite us afhore. The Boats of the
Country came in Crouds to our Ships, to offer
us all forts of Refrefhments ; and we already

Arabs a
good fort
of People.
found the *Arabs* to be a very good fort of
People, and more accuftom'd than we ima-
nine to fee Strangers.

Captain
lands.
Mr. *Champloret* and I, accompany'd by
the Officers of the three Ships, landed
after Dinner. We found arm'd Men on
the Kay, who conducted us to the Gate,
call'd among them the greater Gate of the
Sea, becaufe it looks towards the Port : It
has a Guard-Houfe before it. I obferv'd
in paffing, that this Gate is of a prodigious
Thicknefs, ftrengthen'd with Nails, or rather
great Irons Pins, revetted behind ; and, for
an additional Security, with a Bar alfo of
Iron, which is in Proportion to the reft.

Received
by the
*Amir al
bahr.*
We entred by this Gate into a Place well
vaulted, and five Paces further we found a
kind of Chamber vaulted alfo, and ending
in an Angle. 'Tis there where an Officer of
Figure (whom they call *Amir al bahr*, and

we

we the *Mirabar*, that is, * the Prince of the Sea, but properly the Captain of the Port) receiv'd us very civilly, and made us fit down in an Elbow Chair, of an odd Figure. He ask'd us from whence we came, and the occasion of our Voyage? The Conversation was short, because that Officer had already inform'd the Governour of our coming on shore, and that his Order arriv'd that instant to conduct us to him.

We went out presently through an Iron Gate, which is at the end of that Place, and which led yet to another made of wooden Bars; and we marched between two Ranks of Soldiers, with several others both before and behind us, the *Amir al bahr* being on our left, till we came to the Governour's Palace. *Proceed to the Governour's Palace.*

We ascended by a very fine stair Case into the principal Apartment, where we found him at the further end of a Room, sitting upon an *Estrade* cover'd with magnificent Carpets, and leaning upon Cushions made of Stuff embroider'd with Gold. His Attendants were rang'd on the right and *Manner of the Governour's Reception.*

[* In *Arabick*, *Amir al bahr*, of which *Mirabar* is a Corruption.]

left, fitting on other Carpets, all the reft
of the Hall being cover'd with very fine
Mats. We advanc'd up to his *Eftrade*
without putting off our Shoes, which he
does not ufually permit to any Body; and
having faluted him, the Governour prefent-
ing his Hand to us, bid us fit down by his
Interpreter, who was a *Portugal Rene-*
gado.

He began with asking us feveral general
Queftions about the Country, from whence
we came, and concerning our Voyage; of
which having fatisfy'd him, he affur'd us
of his Protection in all Parts under his Government. After this he treated us with
Coffee of the Sultan*, and he had the
Complaifance to tell us, he had given Orders for our Lodging. And, as one never
fpeaks of Bufinefs in the firft Audience, we
retir'd after returning him our Thanks, and
promifing to return to fee him next Day.

We were conducted with the fame Ceremony by the *Amír albahr* to his own
Houfe, which the Governour had appointed

[* *Coffee ala Sultana,* for fo it is in the *French*, is ex-
plain'd hereafter in the Memoirs of *Coffee.* 'Tis probably
Cahwah al Soltány in *Arabick*, which fignifies the *Sultán's*
Coffee, as much as to fay *Royal Coffee.*]

for

for our Lodging, and where we had the
neceſſary Proviſions and Commodities
brought from our Boats. This Houſe, tho' Lodging. deſcribed.
great and fair in Appearance, had no other
Moveables in it but Matts, which were to
ſerve us inſtead of Beds, Chairs, and Tables. We were pretty much ſurpriz'd at it,
but it is the Cuſtom of the Country. They
brought us Wax-Candles without Candle-
ſticks, which put us to our Shifts to ſupply. We ſupp'd, and afterwards paſs'd the
Night ill enough.

Our Hoſt the *Amir al bahr* made us a Viſit
very early in the Morning, to know if we
had reſted well? I anſwer'd him very in-
genuouſly; whereat, appearing aſtoniſh'd, he
ask'd, What it was that cou'd diſturb our
Repoſe, having given particular Directions
in the Houſe, that none ſhould make a
Noiſe? I reply'd, that we were not us'd to
lye ſo ſoft, which made him ſmile a little;
for theſe People are ſo grave, that they ſel-
dom or never laugh out.

We went afterwards to walk towards Second Audience of the Gover nour.
the Gate, waiting till it was time to viſit
the Governour, who was gone to the Houſe
where he kept his Women. He gave us
there his ſecond Audience. We obſerv'd

in

in the Wall of the Stair-cafe feveral Windows with Lattices, from whence thofe Ladies obferv'd us as we pafs'd. We were introduc'd into an Appartment made and furnifh'd almoft like that we were in the Day
before; the Governour being feated on the
Ground, but his Court was not fo numerous.
We made him a Prefent of Scarlet, and
fome Fufees, which he received very agreeably. He invited us very earneftly to trade
in his Government, giving us Affurances of
his Favour, and fpeaking to us particulaly
about Coffee, which is there very excellent,
and in great plenty, without reckoning the
other Merchandizes of the Country, and
great Quantities of other foreign Commodities which are found there.

Vifit the
Gover
nour of
the *Cita-*
del. From thence we went to vifit the Governour of the *Citadel*, who has a Houfe
in the Town; we gave him two Fufees
and fome Cloth; he treated us with Coffee
of the *Sultân*, and Sweat meats of the
Country. Our Men were ferv'd with Fruit.
This Governour was very affable, and had
the Air of a Man of Quality; he was in
mighty Efteem throughout the Country.

Vifit from
the *Ban-*
yâns. A while after being return'd to our Houfe,
the principal *Banyâns*, who are the Brokers

kers of *Arabia,* came to pay us a Vifit, and to offer us their Services. They de-fir'd us to fend for the Merchandizes which were on board our Ships, or at leaft Sam-ples of them : But as we had only Iron Bars, a little Coral, and Cocheneal, our principal Funds being in Piaftres to buy Coffee, we were content to let them fee Samples of the Stuffs which were found in our *Holland* Prize.

In the Afternoon we return'd the Vifit to the Captain of the *Banyáns,* of whom without Ceremony we ask'd for *Sherbet,* inftead of *Coffee of the Sultán,* which we were not yet accuftomed to drink. We pafs'd from thence to the *Bazar,* where all the Merchandizes are fold. One fees them there fet out to fale in the Shops, which take up feveral little Streets, difpos'd much like thofe of the Fair of St. *Germain.* The *Banyáns* are Merchants that fell them, and there are no Women to be feen there. *Returns it.*

The fame Day a Lord of the Town fent to defire us to come to his Houfe. We found feveral of his Servants who receiv'd us at the Door, and others on the top of the Stairs. Thefe laft defir'd us to put off our Shoes, which I abfolutely re-fus'd *Vifits a Lord at his Re-queft.*

fus'd to do, charging the Interpreter to tell that Lord, that on such Terms I cou'd not have the Honour of seeing him.

Polite Reception.

Thereupon he came himself as far as the Hall Door, and, after putting his Hand to his *Turban*, and then upon his Stomach, he presented it to me very civilly, inviting me to walk in, and welcoming me with many *Arabic* Words. He led us afterwards to the end of the Hall, and made us sit down with him upon the same Estrade, cover'd with very fair Carpets, and rich Cushions, after the Fashion of the Country.

After new Civilities had pass'd, that Lord ask'd me, Whether in so long Voyages, we did not bring along with us in our Ships, some Person skill'd in Physick? He spoke this, because one of his Children was very sick of a languishing Distemper, and none of the Doctors of the Country were able to cure him ; intreating me very earnestly to let him have one of ours. I assur'd him that we were so happy, as to have with us a Man, who was reckon'd to have much Experience and Ability ; and that I shou'd do myself the Pleasure to send him to him. He thereupon return'd me many Thanks;
and

and, after we had been regal'd a second
time with *Coffee of the Sultan*, we took
leave of him, to go see the principal Stoves
of the Town.

I must confess, that there are not to be
seen of the kind, fairer Stoves and Baths
than those of this Town; they are all
lin'd with Marble, or Jasper, and cover'd
with a fair Dome, through which the Light
comes, which is adorn'd within side with
Galleries, supported by magnificent Columns.
All the Building is perfectly well divided
into Chambers, Closets, and other vaulted
Appartments, which all meet at the principal
Hall of the Dome. 'Tis needless to give here
a more particular Description, and to speak
of what passes in these agreeable Places; 'tis
much the same as is to be seen in the great
Cities of *Turky*; of which the Accounts
of the *Levant* make frequent mention.

From thence we were oblig'd to pass
across the ordinary Market, where we found
abundance of Flesh, Fish and other Things,
which appear'd to us to be very good in
their kind; and so we came to our Lodgings.

In the mean time the Reputation of our
Esculapius, nam'd *Lambardier*, who indeed

Stoves
and Baths
of the
Town.
exceeding
fine.

Plentiful
Market

deed was very skilful, and knew more
than many of his Profeffion, had fpread fo
about from what I had faid to the *Arab*
Lord, that the Governour had already fent
to look for him, and we actually found fome
of his Domefticks, who had Orders to bring
him with them. He wanted to confult
him about the Diforders of his Stomach,
and great Loathing, of which he complain'd.
Our Doctor gave him Hopes of a Cure, and

The
French
Surgeon
under-
takes to
cure the
Gover-
nour.

to that purpofe he return'd on board the
Ships to look for Remedies, to compofe
a Medicine which he carry'd to him ; after
which he return'd to fup, and lye at our
Houfe, where they did not fail to laugh at
the Doctor's Expence, congratulating him
upon his new Method of Practice.

Alarm'd
at an un-
feafonable
Meffage
from the
Gover-
nour.

Every one after that retir'd ; but about an
Hour after Midnight, we were pretty much
alarm'd by a great Noife of Men, which
we heard at the Gate, who knock'd at it
with much Violence. Prefently after, they
came to tell us it was the *Amir al bahr*, accompany'd with feveral Soldiers, who demanded Entrance. At this one of our Officers was feiz'd with a panick Fear, which
he communicated to all the reft ; he imagin'd that our Doctor had done fome Hurt

to

to the Governour, and that thereupon they were come to lay fome Impofition upon us.

Tho' that Hour was unfeafonable, and I ʻwas fufficiently furpriz'd at fuch a Vifit; yet I gave my felf the Pleafure of encreafing the Fear ¦of that Officer, by pretending to have had the fame Thought with him. In the mean time the *Amir al bahr* entred with his Company, who acquainted us with an Air blunt enough, that the Governor wanted to fee us immediately. The poor Doctor was half dead, he alledg'd inceffantly the good Qualities of his Drugs, of which he told the Names and the Virtues, not forgetting the Dofe which he affirm'd he had adminiftred with all the Care imaginable. We arriv'd in this Perplexity as far as the *Amir al bahr*'s Houfe, who caus'd us to reft a little till he went and inform'd the Governour. They prefented us with Pipes and Tobacco, but no one had any Stomach to fmoke, excepting me, who was difpos'd to keep the *Amir al bahr* Company.

The Doctor in a great Fright.

A while after we came to the Governour; I went in firft, he gave me his Hand as ufual; and, having caus'd us to fit down with an Air of Tranquility, he told us

Civil Reception of the Governour.

D   in

in a mild Grave way, that he perceiv'd we
had no Defign to trade in his Government,
that notwithftanding we might do our Bufinefs well enough there : But that he wou'd
give us a Letter for his Brother the Governour of *Moka,* by whom we fhou'd be very
well receiv'd, and where we might trade
to as much Advantage at leaft, as in the
Gulf of *Perfia;* for at firft we pretended
we were bound thither.

We return'd him, as you may believe,
very hearty Thanks, and teftify'd much Joy
at the Letter which he promis'd, which
alone was fufficient to carry us to *Moka,*
in hopes of finding the fame Favour from
the Governour his Brother. Afterwards he
caus'd our Doctor to draw near him, to ask
him at what Hour he ought to take his
Phyfic; who having fatisfy'd him, we took
our Leave with all the Content imaginable.

Caufe of the Governours Meffage. We return'd with the *Amir al bahr,*
where every one fmok'd and rejoyc'd, not
without fome kind of Shame, for having taken the Alarm without Caufe. We
underftood there, that the Governour, returning from the Appartment of his Women, cou'd not fleep, and that, not imagin-
ing he cou'd difturb Seamen, who were
accuftom'd

accuftom'd to watch, he took it in his Head to fend for us. We return'd after that to our Lodging, to take fome Repofe during the reft of the Night. I rofe very early in the Morning to walk without the Town, and to obferve it at my Leizure on the outfide, accompany'd by the *Portugal* Interpreter, who explain'd every thing to me.

Aden (*a*) is feated at the Foot of high Mountains, which furround it almoft on all fides. There are five or fix Forts on the Tops of them, with Curtains, and a great many other Fortifications at the Necks of the Mountains. A fair Aqueduct conveys from thence the Waters into a great Canal, or Refervatory, built about three quarters of a Mile from the City, which fupplies the Inhabitants with very good Water; for there is no other at (*b*) *Aden*, and I know not by what Authority our Geo-

Defcription of *Aden*.

(*a*) It is, according to *Abulfeda*, in 70 Degrees of Longitude, [from the Shore of the Weftern Ocean 10 Degrees on this fide the fortunate Ifles] and 12 of Latitude. [But others make it 12º, 35¹, or 12º, 47¹, and 12º, 13¹. I fhou'd chufe the firft, *viz.* 12º, 35¹.]

(*b*) *Abulfeda* fays, that *Aden* has a Gate towards the Land, call'd the Gate of the Water Carriers, and that through the fame they carry the frefh Water elfewhere.

graphers

graphers make a River .pafs through this Town.

Walls in
bad or-
der.
The Place is encompafs'd with Walls, which are at prefent in a bad Condition enough ; efpecially towards the Sea, where neverthelefs there are fome Platforms at certain diftances, with five or fix Batteries of Brafs Canon, fome of which carry a Ball of fixty Pounds weight. 'Tis thought to be the Artillery which *Soliman* II. left there after taking the Town, and conquering

Country
conquer'd
by the
Turks and
aban-
don'd.
almoft the whole Country, which the *Turks* were afterwards conftrain'd to abandon to the *Arab* Princes.

There is only one Road to arrive at *Aden* on the Land fide, which is made along a narrow Piece of Land, advancing into the Sea like a *Peninfula.* The Head of this

Fort at
the Head
of the
Road.
Road is commanded by a Fort, with Guard-houfes at proper diftances; and a Gun-fhot lower there is another Fort, fortify'd with forty Pieces of Canon on feveral Batteries, and a Garrifon ; fo that it wou'd be impoffible to attempt a Difcent on that fide ; and to go from the Town to this laft Fort, there is upon the Road of Commmunication yet another Fort of twelve Pieces of Canon, with a Garrifon.

With

With regard to the Sea, by which this _{Wide} Bay. Town is acceffable enough, it makes there a Bay; which is eight or nine Leagues wide at the Entrance, and which is divided as it were into two Roads, one of which is very large, and a pretty diftance from the Town; the other is lefs and nearer, which is call'd the Port. This laft is about a League broad, meafuring from the Citadel, which commands it with fifty Pieces of Canon, to the advanc'd Point, where are the Forts of which I have fpoken. One anchors in every part of it, in eighteen, twenty or twenty-two fathom Water.

I fay nothing about the Infide of this Town, which is confiderably big, and where there are to be feen many fine Houfes of two Stories, and terrafs'd on Top, but with all, many Ruins and decay'd Buildings. 'Tis eafy to perceive by what remains of it, and the advantagioufnefs of the Situation, that *Aden* was formerly a famous Town, and Town of great Importance, very ftrong, and the formerly very fa- principal Bulwark of the Happy *Arabia*. mous. The Territory, which is about it, is very a-greeable, tho' not large, and affords much Grafs at the Foot of the little Hills nigh the Mountains.

D 3   Re-

Returning from my long Walk, I found at the Sea Gate Mr. *Champloret*, who was ſmoaking with the *Amir al bahr*. He told me, that having a mind to go on Board, they had refus'd to let him paſs through that Gate. I wanted to know the Reaſon of it, and at the ſame time I was arreſted my ſelf in the ſame place, without acquainting me with the Cauſe. This Proceeding, which I cou'd not comprehend, made me bid an Officer of our Ship, who was there by accident, to go forthwith, and order three Shallops a ſhore well arm'd with Soldiers, who were to hide their Arms, and, at a ſignal given, to fire upon the Guard, in order to deliver us out of their Cuſtody, and favour our embarking: But, after much Enquiry, the *Amir al bahr* told us at laſt, that the Governour had given that order, and, that having taken Phyſick, he wou'd needs ſee us. This oblig'd us to enter the Town again, in order to dine at our Lodgings.

Attend the Governour.

Two Hours after, one came from the Governour to look for us, and we went to him attended with a great Train, for our Men were arriv'd from the Ship with the Shallops. At firſt he told us a thouſand
fine

fine Things of the Phyſick which he had taken, and of the Perſon who had prepar'd it. He afterwards ſignify'd the Concern he had at the Reſolution we had taken, repeating all his former Offers, and omitting nothing which might engage us to continue at *Adén*. In ſhort, after many Thanks on our ſide, the Governour left us to go and repoſe himſelf, and caus'd the Letter which he had promis'd to be diſpatch'd. He had alſo promis'd to give us a Pilot, which we had ask'd of him, but he did not come to us, the Governour thinking perhaps that it would make us change our Reſolution,

I went immediately to the Sea Gate with four or five of our Officers, and found no Difficulty iu paſſing out; this obliged me to ſend back the Shallops with Orders to hoiſt Sail next Morning, and to ſend the Boats for us to that Gate, in order to fall down with the Tide in caſe we could not embark at high Water. We ſpent the reſt of the Day in walking along the Shore, and diſcourſing with the *Amîr al bahr*, to whom I made a Preſent of a *Turkiſh* Sabre, which he had ſeen with one of our Men, and had ask'd to buy it.

The

Depart from be- fore *Aden*.

The 27th of *December* 1708, it was scarce Day-light when they brought us the Letter of the Governour of *Aden* for him of *Moka* ; and, having been conducted by the Governour as far as the Shore, we em- bark'd, in order to return to our Ships, which were then about a League and a half from the Town. The Yons or Ships of that Country, which were coming in as we were embarking, were greatly frigh- ten'd, feeing our ftrange Veffels, and went to anchor very near the Shore, at the risk of running a-ground.

Currents at Cape *Aden*.

For our Parts, we were warned in time, to beware of the Currents, which we did in weighing Anchor; for on the fide of the Cape of *Aden*, they fet againft its Point with great Rapidity ; and, notwithftanding all our Caution, we pafs'd within but a quarter of a League of that Cape, which may be about a Mile in height. It is very ftrait and fteep; we obferv'd two Towers with Soldiers on Guard, and thefe Towers are in fight of a Caftle, which is not above half a League from the Town ; upon which, on occafion, they fet up Flags and Signals to give notice, which are anfwer'd again, both from the Town and the Citadel, which

has

has the same Prospect. They say, that from the Top of that Cape one may see the Country for ten Leagues round, and discover the Sea at fifteen or twenty Leagues distance. This Coast in general appears dry and sandy; but a little within Land, the Country is full of Groves and Moisture.

It was recommended to us very much to direct our Course only by the West, and one Point towards the North-west; but the *Pilot* of *Monsieur de Champloret,* whose Ship was a-head of ours, kept steering a Point to the South-west: Nevertheless, next Morning he perceiv'd the top of *Bab al mandel* [*Bab al mandab*] a famous Mountain, which is at the Entrance of the *Red-Sea,* on the *African* side, and did not know it. He continu'd the same Course, saying, he was sure he was well instructed, and that he had very exact Journals. He crouded Sail, so that we cou'd not speak to him, being above two Leagues distant from us. We being of necessity oblig'd to follow him, found our selves soon after at the Entrance of a Bay, above six Leagues wide, in the middle of which there is an Isle.

Monsieur de Champloret perceiv'd from the Place where he was, some Pirogues of Fishermen

Directions for entring the *Red-Sea.*

Mistake *Tagura* Bay for the *Streights.*

Fifhermen upon the Coaft; he fent his Boat to get Intelligence of them, but his Men could not make themfelves underftood. For our Parts, upon examining the aforefaid Bay, and the Iflewhich is in the middle, and comparing them with our Charts, we were eafily induc'd to believe, that this might be the Entrance of the Red fea; prepoffefs'd moreover by the affurance which that *Pilot* gave us of conducting us right ; and by the Report of the Men, whom we fent with the Shallop, who cou'd not difcover the bottom of that Entrance, which agreed well enough with the Account we had of the *Streight* we were in queft of.

As there was but little Wind, we were all of Opinion to enter, and, having got two Leagues within, founding all the way we went, we faw a Bark, which made towards us, and at the fame time we difcover'd a Town; the Men of the Bark, who confifted of two *Pilots*, one *Banyân* and the Ship's Crew, twenty in Number, foon inform'd us, that it was the Town of *Tagora* in *Africa*, in the Kingdom of *Adel* and *Zeila*, formerly belonging to the Empire of the *Abyffins*, and that we were in the Bay of the fame Name. At the fame

time

time they handed me a Letter from the King, which the Governour had fent me ; for they had fpy'd us from the Watch-houfe, and they did not doubt but we had a Defign to carry on fome Trade in their Country, or at leaft ftood in need of Provifions. After that, they gave a particular Account of the Merchandizes, and the great Conveniences and Eafe of Trading, which we fhould find amongft them, crying up at a great Rate the good Qualities of the Governour of *Tagora,* who, they faid, had a great Defire to fee us. In the mean time, they interpreted the *Arabic* Letter before-mentioned, which was as follows ;

The Letter of Soltân Mohammed Ebn Dainy, *from the fecure Port of* Tadgiura, *that is to fay,* Taghora, * *in the Name of the moft merciful God.*

Praife be to God, as is his due.

GOD *give his Bleffing to him, after whom there fhall be no more Pro-*

---

¹ The *Mohammedans* are obliged by their Law to write the Name of God at the beginning of their Letters, and all their Works : to praife him, and in fhort to blefs *Mohammed.*

phets ;

phets; and to his Family and Friends Peace.

This Letter is written by order of our Master Soltân Mohammed, *Son of* Soltân Dainy, *whom the most hgh God preserve.* Amen.

We give you to understand, O Captain of *the Ship, that you have entire Security and Guarantee in this* Port *of* Taghiura, *for taking in Water and Wood, for we are oblig'd to furnish you with it, and we will give you a* Raban *to introduce you into the Town, which you may have a desire to see; if you wou'd go to the Port of* Zeila, *it is nearer the Place where you at present are.   We are People of Fidelity, and we believe in God, and is his Prophet; for our Profession of Faith in this:* I testify that there is no other God but God, *and that* Mohammed *is his Prophet; God give him his Benediction, and shower upon him a great number of pleasing and blessed Greetings of Peace, till the Day of Judgment.   And praise be to God the Lord of both Lives.   You have the Security of God, and the Security of* Soltân Mohammed, *Son of* Soltân Dainy *; and Greeting be*
to

Zeila
Port.

to you, and the Mercy of God and his Be-
nedictions.

On one fide is the Seal of the King, which contains thefe Words: He who trufts in the King of Heaven, *Soltán Mohammed* Son of *Dainy*, in the Year 1117.

That is to fay in the Year 1117 of the *Hegra*, which anfwers to that of *Chrift* 1705, the Year in which the King of *A-del* was advanc'd to the Crown, and the aforefaid Seal was engrav'd.

And on the other fide of the Seal, there is found, after the Subfcription, the Word *Catmir*, which is the Name of the Dog, which the *Mohammedans* pretend, according to the *Coran*, had the keeping of the Sleeping Brothers, during their Nap of three hundred and nine Years. They ordinarily write that Word on the Letters, which are fent far or crofs the Sea, as a fafeguard and kind of Talifman, which keeps them fafe.

In thefe Circumftances, join'd to the beauty of the Country, which appear'd to me very charming, and having but about half a League to the Town, I came to a Refolution to go and anchor near *Tagora*; but for greater Security, in regard Night
drew

drew on, I fent our Boat always before
with the Log to found the Road; and it
prov'd exceeding lucky for us, for our Men
soon found a Ridge of Rock, over which
Dange- we muft of neceffity pafs, with only three
rous Bay. fathom Water; which oblig'd us to turn
back in hafte, and to change our Defign.

I took the two *Pilots* on board my Ship,
and fent back the *Banyàn* with the Bark,
ordering him to make my Apology to the
Governour, to whom I fent twelve Pounds
of excellent *Virginia* Tobacco, two Fufees,
and two Meafures of Powder; affuring him,
that I wou'd recompenfe the *Pilots*, whom
I kept to conduct us to *Moka*.

Leave the   I did not quit the Bay of *Tagora* with-
Bay of out regret, becaufe of the Beauty of the
Tagora. Country, and the ufeful Knowledge with
regard to Trade, which might be drawn
from that Place; of which it feems to me,
that neither the Travellers nor Voyagers
have yet taken any notice: But the prefer-
vation of my Ship was preferable to all o-
ther Confiderations.

We were oblig'd to fteer out the fame
Way we put in, and at Day break we faw
our two Comrades, the *Diligent* at Anchor
at the Entrance of the Bay, and the *Prize*

a good

a good League diftant from her. We made fail to come up with them, and at the fame time I perceiv'd fome a little to the windward of us. I fent an Officer immediately in the Boat to fee what it was, to examine the Channel, and to caft Anchor in the deepeft part of it, with a Grapple, which might ferve as a Signal for us to get out profperoufly. I gave him to underftand that he fhou'd coaft along the Fome, notwithftanding which, he went out of his way, always doing contrary to what we inftructed him by Signs.

Mean time the Ship with its two Foretop Sails, and a little Wind at Stern, carry'd us infenfibly upon a very dangerous Bank, the oppofite fide of which caus'd the aforefaid Fome, by the Seas beating againft it. I had occafion all that time to go down to my Cabin; and, as I was taking up a Shirt in my Hand, I perceiv'd on a fudden a great fhock of the Veffel, which made me conclude it touch'd Ground; upon which I ran upon Deck in all hafte, and there found a ftrange Confufion, every one lamenting and giving himfelf up to difpair, inftead of endeavouring to help themfelves out of the Danger.

Run up-on a Bank.

Then

Then after I had fhot off one Gun, put
out the Flag for a Signal, and taken in the
foretop Sails, I caus'd our Shallop to be
well man'd, and a Jet Anchor put on
board it, under rhe Management of an
Officer, who was order'd to caft that Anchor a Head to the Starboard of the Ship,
in order to draw her off that Bank. The
Shallop being thus loaded and crouded
up, cou'd go but with four Oars, and that
flowly; but by good Luck, our Boat came
back in time, and we fet her to tow the
Shallop; and thus all the Care that cou'd
be was taken.

Ship in
Danger.
In the mean time, the Ship ftruck upon
the fide of the Bank, occafion'd by a fmall
Wave which lifted it up, and let it fall to
the bottom when it was pafs'd; which
caus'd a Shock that made every thing trem-
ble. I went down into the Gunner's Cabin to obferve the Rudder; the Ship ftri-
king upon the Keel, being in fear left fhe
fhou'd bulge, by breaking her Iron Works,
and the Whipftaff. I alfo look'd out through
the Portholes; and, as the Sea was calm, I
faw the bottom of the Bank, upon which we
were, having not above fourteen Foot Water;
whereas our Ship requir'd at leaft feventeen.

This

This Bank was of Sand, interfpers'd with large Rocks, againft which the bottom of the Veffel rubb'd, and ftruck; this at length took off feveral Pieces of the Keel, which I faw floating upon the Water.

But by the great Care of the Men who were in the Shallop, in cafting the Anchor, and the Labour of all the Crew, the Ship foon got clear of this Bank, and every one recover'd from the Fear of the Danger, which we had been in. I fent immediately the Boat to gather the Pieces which had come off the Keel, to difcover whether or no they were off the Bottom of the Ship; but they found it was no more than the Lining of the Keel, which put us out of all Apprehenfion; and as the laft Proof, they pump'd, and by good Luck, found that the Veffel did not draw Water.

Get clear of the Bank.

In the mean time, the Shallops of the other Ships arriv'd to lend us their Affiftance, of which we ftood no longer in need. It was mov'd to fail directly out of the Bay, and for that end, the two Pilots of *Tagora* advis'd to pafs on the Larboard fide of the Ifle, which lies at the entrance of it, tho' there is no anchoring there for want of Bottom.

E　　　　　　We

We then weigh'd Anchor, and crouded all our Sails, becaufe the Wind was very calm; and thus we got out, removing about a League from Land. We pais'd the Night following in a calm, and next Morning a fmall Gale of Wind rifing, we fail'd along the Coaft, and entred at length into the famous *Streight* of the *Red-Sea*, or the *Arabic* Gulf, or the Gulf of *Mekk?*, for Geographers give it thofe three Names.

The Entrance of the *Streight* of the *Red-Sea* defcrib'd. It may not perhaps be amifs, before we go further, to give here in a few Words an exact Account of the Situation of this Gulf, and the nature of its Entrance. Cape *Gardafuy*, of which I have fpoken before, which is in the Kingdom of *Adel*, faces another which is oppofite to it, call'd Cape *Fartach*, in a Kingdom of the fame Name, on the Coaft of *Arabia*. The Diftance from one to the other is but about fifty Leagues; but the Ocean inclos'd within thofe two Lands for the Space of above one hundred and fifty Leagues, is at length fo ftraiten'd by the Coafts, which approach each other, that there remains not above four Leagues of opening, or diftance of one Shore from the other; and 'tis this Opening which forms the fmall Channel, commonly

monly call'd the *Streight*, or the beginning of
the *Red Sea*. This Sea grows wider afterwards, and extends itfelf along feveral
Coafts, under different Names, the fpace
of near two hundred Leagues, running
from the South Eaft, to the North Weft.

As Night drew on apace, and the Sea
fell, we went and anchor'd in a fandy Creek
at the Entrance of the *Streight*, in 10 Fathom
Water, where we faw a Mosk, fome
Huts of Fifhermen, and feveral Bales of
Merchandize by the Water Side. Mr. *de
Champloret* fent thither his Shallop, which
found no body to fpeak to.

Over againft this Creek, is the Ifle of Ifle of
Bab al Mandel, which gives Name to this Bab al
Streight, or receives it from it. This Name Monaub.
is compos'd of three *Arabic* Words, *Bab*,
al Mondub, which our Geographers have
render'd into *Latin*, by *Oftium Luctus*,
the *Streight of Weeping*, without fhewing a
Reafon for this Denomination. The Ifle
lies upon the right Hand in entring it; it
may be about two Leagues long, and a little lefs in breadth. One fees Grafs there
in certain Places, tho' for the generality,
'tis almoft one continued barren Rock, expos'd to the Winds and Waves, and burnt

with

Ill plac'd
in the
Charts.
with the Heat of the Sun ; for the reft I find it very ill plac'd in moft of the ordinary Charts, which put it directly in the middle of the *Streight* ; whereas it is altogether on the *Arabian* Side, and fo near, that between the Ifle and the firm Land, there is only a very narrow Paffage for the fmalleft fort of Veffels.

Good
Anchor-
age within
the
Streight.
Within the Entrance of the *Streight*, and where the Ifle begins to rife, the Anchorage is very good ; and there is another Creek bigger than that, where we anchor'd, about a quarter of a League broad, with low Grounds in the Middle ; where are to be feen little Houfes cover'd with Mats. We faw there People upon the Strand, two Barks at Anchor, and two Pirogues which had run aground. 'Tis there where the Pirates and Rovers are accuftom'd to come, and anchor under Cover from the Winds of the South Weft Muffon.

Moun-
tain of
Mondub.
Upon the high Mountain, which alfo bears the Name of *Bab al Mondub,* * and
bounds

* It is properly this Mountain which gives the Name to the *Streight* and the Ifle of *Bab al Mandel. Abu'lfeda,* a famous *Arabian* Geographer, calls it *al Mondub,* and the *Streight Bab al Mondub,* that is to fay, the Gate of the Mountain of *Mondub. Mondub* fignifies properly
the

bounds with its Foot the *Streight* on the *African* Side. Oppofite to that of the firm Land of *Aden* in *Afia*, there was former-ly a Fort, which fecured the anchoring Place I have mention'd; but at prefent, it lies in Ruins. One may fail along this Coaft as near as one will, and we were not above three quarters of a Mile from it in our Paffage. It wou'd be eafy to procure from thence Provifions, Incenfe, Gums, and other Merchandizes. 'Tis to this Place that they fend from *Moka*, to fee if the *Arab* and *Indian* Veffels may go out in fafety; that is to fay, if there be no *Pirates* hid in that Creek, and if none have been feen cruifing without. In turning out of the *Streight*, they are accuftom'd to fail along the Coaft, and Cape of *Aden*, which, by its Elevation appears, from whatever fide one comes, more than fifteen Leagues diftant; and it is alfo a part of the Sea, in which all the People of *Afia* are in fear of meet-ing Pirates.

Good Harbour for *Pirates.*

We weigh'd Anchor early in the Morn-ing, with a fair Wind, and the four great

the Place of Tears, from the *Arabic* Root *Nadaba, he wept over the Dead,* becaufe formerly the *Arabs* bewail'd, as if dead, thofe who pafs'd through that dangerous *Streight,* to enter into the Ocean.

Sails up, steering our Course for *Moka*,
which is situate in the Gulf of the *Red-
Sea*, twenty Leagues from the *Streight*. From
the Isle, the true Situation of which I
have obſerv'd, for as far as one can ſee, there
are nothing but low Lands, bounded with
high Mountains. We made great way, aſſiſted alſo by the Tyde, which was coming
in, keeping about two Leagues from the
Land, which was to the Starboard of us;
that is to ſay, having the Coaſt of *Arabia*
on our right Hand, where we obſerv'd at
certain Diſtances ſome Groves.

Proſpect
of *Moka*.
At length, when we were about ſix Leagues
from *Moka*, we diſcover'd that Town,
which preſented us with a very fine Proſpect, becauſe of its high Towers, and its
Moſks [Meſgids] which are all white
waſh'd on the Outſide. This Sight rejoyc'd
us very much, *Moka* being the end of
our Wiſhes, the Place on account of which
we left *Europe*, and which had made us
undertake a Voyage of more than nine
Months Continuance. We began from
that time to ſee a great many Palm Trees,
which ſeem'd to us to run along the Shore
as far as the Town, which has abundance

of

of them in its Neighbourhood, affording a very agreeable Profpect.

The Wind was always very frefh, without being tempeftuous, and Mr. *Champlo-ret's* Boat, which was drawn along by a Rope, had like to have perifh'd, the Ship having given a Rowl, which overfet it, and fill'd it with Water, fo that he was oblig'd to put out his Shallop to fave the Sailors.

In the mean time we loaded two of the main Sails, and put them acrofs, to found the Bottom, always keeping at a diftance of two good Leagues from Land for fear of the *Blacks*, which are on that Coaft. We found each of us eight Fathom Water. My Comrade waited after that the Return of the Shallop; after which, inftead of following us, he kept on with his four greateft Sails always up, and continued to fteer his own Courfe.

For our Parts we went on founding, cafting the Log every Minute, and putting further from Land when we found lefs than eight Fathom, to get into the fame Depth again, and into the ordinary Channel: We did it alfo to remove ourfelves from a great Sand Bank, which one meets

two

two Leagues on this fide the Road of *Moka*, and which continues half way in, and is above two Leagues in breadth, from the Coaft to the Channel.

The *Diligent* in danger.
The *P lot* of the *Diligent* made it a fort of Point of Honour to get into the Road firft, neglecting all his Inftructions and Memoirs to compafs his Defign. He had done the fame four Days before, when, in order to enter firft into the *Red-Sea*, he had made us mifs the Entrance of the *Streight*, and carry'd us into the Bay of *Tagura*; but he had reafon to repent it, the Ship having ftruck upon the Bank, as I mention'd before; which oblig'd him to fire a Gun, to take in the foretop Sails, to cut the main and mizen Sails, which he caus'd to be refitted fome time after, and in fhort, to put out a Flag to demand Help.

We were then, as I have obferv'd, wide of that Veffel, about the diftance of half a League, always founding and uneafy enough to have found juft at that juncture but fix Fathom Water; which made us ftand further off ftill. Our *Prize*, which follow'd us, and which it was much our Interefts to preferve, directed itfelf by fteering the Courfe we did.

When

When we had found the eight Fathom
Channel again, we caſt Anchor there with
the *Prize*, and immediately put out the Shallop and Boat, man'd with our beſt Hands,
to go to the Aſſiſtance of our Comrade;
but the Wind, which was encreas'd, and the
contrary Tyde hindred them, ſo that they
were a whole Hour before they could get
on board them. Mean while, as the Sea
ſwell'd, and the Wind blew ſtrong in her
Sails, the Bank being very fortunately of Gets clear
Sand mix'd with Slime, the Ship ſlid over of the
Bank.
it, and at length got quite clear.

Upon the Return of our Shallop, which,
on account of its Loading and the time, cou'd
not get above a third part of the way to the
Diligent, we ſounded again, and did not find
above five Fathom Water, the Sea beginning to fall. Then our *Pilot* made us
weigh Anchor, and hoiſt the foretop Sails;
and in a little while, we came to anchor
near a Point, which runs pretty far out,
forming on the North ſide half of the Port Arrive
of *Moka*, and upon which a Fort is built. near
Moka.
We there found ſix Fathom Water, and
good Anchorage; the Bottom being Sand
mix'd with a few Shells.

LETTER

LETTER III.

Description of the Port and Town of Moka; *of the adjacent Country, and of* Arabia *in general; with an Account of what the* French *did there, during their stay.*

Port of *Moka* described.

I T was the third of *January,* Sir, when we cast Anchor at the Road of *Moka.* The Port is form'd by two Tongues of Land, which bend towards each other like a Bow, and thus represent a perfect half Moon. Upon the two Points are situated Forts, which defend the Entrance: And this Entrance, which is about a League in breadth from one Fort to the other, makes a kind of a Road, where great Ships are oblig'd to anchor. The rest of the Port is not deep enough, and so serves only for lesser Vessels.

As

As foon as we had caft our Anchors, the Forts fet up a red Flag, which carry'd three Crefcents, and * Figure in Saltire: We obferv'd alfo, tho' a great way from the Town, the *Dutch* Flag which the Director of the Factory had caus'd to be difplay'd, in order to do us Honour. And then another Flag like thofe of the Forts, upon a Battery of Canon, which is near the Governour's Houfe.

The Captain faluted from the Town.

We faluted each of them with feven Guns, and they return'd our Compliment with five from the Battery of the Town. The Governour fent immediately one of his *Barks* to our Ship, carrying a Flag and a Streamer, with the *Amîr al bahr*, or Captain of the Port of *Moka*. His Cloathing was of green Stuff, plaited, and with large hanging Sleeves, fhap'd like a *Monk's* Frock, having a ftrip'd Caffock underneath, of a Merigold Colour. He was accompany'd with *Banyân Bira*, who fpoke *Portuguefe*, and was cloath'd in white, with a fine embroider'd Girdle, wearing on his Shoulder a

Amir al bahr fent on board the Governour.

That Figure is the famous Sword of *Aly*, *Mohammed's* Son-in-law, call'd *Zulficar*. It has two Blades, and has done great Execution according to the *Moflemans*. [This fhews they are in *Yaman*, *Shiais*, or of the Perfian Sect.]

filk

Silk-Scarf of feveral Colours; and by a *Dutchman* of the Factory, who had dwelt in *Turky*, and underftood the *French* Tongue very well. This laft was cloath'd after the *Turkiſh* manner.

The firft Ceremonies being over, I gave an Account to the *Amir al bahr* of the occaſion of our Voyage, that we had undertaken it by the Direction and Favour of the Emperor of *France* our Mafter, who was willing that his Subjects fhould contract a Friendſhip, and trade with thoſe of the King of *Yaman*; which the *Amir al bahr* was exceedingly pleas'd with; aſſuring us that the Governour of *Moka* wou'd be rejoyc'd at our Arrival, and the Propoſals we made.

I preſented them afterwards with Liquors, but they wou'd never drink any, contenting themfelves with fmelling to them. The *Banyán Bira* offer'd us his Houſe; They return'd with one of our Officers, whom **Letter from the Governour.** I fent with a Letter to the Governour, and that which I had from his Brother the Governour of *Aden*; and I caus'd them to be faluted with five Guns.

They return'd fome time after with Refreſhments, bringing me a Letter from the Governour, in anſwer to mine, and another from two Miſſionèrs of the *Italian* Recollets, written in *Latin*. That from the Gòvernour was in *Arabic*, tranſlated as follows,

To the *French* Captain.

Monſieur de Marveille, *whom God direct.*

Praiſe to him, to whom it is due,

HIS *high and lofty Excellence, the* French *Captain Monſieur de* Marveille, *whom God direct, if it pleaſes him, bleſs his Merchandize and Effects, and put him in a flouriſhing Condition. We have receiv'd your Letter by your Envoy, by which you have given us notice of your happy Arrival in the bleſſed Port of* Moka, *always flouriſhing by the grace of God, and by the Juſtice of* * *the Commander of the* Faithful, Almahdi † liden illah, *whom God make triumphant. You conduct your*

---

* It is in the *Arabic, Amir al muminyn,* that is to ſay, the Commander of the Believers, or the Faithful.

† That is to ſay, the Conductor to the Religion of God. The King of *Yaman* aſſumes the Names and uſual Titles of the *Chalifas,* which all end with the Name of God. [It ſhou'd rather be written *Al mòhdi-ldˌni'llah.*]

felves according to the moſt excellent Max-
ims, and the moſt perfect Cuſtoms. To-
morrow, if it pleaſe the moſt high God,
we will go and ſee you, and inform our-
ſelves to the bottom of your Affairs. We
implore God for his Grace, being our ſure
Hold, and laſt Support.

> *By the Governour of the* Port *of* Mo-
> ka, Saleh, *the Son of* Aly, *whom*
> God *preſerve.*

Recollets viſit us.

Next Day which was the fourth, the Fathers Recollets came on board, and I deſir'd the Favour of them to procure a fiſt
Audience of the Governour, which was
diſpatch'd the ſame Day. 'Tis true he
wou'd have put it off till next Day, having
a Deſign that we ſhou'd make a publick
Entry, as being the firſt *French* Officers that
had arriv'd in his Government; but we
pray'd him to diſpenſe with that Ceremony,
and to permit us the Honour of paying
our Reſpects to him off hand.

Captain lands.

We embark'd therefore in our Boats,
Mr. *de Champloret* and I, accompany'd by
ſome of our Officers in proper Habits, and
with a Retinue very neatly dreſs'd, and
landed at the Key belonging to the Port.

After

After we had pass'd from that Key to the Gate of the *Marine*, we found twelve Horses nicely well equip'd, and about two hundred Soldiers with Timbrels before them. The *Amir al bahr* receiv'd us at that Gate, and conducted us to the Palace of the Governour, which is not far from it, follow'd by a great Concourse of People.

Conducted to the Governour's Palace.

We were scarce got into that Palace, when one desir'd us, by our Interpreter, to put off our Shoes, in order to be introduc'd into the Hall of Obedience; a Compliment which they had already made us at *Aden*, and which I return'd in the same manner by a Refusal, which I grounded upon our Customs, which did not exact that Formality from us, even at the Court of our Emperor, the greatest Prince in *Europe*; adding, that I was ready to return without having an Audience; and, as I made a shew of doing as I said, they call'd me back, and brought us all into a large Hall, cover'd with Foot Carpets, and dispos'd like those of the *Turks* in the *Levant*, with a Sopha or Estrade rais'd upon the Floor.

Refuses to put off his Shoes.

The Governour was seated upon two Carpets embroider'd with Gold, leaning upon Cushions of the same Stuff. He receiv'd

Audience of the Governour.

ceiv'd us very civilly, and gave me his Hand. I made him my Compliment, which was, that our Emperor, the moſt powerful, and moſt magnificent, and the moſt ſhining with Glory of all the Princes in the Weſt, always full of Goodneſs, and Juſtice, had given Permiſſion to his Sub-jects, of a Company honour'd with the Name of * Royal, to come for the firſt time to open a Trade in the Kingdom of *Taman*, the Prince of which he had a great Eſteem for; and that, if they favour'd our Undertaking, he wou'd ſend others to ſuc-ceed us, who might continue a uſeful Com-merce between the two Nations.

The Governour, before he made any An-ſwer, put his Hand to his Forehead, and after that upon his Breaſt, bending forward as it were, to teſtify the Reſpect which he had for the great Monarch I had ſpoken of;

Gover-
nour's
Anſwer. and then, ſpeaking, he told me that he was very well pleas'd with our Arrival, and that he wou'd give notice of it to the King his Maſter; adding, that he was an excellent great and beneficent Prince; that he was a lover of Juſtice, and took particular Care

* This is to be underſtood on Account of the *French Eaſt-India* Company.

to

to ufe the *Europeans* well, and that we
fhou'd be fenfible of the Diftinction which
he wou'd make of a Nation fuch as ours.
We were ferv'd afterwards with *Coffee,*
which ended this firft Audience.

We went from thence to the *Banyân
Bira's* Houfe, who is the Interpreter (*b*) and
principal Factor of the *Europeans,* and we
took up our Lodging there for fome time.
Next Day, the Director of the *Dutch* Factory came to fee us, and invited us to Dinner.
We went there after returning his Vifit,
and he treated us very handfomely This
Factory is fettled there, becaufe the *Dutch*
fend every Year a Ship of feventy Tuns
from *Batavia* to *Moka,* to be loaded with
Coff.e and other Merchandizes of *Arabia,*
which they Tranfport from that firft Place.
Which is their general Magazine, and the
Depofitory of all the Merchandizes, in order to fend them into *Europe,* or to export them elfewhere into the *Indies* themfelves.

We began fome Days after to fpeak a-
bout Bufinefs, and to treat with the Go-

Vifits from the Dutch Director.

Treat with the Governour bout fettling a Trade.

(*b*) [The *French* Word is *Truchement,* which as well
as the *Englifh* Drugerman, is a Corruption of *Torjamân.*
as the *Turks* and *Arabs* exprefs the original *Syriac Targmân*]

F   vernour

vernour in reference to our Trade, which
fhou'd induce us to make a long Stay in
his Government. I fhall here give you the
Treaty which was made on this Occafion,
and which the Governour caus'd me to put
into Form, when the Conditions were agreed
upon on both Sides.

<table><tr><td>Article:
of Trade.</td><td></td></tr></table>

*A Treaty made between the Go-
vernour of* Moka, *and the
Captains of the* French *Ships,
the fixth of* January, 1709.

In the Name of (*a*) the moft Merciful God.

*Praife be to God the Lord of this Life and the
next,* Saleh Ebn Aly, *whom God preferve.*

His Seal is in this Place.

' **A**Fter the praife to God, who begins
his Difcourfe to Men, by giving
' praife to himfelf, to teach them to enter
' by that Gate of Praife, into whatever they
' begin ; and after rendring Thanks to him

(*a*) [The literal Senfe of the *Arabic alrahmâni 'lrahimi*
is *Clement and merciful,* as rendred in the *French,* but it
ftands for moft merciful always on this occafion.]

' **for**

‘ for his great Benefits, and having bless'd
‘ his holy Name, the Truth of his Promi-
‘ ses, and the Elevation of his Word and
‘ wish'd his Benedictions and his Salutati-
‘ ons upon his Prophets, who have truly ful-
‘ fill'd his Will, when they have directed his
‘ People in the right Way,

 ‘ We declare, that in the Year 1120,
‘ under the reign of our Master, the Prince
‘ of the Faithful (*a*) the Lord of the *Muffle-*
‘ *mans* (*b*) *Al Mohdi lidîni 'llah Ruvbi*
‘ *'àiamîna.* whom God protect, there
‘ have arriv'd in this Port, flourishing by the
‘ good Conduct of his Majesty, three Ships
‘ of the *French* Empire, according to the
‘ Account given by the illustrious Captains
‘ of the aforesaid Ships, who have demand-
‘ ed of us a Writing, which is left in their
‘ Hands, in manner of a Certificate ; thro'
‘ which they have had Confidence in us ;
‘ and on their side, they are to observe the
‘ Conditions which relate to them.

 (*a*) [*Amir al mumenin.*]
 (*c*) That is to say, the Conductor to the Religion of
God, Lord of the Worlds. [in the *French* it is of the two
Worlds, by mistaking the *dual àlamay·a,* for the plural
àlamîna, as it stands in the *Koran,* from whence the Expression is taken]

' I. They may have the Exercife of their
' Religion, in which they believe, both with
' regard to the Living and the Dead, which
' cannot be refus'd them : and, as it is the
' Cuftom.

" II. Their Shallops may load and un-
' load from Sun rife to Sun fet, but their
' Men muft always pafs the Night on board
' their Ships, or at the *Daka*, and may land
' and embark, except at high Tides, which
' hinders them from working, they may not
' land but with Permiffion.

' III. They may fet up their Flag on the
' Houfe where they lodge.

' IV. With regard to Merchandizes
' which they unload, they fhall be laid near
' the Gate *Alforfa*, until the *Land-Waiters*
' have notice of it, and from the Gate of
' *Alforfa*, they fhall be carry'd into their
' Houfes, and open'd according to the Cu-
' ftom towards Strangers.

' V. As to what regards the Cuftom-
' Houfe, they fhall pay three *per. Cent.* and
' only for thofe Merchandizes which fhall
' be fold, and whatever fhall come back
' again from *Ayn al mal*, fhall pay no
' Cuftom.

VI.

' VI. When they have occafion for the
' Shallops of *Beyt al mal* (*a*) they fhall
' pay for unloading two Piaftres, and for
' loading as much; and for the fmall (*b*)
' Oars one Piafter only.

' VII. And when they land, they fhall
' pay fo much a Man, as has been all along
' practis'd with regard to the like Perfons.

' VIII. If any of the Inhabitants of the
' Port of *Moka* infults any of them, we
' we fhall take care to do him juftice.

' IX. The Merchandizes fhall be put to
' the Account of the Broker, if they are fold
' in his Prefence, and with his Knowledge.
' We fhall take care to do juftice to thofe
' who revolt againft them, or who fhall
' become Bankrupt, or who fhall run away
' from them with any Goods, which they
' fhall have fold themfelves, without a
' Broker.

' X. And for as much as the Men of
' thefe three Ships, which have come di-
' rectly from their own Country, namely,
' Captain *Monfieur de la Merville*, and Cap-
' tain *Monfieur de Champloret le Brun*, are

(*a*) The Government's Shallops of fourteen Tons.
(*b*) Leffer Barks of feven Tons.

F 3   ' Guefts

' Guefts in the Country of *amir almu-*
' *menîn*] the Commander of the *Faithful,*
' Lord of the *Muflemans,* (*a*) *Chalîfa* of
' the Lord of the Prophets, *al mohdi li*
' *dîni 'llah Rabbi àlamina,* whom God
' preferve. And whereas they have ask'd of
' their own accord fome Favour, whereby
' they may be honour'd; we therefore
' grant them a fourth part of the Cuftoms
' of the Merchandizes which are in their
' Veffels, which they fhall land during this
' Year only. And at the Time this Writing
' was drawing up, they affurr'd us
' that they had inform'd the People of their
' Country, that they were exempted for
' this Year, from what fhall be landed or
' put on board them : For which reafon,
' we have regulated that Matter, both with
' regard to Loading and Unloading, for this
' Year only, becaufe they are the King's
' Guefts, on Condition that they forbear

(*a*) That is to fay, the Vicar or Lieutenant of their
falfe Prophet *Mohammed,* as well in Spirituals as Tempo-
rals. [*Chalifa* is us'd at prefent in this Senfe on the *Barbary* Coaft, and perhaps in other parts of the *Mohammedan* Dominions ; but the original Senfe, in which it was
us'd in the Perfon of *Abubecr,* the firft who bore that
Title, feems to have been that of Succeffor.]

' to

' to attack any of the Ships arriv'd in this
' happy Port, whatever they be Friends or
' Enemies; and that they do not affault the
' Nations, which are accuftom'd to fet up a
' Flag upon their Houfes; and that their
' Men commit no Infult to the Intendant
' of the Sea in the *Daka*; and at the
' Place where they take in Water from the
' other *Daka's*, the firft that comes fhall take
' in Water firft, and at the Scales the
' fame is to be obferv'd; the Rule for all thefe
' things being already known. They fhall
' alfo do Juftice upon fuch of their People
' as fhall infult any one; and if by chance
' their Ships happen to meet in the Road
' of *Moka*, with thofe of other Nations,
' the one fhall not be fuffer'd to infult the
' other; the Road being a facred Place,
' where there is the Security of God, and
' of the Commander of the *Faithful*, whom
' God preferve; for which reafon they are
' oblig'd to forbear, and it is for their Ho-
' nour. To conclude, when they depart
' they fhall fail out with Colours flying,
' Trumpets founding, and Guns firing, accor-
' ding to the Cuftom of other Nations;
' and if any of their Men efcape afhore,
' we fhall deliver him up; and if any of

' them

'them has a mind to change his Religion,
'we fhall not receive him till he has ob-
'tain'd the Confent of his Captains; and
'if any *Mufleman* or other is willing to
'make his Paffage in their Ships, they fhall
The 16
of *Jan.*
1709.
N. S.'convey him in Safety.   Written the 30th
'of the Month of *Zilcade* [*Thu 'lkaadah*]
'in the 1120th Year of the *Hegra* of the
'Prophet, to whom God give his Bene-
'diction.

Obligati-
on of the
French
Direct-
ors.'We the Directors of the Company
'Royal of *France*, promife the Lord
'*Sheich Saleb al Hareby*, Governour of
'this Town of *Moka*, that our three Ships
'which are in the Road, fhall not infult
'or offend any of thofe which belong to
'his Friends in the Red Sea, regarding him
'as our Allie and good Friend, and oblig-
'ing ourfelves to defend him, as he is ob-
'lig'd to defend us upon all Occafions. Gi-
'ven under our Hands and Seals at *Moka*,
'the 16th of *January*, 1709.

Both before and after the Conclufion of
this Treaty, I was very well receiv'd by the
Governour, and honour'd much with his
Confidence. Neverthelefs, when Mr. *de
Champloret*

Champloret and I had a mind to go to our
Ships, we were oblig'd to pay him a fort
of Compliment, at leaft to give him notice of it, according to the Ufage of the
Country with regard to Strangers, which
has been fettled in order to fecure the Duties of going out, (which are never paid till
one is on the point of departing,) and the
Debts contracted in the Country.

This Governour has under him in divers
Places, feven other Governours or Lieute-
nants; he is abfolute and exceeding rich,
being concern'd alfo in Trade. He pays
the King of *Taman* thirty thoufand Piaftres, which he levies upon the People, as
do the *Bafhas* in *Turky*.

For the reft, the Town of *Moka* (a) is
not fo confiderable as that of *Aden*, but is
become a greater Place for Trade; having
for fome time pafs'd very much diminifh'd
the Commerce of that Town. It does
not contain above ten thoufand Inhabitants,

None can leave the Place without giving the Gover- nour no- tice.

Gover- nour's Ju- rifdiction and Power.

Moka or Mokha defcrib'd.

(a) In *Ptolemy's* Table of *Arabia* tranflated by *John
Greaves* an Englifhman, the Port of *Mofcha* is plac'd in
Arabia Fœlix, and the Country of the *Adramitæ*, at 88,
30 Long, and 14 Latitude; the City *Moka* alfo is fet
down in *Arabia Petra*, whofe long is 67, 50, and Lat.
30, 10.

almoft

almoſt all of them *Mohammedans*, with
ſome few *Armenians*, and a great many
poor Jews in a ſeparate quarter, or a kind
of Suburbs without the Town ; they are all
of them a ſwarthy People, very well ſhap'd
and exceeding civil. The Town is ſurround-
ed with Walls, after the antient manner,
one half Stones and the other half Earth
work'd with Straw. It has four Gates without a Ditch, and ſeveral Towns with Canon
on each of them.

Towers with Canon.

Theſe Towers are inhabited by Soldiers, who patrole all the Night, and who
during the Day keep upon the Port, and in
the *Bazar*, to prevent Diſorders and Thie-
veries ; for in this Country they are very
zealous for the publick Quiet and good
Regulations: They bring the guilty Perſons before the Governour, who upon the
Report of an old Officer, who commands
his Guards, cauſes them to be puniſh'd ſe-
verely.

GoodRe-gulations.

All theſe Soldiers to the number of five
or ſix hundred, aſſemble every Day, from
Noon till two, in the great Place, to conduct the Governour to the *Mosk* [*Maſged*]
whither he goes with a great deal of State
and Preparation, accompany'd by his Sons,
and

Order of the Governour going to the Maſged.

and with all the confiderable Perfons there,
nobly mounted, caufing the Colours of the
King, and thofe of *Mobammed* and *Aly*
to be carry'd at the found of Kettle drums.
Coming from the *Mosk* [*Mafged*] all
the Infantry make a Difcharge, and always
with Ball ; which oblig'd the Governour
one Day, who in his Paffage perceiv'd me
upon the Terras of our Lodge, to fend one
to defire me from him to retire, for fear of
any Accident.

The Women, excepting a fmall number of the common fort, never appear in
the Day in the Streets of *Moka*. In the
Evening they have a little more Liberty,
which confifts in vifiting one another: By
this means we have met the Governour's
Wives, fometimes at one a Clock at Night,
going from one Houfe to another, lighted
only by one Link, carry'd by a Slave, and
follow'd by their Women. When they
find any Men in their way, they immediately range themfelves all on the fame fide
againft the Houfes, to let them pafs, obferving Silence and a great deal of Modefty.

Their Cloathing is much the fame with
that of the Women of the Eaft in general,

Women
never ap-
pear but
at their
Evening
Vifits.

ral, whofe Habits are defcrib'd by Travellers; having over all a great Veil of a fine colour'd Cloath, which hides their Faces without hindring them from feeing through them; they wear alfo little *Spanifh* Leather Buskins.

Hand-
fome.

There are among the better fort of People very handfome Perfons, who are not fwarthier than the *Spaniards,* with very fine Features, capable of infpiring Love. It may alfo be imagin'd that they are neither unfociable or infenfible, by what happen'd to us at *Moka.* The Digreffion, if it be one, fhall not be tedious.

Story of
the
Captain's
Gallan-
tries with
the *Ara-
bian* La-
dies.

After I had ftaid for fometime at the Houfe of the *Banyán Bira,* I took one in the Town: I had for my Neighbour a young *Arabian* Lord, whofe Father had feveral times been on Embaffies for the King of *Yaman.* Our Houfes were feparated only by a Court, both belonging to the fame Landlord, who was a great Merchant of *Surat.* All the Windows of this Houfe were grated in the form of Latices, which open'd, after the manner of the Country, with a jutting out. There the Women us d to come and place themfelves in the Evening, as in a fort of Balcony, to take the
fresh

frefh Air; they fat upon Cufhions either working at fomething, or reading
Romances. At the beginning, the Ladies
hid themfelves with a great deal of care,
and never open'd their Latice; but feven
or eight of our Voluntiers, young Men of
good Families, which I took on board my
Ship, and whom I caus'd to lodge with me
in the fame Houfe, for greater Security,
took a fancy to divert the Evening in the
Court, when every one was retir'd, and
the firft Gate of the Paffage fhut, which
was always done early. This Diverfion confifted in Dancing and Singing, which they
practis'd frequently under the Window of
thofe Ladies. This was enough to bring
them to be fociable.

At firft they open'd the Latice a little,
as if to fee the Dancers better, and afterwards they open'd them quite. Prefently
the Ladies were heard finging the fame
Tune, and, to fhew the thing pleas'd them,
they clap'd their Hands often At length
they danc'd themfelves, to the found of one
of their little Drums, accompany'd with a
very agreeable Tune. Thus accuftom'd by *Arab*
little and little to fee Strangers, and to be ^tune a-
feen, their Latice was fet open in the Day ^greeable

time,

time; fo that from our Terras, which was
a Story lower than that of their Houfe, we
cou'd fee every thing which was done in
their Appartment, which was level with it.

I had caus'd a little Lodge to be made
upon that Terras, and cover'd with Mats,
that I might have more of the frefh Air
than I had in the Houfe, where I was almoft ftifl'd with the Heat. I cou'd eafily
obferve that thofe Ladies were four in number, the oldeft of which was Miftrefs of
the Houfe, and was not above twenty five,
very well fhap'd, tho' a little too full. The
three others were younger, and fhe, which
was the youngeft of them, appear'd to be
not above fourteen or fifteen. They were
all very handfome; and. in that fmall number, there was one to be diftinguifh'd, which
eclips'd all the reft.

That Lady appear'd oftener at the Window
than her Companions, and affected much to
fhew her felf. She appear'd one Day with
her Head drefs'd up, her Hair curl'd and fet
with Ribbons. She had on a Flame colour'd
Silk, and turn'd herfelf firft on one fide,
and then on the other, that fhe might be
obferv'd. Some time after fhe went and
put on another Suit, which fhe came to
fhew

Airs of a
young
Arabian
Lady at
her Win-
dow.

ſhew in the ſame manner. This ſhe repeated no leſs than five times, appearing ſtill finer and finer. The laſt time ſhe put a Ribbon on her Head, and, advancing her Hand towards the Side where I was, gave me to underſtand, by ſeveral Signs which ſhe made, that ſhe lik'd that ſort beſt. Afterwards ſhe ſtrok'd up her Arms with her Hand, affecting to ſhew them as far as her Elbows, and adding ſeveral pretty Motions with her Fingers, which paſs in that Country for ſo many Marks of Eſteem and Friendſhip. To end the ſcene, this pretty Creature went to put on her firſt Habit, and appear'd once more at the Same Window, with a little Girl of ſix or ſeven Years of Age, her Countenance always pleaſant and agreeable.

I was then lying on the Bed to reſt, very much incommoded with a Diſorder to which Strangers are pretty ſubject, when the great Heats come on. But to anſwer in ſome meaſure ſo many Gallantries, I caus'd to be brought to me a *China* Cabinet, fill'd with little Curioſities, out of which I took ſome Ribbons and Fans, which I ſhew'd that Lady, which, by reaſon of the nearneſs

and

and difpofition of the Houfes, was no difficult matter.

Great
Decorum
and Po-
litenefs of
a Child.
At the fight of them fhe leap'd for Joy,
and immediately fent me by a Slave the
little Girl, who had only a Court to crofs,
entring by a little Door which made the
Communication, which I had not obferv'd
before. I receiv'd her with all the Carref-
fes imaginable. She was very neatly drefs'd,
and taught to make her Compliments,
which fhe did very well. I fhew'd her firft
the *China* Cabinet, and all that was in the
Drawers. She feem'd moft taken with a
very neat Fan, finely gilt, and a Gold Ribbon, the Ground of which was blue, which
I gave her. After which, I fhew'd her by
degrees all the Appartment, which was
pretty neatly furnifh'd. Nothing pleas'd her
fo much as the illuminated Prints, which
reprefent the Royal Family, and all the
Court of *France*, with which I had adorn'd
my Chamber; and the Ceiling with the
King's Arms, fet out with a large Border
of blue Cloth, ftrew'd with Flowers de Luce.
She did not fail alfo to look at herfelf in
two great Looking-Glaffes, and carefully
to examine a Toilet edg'd with Gold Lace,
and a Buffet, in which there ftood a good

deal

deal of Plate; in fhort, all the Moveables, and efpecially the Chairs, which they know not the ufe of in this Country, were Matter of Admiration to this Child. I wou'd have had her reft herfelf upon Cufhions laid on purpofe, with *Turky* Carpets, for the People of the Country; but fhe cou'd not leave off admiring, and I had much ado to get her to eat fome Comfeits.

At length fhe took her Leave of me, with Compliments and a Politenefs which furpriz'd me. The Slave inform'd me, that fhe was the Daughter of the principal Lady of the Appartment. I gave that Slave a Pot of preferv'd Cloves, after the *Indian* manner, for the Lady who had fhewn herfelf to me a little before drefs'd, as I have defcrib'd, which the Slave underftood very well.

The little Girl was fcarce got back again, before I heard great Acclamations and Expreffions of Thanks feveral Times repeated. After which, the Lady beforemention'd appear'd feveral times at the Window, holding her Fan open, and fignifying feveral ways the Joy which fhe had conceiv'd. Some Days after, that pretty Creature growing daily more fociable, came to the Window

Young Lady appears again at the Window.

G   of

a Chamber which join'd our Terras, and very obligingly gave me, acrofs the wooden Bars, a handful of little white Flowers, much efteem'd in *Arabia*, which have much of the fmell and form of the *Spanifh* Jafmin.

Here ended all the Gallantries between thofe Ladies and me. 'Tis true, that being well acquainted with the Lord who liv'd in this Houfe, whom I vifited two or three times a Week, I took the Liberty one Evening to go fee him, juft as the Ladies were come from vifiting in the Town: I found them in the Entry, and Compliments were begun on both Sides, when that Lord enter'd, who with a Word only made them retire very quick, treating me at the fame time with his ufual Civility.

Country about *Moka*.

After giving you an account of the Town of *Moka* and its Inhabitants, I muft tell you that the Country in general is very dry, having no Water but what is brackifh, and almoft Salt, as is almoft all the Water near the *Red-Sea*; but the Territory of *Moka* is the worft of all: It is fubject to an ex-ceffive Heat, and there fcarce ever falls any Rain; infomuch, that, for two Years before our Arrival, there had not fallen a Drop. And it is as hot in the Month of *January*,

Great Heat.

as

as it is ordinarily at *Paris* in *July*. Nevertheless, the People of the Country, accustom'd to still greater Heats in *June* and *July*, when the South Wind blows, sometimes say it's cold, and the best to pass among them wear a Cloth Vest, which they do not leave off ordinarily before *March*. It rain'd twice during that Month while we staid there. We observ'd also, that, about nine or ten in the Morning, there blew a North Wind from the Sea, which refresh'd very much, without which there wou'd be no enduring the Heat; for one sweats very much without doing any Exercise.

One sees without *Moka* some Palm-trees planted in the Sand, which they take care to water, by means of Pits they have dug, and which bear Dates in abundance. There also comes up Millet in some places, which is very white, and three times larger than ours. After the Rain, the earth is cover'd with a sort of salt Crust; that which they make use of in the Country is made almost without any trouble, by means of Trenches and Drains which receive the Water of the Sea, at spring Tides; and the Salt hardens in them to that degree, that in order to take it out, they are oblig'd to break it as if it was stone with Pick-axes. G 2 LET-

(margin note: Palm-trees.)

(margin note: Salt.)

LETTER IV.

A Continuation of the fame Subject, together with fome Hiſtorical Obſervations relating to the Deſcendants of the falſe Prophet [Mohammed] and the Sharîfs of Mekka and Medina.

SHALL now Sir reſume the Subjeƈt of our Voyage, relating to the Buying, the Carriage and Loading of *Coffee*, which we were to bring into *Europe.* But firſt it is neceſſary, before we go any further, to make you acquainted with the Country which produces a Plant ſo much belov'd, and which one goes ſo far in queſt of.

General Deſcription of *Arabia.*

Arabia in general, as every one knows, is that vaſt Country which extends from

the

the *Streight* of the *Red-Sea,* as far as the Gulf or Bay of *Perſia,* and from the eaſtern Ocean, or the great Sea of the *Indies,* to the Frontiers of *Syria, Paleſtine* and *Ægypt,* forming the greateſt Peninſula in the whole World. Every one knows alſo the ordinary Diviſion of this Country into three *Arabias,* which are the *Deſert,* the *Stoney,* and the *Happy:* a Diviſion which has not been follow'd by the oriental Geographers and Hiſtorians, who have divided *Arabia* into ſeveral Kingdoms and Regions or Provinces, which are at preſent poſſeſs'd by particular Kings and Princes, who are dependent neither on the Grand Seignior, nor the King of *Perſia.*

One of the moſt conſiderable of theſe Kingdoms is that of *Yaman;* it contains the greateſt part of the Country, which has been nam'd the *Happy Arabia.* This Country extends eaſtward along the Coaſt of the Sea from *Aden* as far as Cape *Ras al gat,* that is to ſay, from one Gulf to the other. One part of the *Red-Sea* bounds it on the Weſt and South ſide; and the Kingdom or Country of *Hegaz,* which belongs to the Sharîf of *Mekka,* is its northern Boundary.

Kingdom of *Yaman.*

G 3   The

The Kingdom of *Yaman* only, exclusive
of all the other parts of *Arabia*, produces
the *Coffee* Tree; nor is it found there in
any plenty except in three principal Quarters, which are those of *Betelfaguy*, *Se-
nan* or *Sanaa*, and *Galbany*, taking their
Names from three Towns which are in the
Mountains, and of which, *Sanaa* passes for
the Capital of the whole Country. 'Tis
true, 'that from the Mountains proceed all
the Agreeableness, Plenty, and Riches of
the Kingdom of *Yaman*; for, as I have already observ'd, all that lies along the Sea
Coast, is nothing but a dry flat Shore, almost quite barren, which in some Places
is ten or twelve Leagues in breadth, but
which, to make amends, is bounded by these
Mountains which, besides the *Coffee*, produce many other Trees and Fruit in abundance; and where, in short, is to be found
wholsome Water, an agreeable fresh Air,
and almost a continual Spring.

It was in our Power, when we were at
Coffee of
Sanaa and
Galbany
not so
good as
that of
*Betelfa-
guy.* *Aden*, to have loaded ourselves with *Coffee*
of *Sanaa* and *Galbany*, which are pretty
near at hand: But they are not so much
esteem'd or enquir'd after, as those of *Betelfaguy*. This Consideration and the hopes

of finding *Coffee* cheaper, made us go to
Moka, where after we had concluded our
Treaty with the Governour, and provided
every thing which concern'd the safety of
our Ships, we went to *Betelfaguy* to settle
a House there also for our Trade, and transf-
port our *Coffee* to it, which might be carry'd by land from that Town to *Moka*.

 Betelfaguy lies from *Moka* about thirty *Betelfa-*
five Leagues drawing towards the bottom *guy.*
of the *Red-Sea*, from which it is ten
Leagues distant. We made two small Days
Journey of it along the Foot of the Mountains, and about two thirds of the Way we
found the Town of *Zebit.*

 Zebit or *Zebide*, where we usually lay, *Zebid.*
appears to have been formerly great and
considerable. There is almost no Water in
the Town, tho' some Geographers describe
a River by it. 'Tis true that all along that
Road one finds divers little Bridges, which
serve for a Passage to the Brooks, or rather
Torrents, which at certain times fall from
the Mountains, but which never arrive at
the sea, loosing themselves in the burning
Sands which are on that side.

 The Town of *Betelfaguy*, tho' bigger *Betelfa-*
than *Moka*, is in the same Government, *guy* in the
     G 4   the *Govern-*
              ment of
              Moka.

the Governour of *Moka* fending a Lieutenant thither, who takes alfo the Title of
Governour. It is beautify'd with very fair
Mosks [Masgeds] the high Towers or
Menâras of which are whiten'd, as well
without as within. The Houfes are of
Brick, one and two Stories high, with Terraffes. The Town has no Walls, but, at a
Musket-fhot diftance, one fees a very pretty
Caftle, where there is no other Water but
that of Wells, which are exceeding deep·
the Water of which, being drawn out by
means of Camels, fmokes when it is taken
up as if it boil'd, fo that there is no drinking it immediately ; but, letting it ftand all
Night, it becomes the beft and moft re-
frefhing Liquor that can be.

Large Ba-
zar or
Market
for *Coffee.*

There is in this Town a very large Bazar, or Market for *Coffee*, which confifts
of two great Courts with cover'd Galleries.
Hither the *Arabs* of the Plain come to
fetch away their *Coffee* in great Sacks,
made of Mats, loading two upon each
Camel. The Merchants, who have a mind
to buy, employ *Banyâns*, People who
perform in *Arabia* all the Functions of
Jews in *Turky*, and Brokers in *Europe*,
efpe-

especially for the *Coffee* Trade, which they underftand perfectly well.

In the middle of the *Bazar* there ftands a Diwan or Sofa, rais'd about four Foot from the Ground, where the Officers of the Cuftoms, and fometimes the Governour in Perfon fit upon Carpits. Thefe Officers keep an account of the Weight and Price of all the *Coffee* which is fold in their Prefence, in order to collect the King's Tax. The Weighers make ufe of great Scales, and for Weights huge Stones wrap'd up in Cloth.

All the Tax upon *Coffee* is paid by the Seller only, at the Rate of one Sol out of every Piaftre that it is fold for; and the Purchafe muft always be paid down upon the Nail, the *Arabs* of the Villages giving no Credit. Payment is made in Piaftres of *Mexico*, thofe of *Peru* and *Seville* not paffing, fince the *Portugals*, as they fay, mix'd falfe Pieces with them of the fame fort; which they have not yet forgot. They alfo take Shekins of Gold.

They daily bring *Coffee* to *Betelfaguy* from the Mountains, which are but three Leagues diftant. The Market is held there every Day, except on Fridays, when the

Gover

[marginal notes:] Tax paid by the Seller only.

Money current.

Governour and the Cuftom-houfe Officers go to the Mosk [Mafged] in the Afternoon, accompany'd by their Officers and Soldiers, carrying the Colours of *Mohammed,* and and thofe of the King. The Peafants have the Trick of bringing no *Coffee* to Market, when the Price is not that which they like.

Coffee bought up there. 'Tis at *Betelfaguy* that the *Coffee* is bought up, which fupplies all *Turky.* The Merchants of *Egypt* and *Turky* repair thither for that end, and, loading a great Quantity of it upon Camels, each of which carries two Bales of 270 Pound weight each, to a little Port on the *Red-Sea,* in much the fame Latitude, ten Leagues diftant. There they put it a board fmall Veffels, which carry it one hundred and fifty Leagues farther up in the Gulf to another very confiderable Port, call'd *Gedda,* or *Zieden,* which is properly the Port of *Mekka.*

Whither tranfported. At this Port, the *Coffee* is again fhifted on board *Turkifh* Ships, which carry it to *Sues,* the laft Port at the end of the *Red-Sea,* belonging to the Grand Signior, from whence it is tranfported by Camels into *Egypt,* and the other Provinces of the *Turkifh* Empire, by different Carawans, or by the *Mediterranean* Sea ; and it is, in

fhort,

fhort from *Ægypt*, that all the *Coffee* confum'd in *France* was brought, to the time
that we undertook the Voyage to *Arabia*.

The Purchafe which we made rais'd the
Rates of *Coffee* every Day ; the arrival of
our Ships at *Moka*, having befides rais'd
the Price of it, which was ftill encreas'd
by the Quantities which were bought up
at the fame time for *Ægypt* and *Turky*.

And, with regard to the Price in general, Price of
things are much changed from what they *Coffee*
much
were, and it is eafy to fee that the Con- rais'd.
fumption of *Coffee* was never fo great as it
is at prefent ; for, not above twenty five Years
ago, the *Bohor* of *Betelfaguy*, which is a
Weight of feven hundred and fifty Pounds
of *France*, went for ten or twelve Piaftres,
which coft at prefent one hundred and fifteen Piaftres, and fometimes more.

But to return to *Moka*, which was always the Place of my Refidence, as having
the Direction of the principal Affairs during
the whole time our Ships continued in that
Road. I had defir'd of Mr. *Champloret* to
make his Abode at *Betelfaguy*, for the
better convenience of Buying and Sending
the *Coffee* by Land, from one Town to the
other. I was always very well with the
Gover-

Governour, with whom I took great care to cultivate a Friendſhip in favour of our Trade, and eſpecially with a view to make our Piaſtres of _Peru_ current, of which we had a good Quantity. He invited me often to come to ſee him at the Cuſtom-houſe, where he uſually went in the Morning, cauſing all the Merchandizes to paſs before him, and deſiring me to chuſe what I lik'd.

Adven-
tnre.
at _Moka_
with _Sidy_
Moham-
med. Nevertheleſs there happen'd an Affair which had like to have ſpoil'd all, and broken the good Underſtanding which was between us. The _Italian_ Fathers, which often ſerv'd me for interpreters, had introduc'd a Merchant of the Town to my Houſe, named _Sidy Mo-_ _hammed_, who became our Friend, and ac-cuſtom'd himſelf to drink our Wine. He paſs'd for a rich Man, and one that had great Knowledge in Trade. He made me an Offer one Day by the Fathers, to help me to the beſt _Coffee_ in the Country, which he wou'd cauſe to be bought upon the ſpot, without coſting me any thing but what I laid out for the Goods, provided I furniſh'd him with Money, which he was not in a Con-dition to advance.

That

That very Day I fent him two thoufand five hundred Piaftres, intreating him to difpatch Perfons to the Mountain, and employ that Sum according to his Promife. He fent indeed to make his Markets, which having given me an account of, I was fo eafy as to let him have fix thoufand Piaftres more : But I expected to be fo much the greater Gainer. After long Expectation, there came a fmall Quantity of *Coffee*, and that very ill cleans'd, fo that confequently it was fubject to very great Wafte ; not to mention feveral Bales which were perfect Refufe.

Ill fatisfy'd with this proceeding, and ftill more vext to fee the *Coffee* did not come as was promis'd for my Money, I began, with good Reafon, to diftruft fome foul Play, which made me confider of the beft Method to take, to help me out of the Scrape. I was well perfuaded of the Juftice of the Governour ; but, as the Cafe ftood, I had reafon to fear a Reproach from him, for having acted without his Knowledge, which in fome meafure excluded me from the Guarantee provided by our Treaty. On the other fide, by taking the Method of fuing him, I gave my Debtor Time

and

and Means to invent Contrivances to pro-
tract the Bufinefs, and it may be an Inclination to quit the Country. In this Perplexity, and continuing every Day to be
amus'd by him, I took this Courfe at
laft.

Captain
detains
Sidy Mo-
hammed.

I fent to defire the *Banyân Bira,* whom
the Governour had affign'd me, as a Man
whom I cou'd confide in, to be my Broker,
to come to my Houfe accompany'd by *Sidy*
Mohammed. They both came in the Evening; I caus'd him to be told by the *Banyân*
himfelf, that fince, after fo long Expectation,
he had not fent me the *Coffee* as he had promis'd, I wou'd pofitively have my Money
back again without waiting one Moment,
or that he fhou'd remain as a Pledge in my
Houfe, till the whole was paid, or he had
given me fufficient Security. Then, directing
my Difcourfe to the *Banyân,* I ask'd him,
if he cou'd engage for it? But the *Banyân*
excus'd himfelf, defiring me not to intangle
him in that Affair. Sometime after Supper was ferv'd up, during which time they
never ceas'd looking at each other, and now
and then fpoke together, I offer'd Wine
to *Mohammed,* who had no Inclination to
drink; contrary to his Cuftom.

After

After Supper we all enter'd into Discourse again, the result of which was, that *Mohammed* resolving on nothing, and the *Banyan Bira* not being able, as he said, to quit him with Honour, for fear he shou'd accuse him of Treachery. They sent Home for what they wanted, in order to pass the Night at my House. I call'd for the Key of the great Gate of the Entry, and plac'd Guards in the Chamber, where they lay, and where I understood they were very uneasy all the Night.

The *Banyân Bira* stays for Company.

Next day we argu'd further about the Matter, without doing any thing to the purpose; so that *Bira* was oblig'd to go about his Affairs, and *Mohammed* remain'd under a Guard of two Men, which I plac'd upon him. About nine a Clock, the *Amir al bahr* and the King's Merchant came to pay me a Visit; I sent for my Interpreter, and, after some Discourse, they told me, they had heard of my arresting *Sidy Mohammed*, desiring me to let them know the Occasion of it.

Visit from the *Amir al bahr.*

It was very easy to see that they had been already well instructed by the *Banyân*, and that they came from the Governour. I thereupon sent for my Debtor before them, and

gave

gave them a brief History of the Affair.
They heard me with a great deal of Patience, and afterwards, with that Moderation
and Gravity which are so natural to those
People, the *Amir al bahr* made me a
long Speech, the Purport of which was,
That this manner of acting was violent, and
altogether unusual in their Country; that
the Governour had the more reason to be
surpriz'd, as he was a just Man, and sufficiently in my Interest; that in this Action
I wounded exceedingly his Authority, being the first Minister of Justice, to whom
only it belong'd to have Prisons, and to
commit thither the Subjects of the King his
Master; that in short I was wanting in the
Obligations I ow'd him for his kind Offices,
and made an ill Return for all the Civilities he had shew'd me.

His smart Remon-strance.

I knew very well, that the Action was
rash, and the Affair very nice; but the Difficulty I was plung'd in made me take that
Course: wherefore I answer'd off hand
to this Effect. I began by praising the
Governor, and acknowledging the Obligations I ow'd him, adding, that, far from in-
fringing his Authority, I was going to him
to give an Account of the Affair just as
they

Captain's Apology.

they came in, defiring them to inform him rightly of it, till I had the Audience which I was going to demand of him, not thinking it proper .to difturb him at fo late an Hour.

Thefe Reafons which, as you may fee, were weak enough, did not hinder the Envoys from replying, that I ought not to fail fending my Prifoner to the Governour, who certainly would do me true and fpeedy Juftice. Then, being fatisfy'd of the Boldnefs of the Action, and loath to let go my Security, I reply'd, that I was fenfible what they told me was Fact, but that unluckily happen'd, in this Affair, that the Moment the Perfon in Queftion was arrefted, in the Houfe of the * Royal Company of France, I had neither the Power nor Authority to let him go, till all the Money which belong'd to that Company was brought in again, unlefs I paid it my felf for the Debtor; that befides it was one of the Privileges of the fame Company, infeparable from the Superiority and Liberty of the *French* Nation ; a Privilege acknowledg'd and put in practice in all the Places of the Eaft,

* Always with regard to the Company of the *Indies*, &c.

H   where

where they have Houſes to arreſt their Deb-
tors without any Formality; that it was
in my Power, according to that Uſage, to
have ſent Soldiers to ſearch for *Sidy Mohammed*, but that 1 had manag'd Matters
otherwiſe, out of regard to the Governour
and the Country; and that in ſhort, no one
cou'd take it ill that I made uſe of our Privileges on ſo important an Occaſion.

As we were the firſt *French* Men that
had arriv'd in *Arabia* by the *Red-Sea*, on
account of Trade, and that with our great
Ships, our Houſes, and all our Equipage,
we made a very good Figure in the Country, they did not think fit to diſpute with
me the Privilege which I alledg'd; on the
contrary, I believe thoſe Perſons took great
notice of it. But, becauſe the Authority of the
Governour was expos'd, which was the thing
that gave them moſt Concern, the two
Envoys, after arguing the Caſe a full Hour,
deſir'd me to take themſelves for Bail.

I foreſaw this Propoſal, and without
looſing that Preſence of Mind, of which
they ſet me an Example, I anſwer'd without heſſitating, that I knew very well the
Value of ſuch Security, but that, looking
on the Perſon in my Houſe from thence

forth

forth as ready Money; he cou'd in no fort
be let go, till the Company was paid every
Farthing; that, in cafe it was not paid, I
wou'd carry him into *France* to the fame
Company, who wou'd approve of my
Conduct.

This Declaration feem'd to baulk all their
Meafures; I eafily perceiv'd they were
piqu'd at it. They got up, faying they
wou'd go to the Governour, in hopes that
if he wou'd give me his Word that I fhou'd
be paid without delay, and take the whole
Affair upon himfelf, I wou'd not affront
him fo much as to refufe him.

I thought then it was high time to yield
a little, which I did, by faying, that I re-
fpected the Governour too much to refufe
him any thing, and that I depended upon
the exact Performance of his Word, the
more for having already engag'd, that all
our Creditors in general fhou'd pay us before we departed.

The Negotiators return'd fhortly after, *Gover-*
bringing with them the Commander of the *nour of*
Governour's Troops, who faluted me, and *Moka en-*
defir'd me in his Name to fend him my *gages for*
Debtor, giving me his Word, that in ten *the Debt.*
Days at furtheft I fhou'd be paid all, either

H 2   in

in Merchandize, or otherwife.   The *Amir al bahr* and the King's Merchant told me the fame thing, adding, that they wou'd become Security jointly with the Governour, which appear'd to me more than fuffi- cient, knowing the Probity of the Gover- nour, whom befides it was much my In- tereft to oblige.

Sidy Mo-hammed deliver'd up.

I then deliver'd my Prifoner into their Hands ; the Commander put him under a Guard of four Soldiers ; and they all left my Houfe, carrying him to the Governour's Palace.   I underftood at firft, that they put him in Prifon and in Irons, and that af- terwards he had been baftinado'd on the Soles of his Feet.   Neverthelefs the Go- vernour's Word was foon difcharged ; for in eight or nine Days, that the unhappy *Mohammed* lay in Prifon, thofe who ne- gotiated his Releafe at my Houfe, got to-

And the Debt clear'd.

gether the Coffee themfelves, and fent me as much as came to the whole Money, or very near it : And thus, with a little Ma- nagement and Refolution, I got out of this Affair, which was pretty nice, both with regard to Honour and Intereft.

A Shàrif of Mekka fled for Refuge to Mokha.

During our Stay at *Moka*, we faw one of the Sharifs of *Mekka*, of the Race of of the falſe Prophet *Mohammed*, who was fled for Refuge to the King of *Taman*, after loſing the Battle which he gave the other Sharif, his near Relation, who remain'd Maſter of all the Countiy. The King had aſſign'd him 100 Crowns a Day for his Maintenance, and the Town of *Moka* for the Place of his Abode; the whole Attendance of this diſpoſſeſs'd Prince was twenty Men, well mounted; he was cloath'd in Green, with a Turban of the ſame Colour, the Ends of which were ſtitch'd with Gold, and adorn'd with a Fringe of the ſame. We ſaw him often go to the Mosk [*Meſgid*] with his ſlender Retinue, cauſing the Standard of *Mohammed* to be carry'd before him, and affecting an extraordinary Gravity. He alſo went ſometimes to a kind of Chappel, which ſtands without *Moka*, where they ſay there are Prophets bury'd. The People go thither in great Devotion, and ſtop on the Road to pray at the Tombs, which are out of the Town.

The Sharif ſtaid five Months at *Moka*; Oblig'd to at the end of which time the Sharif of depart. *Mekka* let the King know, that if he continued to give ſhelter to his Enemy, he

H 3   would

wou'd carry the War into his Country.
This was enough to caufe the unhappy
Sharif to depart out of his Territories.
We faw him leave *Moka*, accompany'd by
much People of Diftinction of the Town,
to feek an Afilum further off.

Captain
freedfrom
feveral
Prejudi-
ces rela-
ting to
*Moham-
medifm*
and *Ara-
bia.*

As *Arabia* is the Country which gave
birth to *Mohammedifm*, one has a better
Opportunity of being inform'd there than
elfewhere, relating to feveral Points of Hiftory and Religion which concern it ; and
I can affirm that I got rid in that Country
of feveral falfe Prejudices touching the
fame: I have made, efpecially on Occafion
of the aforefaid difgrac'd and fugitive Sharif, two Obfervations, which none, it may
be, will be offended to find here.

The firft is, that it is an Error among the
greateft part of *Europeans*, an Error which
is alfo to be found in very good Authors,
that the grand Seignor is the Sovereign of
Mekka and *Medina* ; and that the Sharifs,
that is, the Princes of the Race of *Mohammed*, who command there, are only Governours or tributary Vaffals.

Shàrifs of
Mekka
and *Medi-
na* inde-
pendent.

It is true, the *Turks* having deftroy'd the
Empire of the *Chalifas*, and fucceeded
them by right of Conqueft, the *Soltàn* has
alfo

allo fucceeded to the Dignity, and all the *The Sol-*
Authority of the antient *Chalifas* (*a*), the *tán* of the
Turks ac-
firft Succeffors of *Mohammed*, a very emi- know-
ledg'd
nent Quality, which conftitutes him Head *Chalifa* by
of the Religion and the Empire, and which *Moham-*
medans.
is acknowledg'd to be in him by the four
principal Sects of *Mohammedifm.*

But it is alfo true, that upon the Decay *Shârifs of*
and Divifion of that Empire, the Race of *the Race*
of Mo-
the pretended Prophet preferv'd the Sove- *hammed.*
reignty and Poffeffion of thofe two famous
Towns, and of the Country where they
are fituate, without Oppofition from the
other *Mohammedan* Princes, or being de-
pendant on any one. On the contrary,
the moft powerful among thofe Princes
have an exceeding great Veneration for the
Sharifs, and the Places which they poffefs;
fending them often Offerings and confiderable Prefents. Befides, in the Titles which
they give themfelves, and which are, as eve-

(*a*) [It is not to be underftood here of the *Chalifas* of
Baghdad, whofe Empire was deftroy'd by *Hulaku* the
Tatar in 1258, but of the *Chalifas* of *Egypt*, the laft of
whom upon the Conqueft of that Kingdom by *Soltân*
Selim, in the Year of the *Hejrah* 922, *Ann. Dom.* 1516,
was carry'd to *Conftantinople*, which put an end to the
Chalifas of the Family of *Abbas.*]

ry body knows very haughty, they take only the humble Quality of the Servants of the two facred Towns of *Mekka* and *Medina*; which in particular is true, with regard to the grand Seignor, who assumes also the Quality of Protector of the *Holy Jerusalem*, of which he is indeed the Lord and Master, which sufficiently shews the Difference there is between those two Cities with relation to him.

Descended from *Fâtema*.

In short, this Race of the Children of the Prophet, to speak like the Orientals, draws its Original from *Fâtema*, the Daughter of *Mohammed*, the Wife of *Aly*, by whom he had two Sons, *viz. Haffan* and *Huffein*, who have founded two great Houses in *Mahommedifm*, and who are the Fathers of all the Sharifs or Descendants of *Mohammed*, which are at present in the World.

Branches of the House of *Haffan*.

The House of *Haffan* has been divided into two principal Branches, the first of which remain'd in *Arabia*, and has given Kings or Soverejgns to *Mekka* and *Meaina*. The second Branch pass'd into *Africa*, and has given Birth to the Kings of *Morocco*, and to the other Sharifs, which are in that Quarter of the World.

I say

I fay nothing in this Place of the Houfe or the Defcendants of *Huffein*, the fecond Son of *Fâtema*, which are, according to the Orientals, the prefent Kings of *Perfia*, and the other Sharifs of *Afia*, becaufe that does not belong to my Subject, which is confin'd to the Sharifs of *Arabia* only.

Neverthelefs, tho' the eldeft Branch, of the Houfe of *Haffan*, has multiply'd into numberlefs Houfes, or different Families, in *Arabia*; there never were but four principal Houfes, which have reign'd at *Mekka* and *Medina*, which are thofe of *Banu Cayder* or *Kader, Banu Muffatany*, otherwife *Banu Haffan, Banu Hafhem*, and *Banu Kitada*.

Four Houfes that have reign'd at *Mekka* and *Medina*.

The Sheriff who reigns at prefent at *Mecca*, is of this laft Houfe, which, as they pretend, has held the Dominion above five hundred Years; and he who reigns at *Medina*, is of the Houfe of *Banu Hafhem*, which reign'd alfo at *Mecca* before that of *Banu Kitada*.

Prefent Sharif of *Mekka* of the Family of *Kitada*.

But this laft being yet multiply'd and divided into many other Branches, the Kindred, which is among all the Sharifs of the fame Houfe, becomes often a Subject of Difcord;

cord; they take Arms one againſt the other
for the Sovereignty, and wage cruel Wars.

Sometimes Diſcord ariſes between the
two Sharifs themſelves, who reign at
Mekka and *Medina*; they make War upon each other, and all is in Confuſion in
their Dominions.

Soltán of the *Turks* interpoſes to ſettle Differences between the Shârifs. Then the grand Seignor in Quality of
Sharif, never fails to take cognizance of
their Differences, to talk to the Sharifs with
Reſolution, and ſometimes to fix by force
one Sharif in the Place of another: But
this favour'd Prince muſt always be of the
reigning Family, all the Authority of the
Soltán not being able to interrupt that ſettled Order.

There is one famous Example of thoſe
civil Wars, between the Sharifs of *Mekka*
and *Medina*, and of the part which the
Grand Seignor acted in it, which deſerves
to be related. I was furniſh'd with it by a
Perſon, exceeding well vers'd in the oriental Languages and Hiſtories, who gave me
alſo the Tranſlation of the Piece which
treats of it, in the following Words.

His Letter to the Shârifs who were at War. *Praiſe be to God. when the Kings of
the two ſacred Cities made War upon each
other,*

other, after several Battles, in which the Blood of the Moslemans *was spilt in their Quarrel : The News of it came to the Prince of the true Believers,* Othoman, *whom God assists, who wrote them this Letter.* —— After giving Praise to God, and saluting the Kings of the two sacred Cities, *it goes on.* —— *Children of the House of the Prophet, know that good Works are good of themselves, but that when they are done by the Children of the House of the Prophet, they become more pure and excellent. And, on the contrary, Iniquities are evil in themselves, but when they proceed from the Children of the House of the* Prophet, *they are still more pernicious and criminal. I conjure ye then, by the holy Temple of God, by the sacred Angel, and by the* Makâm, *or Habitation of* Abraham, *to put an end to this scandalous Indecency, and to withdraw yourselves towards your Grandfather; if not, I will draw his Sword from the Scabbord, and discharge it upon you.* Moham-med.

The Soltân *sent them this Letter, they read it with Attention, and it put them into*

into such Confusion, that they agreed off-hand to make Peace, and they wrote the Answer in these Terms.

After the Praise to God, and the Salutation. the Servant acknowledges his Fault, and repents before his Creator. If you will chastise, in your Hands is the Power; but if you will pardon, it will be more becoming your Piety.

Port of *Taman* subdu'd by *Soltân Selim* I.

But this Haughtiness of the *Soltân,* and the Submission of the Sharifs, does not however destroy their Sovereignty. 'Tis true, it has at certain junctures receiv'd some considerable Shocks; especially in the time of *Selim* I, and of *Soliman the Magnificent* his Son, whom nothing cou'd resist, and who, by means of a Fleet, which he caus'd to be equip'd at the bottom of the *Red. Sea,* made himself Master of the Coasts of *Arabia,* and one Part of the Kingdom of *Taman:* But his Successors did not long maintain those Conquests; for, excepting *Jedda,* which is properly the Port of *Mekka,* and where the *Turks* still have a *Basha,* whose Authority is but small, they possess nothing considerable in *Arabia;* 'tis not the same on the opposite Coast, which they

have

have almoft intirely ufurp'd from the *Abyffins,* who by that means have not one
Port in their Poffeffion on the *Rea-Sea.*

The fecond Obfervation which may be
made is, that *Mecca* and *Medina,* together with the Country depending on them,
are not fituate in the *Happy Arabia,* or in
Taman, as many Authors have written, but
in a Province of *Arabia* in general, which
is contiguous to *Taman,* to which the *A-
rabs* give the Name of *Hejaz* and *Taha-
ma.* Thus we fee thefe two Countries
have their Bounds which divide them, and
that they obey Princes who are diftinct,
and independent of one another

After the Departure of the Sharif, who
has occafion'd this Digreffion, there ran a
Report, that the Governour of *Moka* had
been call'd to Court, and that he had Reafons for putting off that Voyage. Neverthelefs he fent to the King his Mafter very
fine Prefents of the moft curious Things,
which came from the *Indies,* excufing
himfelf on account of the great number
of Ships which were at *Moka,* the moft
confiderable of which were *French,* which
he was very defirous to fee difpatch'd before his Departure, which gave him an Opportunity

*Mekka
and Medi-
na* not in
Taman.

Gover-
nour of
Mokha
fent
for to
Court.

portunity of making other Prefents of feveral *European* Rarities.

Is excus'd
from go-
ing.

The King having favourably receiv'd the
Prefents and Excufes of the Governour, he
fent him by one of his principal Officers,
a Veft, a Sabre, and a beautiful Horfe, as
a Mark of Diftinction, and of his Favour.
When the Perfon, who had the Charge of
that Prefent, was arriv'd within a League
of *Moka*, he fent to give Advice of it to
the Governour, who prefently fet forward,
accompany'd by his Sons and all his Hou-
fhold, follow'd by all the Horfe and Foot
which were under his Command, which
made a Train of two or three thoufand
Men. The Director of the *Dutch*, to whom
he had fent Horfes, was there carrying the
Colours of the Company along with him,
and an Efcort of twenty Soldiers.

Ceremo-
ny of re-
ceiving
the Veft.

The Meffenger of the King, and the Governour met half a League from the Town,
and the Veft was receiv'd with a great deal
of Ceremony. The Governour alighted
firft, to receive the King's Letter and kifs the
Veft, which the Officer held aloft, without difmounting. After that the Officer
alighted, put it on him, girded him with
the Sabre, and prefented him with the Horfe
                                    which

he had brought. The Governour mounted it, and return'd towards the Town by beat of Kettle-drums; the King's Meffenger being on the Governour's left Hand. There was a great Concourfe of People from *Moka* to fee that Ceremony.

It always gave me much Concern, that the Throng of Bufinefs, of which I had the fole Care, was fo great, that I had not time to go to the Court of the King of *Taman*, whofe ordinary Refidence is at *Muab*, a Town and Caftle fituate in the Mountains, above one hundred Leagues from *Moka*. They reckon it the moft agreeable Situation in all *Arabia*, and that the King is more fecure there, than in the Maritime Places.

This Prince exercifes an abfolute Sovereignty in his Kingdom, not acknowledging even the Grand Seignor as (*a*) *Chalifa*; Moreover, the King of *Taman*, befides the Grandure of his Houfe, the Antiquity of which they run very high, affumes the Title of *Imâm* by way of Excellence; a Quality of great Diftinction in *Mohammedifm*, which the *Chalifa's* had firft born, and which

King of Taman independent.

(*) This King affumes himfelf the Title of *Chalifa*.

con-

constitutes them Heads and sovereign Pontiffs of the *Mosleman* Religion

Kingdom of *Fartach*.

However the King of *Yaman* does not possess all the *Happy Arabia* ; for in *Yaman* itself, and on the Sea Coasts, there is a great Extent of Country, which is not under his Sway. In this Tract particularly we find the Kingdom of *Fartach*, where grow the Frankincense, Gums, and all the most esteem'd Spices. The Town of *Fartach* is the Capital of this Kingdom, its principal Port at present being that of *Sheer*, a Town situate between *Aden* and Cape *Fartach*.

Coffee-trees.

I said before, that only the most fertile Lands of the Kingdom of *Yaman*, or, to speak more properly, the Mountains of the *Happy Arabia* produce the Coffee. Those who have frequented them most assur'd me, that in those Mountains, and in the Plains

Vines.

beyond them, there are also Vines and beautiful Fruit-Trees in abundance ; and especially Orange-Trees, the Fruit of which we saw at *Moka*, as well as excellent Grapes; whereof the *Arabs* do not make Wine, which is only allow'd on account of the *Jews*, who make it privately. There is also very good

Gums.

Corn in those Parts, as also much Gums and

Spices.

Spices.

The

The Annimal which is moſt common and uſeful in *Arabia*, is the Camel, eſpe- Camel. cially that ſort which is ſet apart for Racing, call'd the Dromedary, and which does not uſually bear Burdens. They teach them when they are young to march with extreme Swiftneſs, by taking a great deal of Pains with them; and beating them on; ſo that no pacing Horſe can keep up with them; one of theſe Camels travelling very well twenty Leagues in a Forenoon, a Thing almoſt incredible, conſidering the Heavineſs and Largeneſs of that Animal.

At the beginning of *March*, the Governour of *Moka* caus'd ſome of theſe Beaſts, together with a certain number of Oxen and Sheep to be ſlain, according to Ceremony, and diſtributed the Fleſh to ſeveral Women aſſembled in the great Square, which is before the Palace. He that diſtributed it receiv'd from each Woman a Commaſſi, which is the ſmalleſt Money of Commaſi the Country, of the value of about two Silver Sols; it is of Silver, with ſome *Arabic* Coin. Characters on it. Thoſe Women afterwards made another Diſtribution of the Fleſh among the reſt of the People, who ſpent the Day in great Rejoycings. It was

I   to

to celebrate the Great *Mohammedan* Feaft,
nam'd by the *Arabs*, *Aid al adha*, the

Feaft of the Sacrifice *Dhu'l-hajjah*. Feaft of the Sacrifice, or of the *Victimes*.
This Feaft falls on the 10th Day of the
laft Month of their Year, on which Day
the Pilgrims, affembled at *Mekka*, affift at
a folemn Sacrifice, which is made to God
in behalf of all the *Moflemans*.

Diforder rais'd by the *French*. There happen'd during that Feaft fome
Diforder in the Town, occafion'd by the
Eafinefs of Mr. *de Champloret*, in fuffer-
ing his Men, contrary to my Advice, to
keep a fort of Tavern at the Gate of his
Houfe, for the Conveniency of our Seamen. Firft and foremoft a Gunner of his
Ship, after getting himfelf drunk with *Spanifh* Wine and *Aqua Vitæ*, had gone to
take a Walk without the Town in the
Heat of the Day, and was found dead in
the open Plain. Afterwards a *Banyân* having made himfelf drunk in the fame Place,
wounded feveral of his Companions with
a Sabre; fo that, Complaint being made
of it to the Governour, he fent an Officer and fome Soldiers to feize him; but
that furious Blade fhut himfelf up in his
Houfe, which he wou'd not open to any
Body. The Soldiers, entring at a Window,
found

found him with the Sabre in his Hand, with which he kill'd three of them, one of whom dy'd the fame Evening: they took him at length by Force, and the Governour order'd his Head to be ftruck off the next Morning.

This unfortunate Perfon puts me in mind *Banyâns.* of faying fomewhat in this Place concerning the *Banyâns* in general, by the Affiftance of whom all the Trade in *Arabia* is manag'd. They are all originally from the *Indies*, and particularly of the Ifland of *Diu* [*Dîv*] * in the Kingdom of *Cambaya*, not far from *Surat*. They come into *Arabia* in their Youth, to feek their Fortune by Trade; on which Account they alfo fpread themfelves over the other Parts of the *Indies*.

There are among them very rich Merchants, many Weighers of Gold and Silver, and Men in fhort of all forts of Trades: For the reft, they are the clevereft Arithmeticians in the World; for, out of three or four Chara&ers traced upon the Thumb

[* *Dîv*, in the *Malabar* Tongue, fignifies an Ifland, and is given by way of Eminence to *that*, which, by corrupting the Term, the *Portugals* call *Diu*. The *Arabs* for want of the 5 Confonants write *Dib*, as *Stran*, or rather *Selandib* for *Selandiv*, i. e. the Ifland of *Selan*, or as we call it *Ceylon*.]

Nail, when they are in haste, they sum up an exact Account in the twinkling of an Eye. Nevertheless, it behoves one to be upon the Guard with them, for they cheat with a wonderful deal of Skill. For my Part, I believe that the Commerce of these People has spoil'd the *Arabs*, who are naturally sincere and honest, making it a point of Honour to appear such; but they have found the way to cheat also, when they can do it with Safety.

Their Re-ligion. The Religion of the *Banyáns* is a fantastical and gross Idolatry; for, 'tis said, they adore all sorts of Animals, but principally the Cow, which is the great Object of their Devotion and Love. So strongly possess'd with the Notion of the Transmigration of Souls, that they never hurt any living Creature; and one cannot displease them more, than to kill in their Presence any Animal, let it be what it will. Their greatest Desire, when they are dying, is, to hold a Cow by the Tail, to the end, as they say, their Soul may enter into the Body of that beloved Animal.

Customs. Besides, among many superstitious Practices, as of washing the whole Body when they get up in the Morning, and before and

after

after Meals, of eating nothing at all that had Life, and of going every Evening to the Sea Side to fay their Prayers, wetting their Forehead with the Hand; they take every Morning a certain Compofition of Cow Dung, mix'd with Saffron, with which they mark the Tips of their Ears, and then the Forehead, proftrating themfelves, and touching the Ground with it.

Among fo many Abfurdities, they have this one thing good, that they eafily pardon Injuries, and never do ill to any Body. In fhort, their Manners in Appearance are very innocent; 'tis faid alfo, that the Name of *Banyân,* which they bear, fignifies no more, but a fimple innocent Man. They have a peculiar Language and Character for Writing, of which I have brought away Pieces, and which I believe to be no other than the *Malabar.* Morality.

Their Habit is very odd, efpecially that of the Head, which is a kind of *Turban* of white Muflin, made up in a Form refembling the Head and Horns of a Cow; and for the reft, they wear a fort of Cotton (*a*) *Albe,* which falls down very low, and un- Habit.

(*a*) *Albe,* a Veftment worn by Priefts in *France.*

I 3   neath

derneath a kind of pretty long Scarfe to gird them round the Body, and which paſſes alſo between the Thighs, wearing neither Stockings nor Drawers, and the moſt part of them going barefoot. The better Sort, have a white Silk Scarfe, embroider'd at the Ends with Silk of different Colours.

Abhor'd
by the
Arabs.

The *Arabs*, who abhor theſe *Banyâns*, and ſuffer them among them only on account of Trade, do not permit them to marry in *Arabia*, nor to have any Correſpondence with their Women ; ſo that they are oblig'd to return to the *Indies*, when they have a mind to marry, and have made ſome Fortune in *Arabia*.

Our Ships had been now ſix Months at *Moka*, and the Time for our Departure approach'd; we had no more to do at *Betelfaguy*, all our Markets there being made, and our *Coffee* ſent in. Mr. *de Champloret*, who had made that his principal Abode, was alſo already embark'd on board his Ship, (which the Governour was very loath to conſent to) leaving behind his Writer, to regulate whatever might concern him in particular. In ſhort, all our Money was employ'd in *Coffee*, to the Value

lue of above two hundred thoufand Piaftres, including the Price of the Merchandizes of the *Dutch* Ship; and nothing remain'd but to fettle fome Accounts with the Offi- cers of the Cuftoms, and with fome pri- vate Perfons about other Affairs.

At that Juncture, I was oblig'd to rectify a wrong Proceeding of the aforemen- tion'd Writer, who being tir'd of *Moka*, thought fit to quit it without Leave, dif- guis'd in a Sailer's Habit. He was difco- ver'd by the *Amir al bahr* himfelf, who made a great Buftle, and told the Gover- nour of it, having firft arrefted him : But, at the Intreaty of the Writer, who was terribly frighted, as well as for the Honour and Intereft of Mr. *Champloret*, who blam'd much the Proceeding of the Wri- ter, I accommodated his Affair.

Affair of the Writer.

I began by difcharging the little Debts which he was engag'd in; afterwards I told the *Amir al bahr* what I thought con- venient; and prefently after I went to the Governour, who was at his Lieutenant's Houfe, where I found him fitting at the end of a great Balcony with feveral Per- fons of Diftinction; among whom was that Lord whom I had already mention'd,

I 4

on

on occasion of the Ladies who were our Neighbours.

He made me first sit down, and, before he heard my Business, he began to chide that poor unhappy *Mohammed*, whose History I have already related; and, falling in good earnest into a Passion with him, struck him hard with a Switch he had in his Hand, and threw his Turban upon the Ground, which is a great Ignominy among them. I then took the Liberty to intercede for that unfortunate Man, finding it was my Presence which put the Governour in mind of his Offence. The Governour grew calm, and then heard me upon the Affair of the Writer, which I blam'd sufficiently. He had regard to my Remonstrance, and consented to his Embarkment, tho' not till after he had brought an Acquittance from the Serrâf, that is to say, his Goldsmith or Banker, a Formality necessary for all Strangers who depart from the Port of *Moka* after trading there. That was easily obtain'd, since Mr. *Champ'oret* and his Writer ow'd nothing then, I having paid for them about two hundred Piastres before I went to the Palace.

Leave obtain'd of the Governour for his Embarkment.

I staid

I ftaid a good while longer with the
Governour, who was in a Humour to difcourfe me concerning the Cuftoms of *Eu-*
rope, inquiring particularly about the King's
Armies, and the Marine of *France*. We
fell afterwards, I know not how, upon the
Subject of the Women; he thought our
Cuftoms very ftrange, on account of the
Liberty which they enjoy'd among us, and
the Familiarity which the Men have with
the Women. A Familiarity, he faid, which
the *French* had brought with them even
into *Arabia*, (and about which, he had receiv'd Complaints from the moft confiderable Inhabitants of *Moka*) not fcrupling
to pry into the moft private Appartments of
the Women from the tops of their Terraffes;
not to fpeak, added he, laughing, of a Hiftory gallant enough, which happen'd at *Be-*
telfaguy, and which one of our Officers
was charg'd with.

In fhort, the Converfation between the
Governour and me was perfectly gay; and
one cou'd not be more agreeably entertain'd
at the Conclufion of two pretty nice Affairs. He did not fpeak a Word to me
about *Sidy Mohammed*, who had given him
fo much Trouble, either being willing to
forget

forget it, or loath to expofe his Authority any more.

All our Affairs and Trade being at length finifh'd, and the Day fix'd for my Embarkment arriv'd, I went to take my Audience of Leave of the Governour, who redoubled all his Civilities towards me. He wou'd alfo have engag'd me to make a longer Stay in *Arabia*, promifing to furnifh me with the means of buying more *Coffee*, and other Merchandizes of the Country, at a Price which wou'd fatisfy me ; and affuring me that it was in my own Power to inrich myfelf at *Moka* ; and, upon letting him know, with Thanks for his Civilities, that all my Stock of Piaftres was laid out, he reply'd, he wou'd furnifh me with as much as I pleas'd, and that I needed only depend upon him.

I then perceiv'd that the Governour had a mind to make ufe of me to ferve his private Intereft ; for he was very fond of the Profits of Trade, and concern'd himfelf in it a little too openly, at which they began to murmur in the Country. I might have found my Account in his Views, but I judg'd I ought to prefer the Benefit of the Company in general, which had confided

in

in me, to all other Confiderations. A longer Stay was attended with Inconveniences; the Fortune of the Governour might
change, and there was an abfolute Neceffity
for our Ships to quit a Sea, whofe Waters
were of fuch a Quality, as in time to en-
gender dangerous Worms in the beft Wood
of *Europe*. I then, in the moft complai-
fant manner I cou'd, declin'd the Offers of
the Governour, and I retir'd very well pleas'd
with him in all Refpects.

My laft Care was to pay all that remain'd,
for the principal Houfe where I dwelt in
Moka, and to get a fort of general Acquittance, in the Name of him who had let
it to me. Here follows the Writing which
was given me, and perhaps is not unwor-
thy the Attention of the Curious.

Praife be to God,

This Writing is to teftify, that the Mul-
la or Doctor Aly Ebn Abd-alwâheb, *has*
paid all the Rent of the Houfe of the
Rofary *of* al Fakîh (*a*) Khader, *which*

(*a*) *al Fakih Khader*, is the Name of a Doctor in Law,
call'd *Elie*, who had built that Houfe, to recite the daily
Prayers there in Publick. They give to thefe Prayers
the Name of *Rofary*, from the Word *Werd*, a Rofe.

Khader, fignifies properly green or flourifhing; the *Mo-*
fleman's give that Name to *Elias*, becaufe they believe he
is ftill alive and blooming, &c.

he

he had taken absolutely in his Name for the Sum of twenty-four Ducats in Gold, and that there remains nothing behind of the said Rent on his Account, which I declare this 16th *Day of the Month of* Moharram, *in the Year* 1121 ; *written by him who is poor in the Eyes of God,* Kasem Alwajîh.

A Brangle with the *Banyân Bira*.   Just as I was going to embark, there happen'd an Affair with the *Banyân Bira,* who, instead of returning me above one thousand Piastres which remain'd due, upon balance of all Accounts between us pretended he ow'd me nothing. He was supported by the *Amir al bahr* and some Officers of the Governour, who cou'd not take the Examination of this Affair upon himself. An *English* Captain newly arriv'd from the *Indies,* whose Ship lay at Anchor near ours, undertook very civilly to adjust the Matter, and I left it to him; but he cou'd not prevail on the Avarice of the *Banyân* to come to any thing; so that I was oblig'd to embark under a good deal of Resentment; telling the *Amir al bahr,* that, since they did me so much injustice, I wou'd remedy my self by some Reprisal before I quitted the Road.

This

This was not my Intention, but I had a *Kind Office of an English Captain.* mind to fee what Effect Fear might have upon them; and to augment it, being got on board my Ship, I order'd |the Shallops to be arm'd, and fent them to found the Port in feveral Places. This Step at firft caus'd them to fire five Guns from the Forts; and a while after we faw a Bark, carrying a white Flag, which came directly to my Ship; there ftept out of it a Man, who deliver'd me a Letter from the *English* Captain, with a Bag of five hundred Piaftres, which was all that obliging Gentleman was able to do for me; advifing me to be fatisfy'd with it. He beg'd of me alfo to add to that Favour another, which the *Banyân* was very earneft for, *viz.* to fend him Cloth to make a Veft, in Token of Reconciliation and Friendfhip, and to fave his Honour in the Country, where our Difference had made a Noife.

I was fo well pleas'd with the Behaviour of the Englifhman, and I had fo many Reafons for departing without Delay, and in Friendfhip with every Body, that I agreed to every thing he demanded; not without admiring the more than pharifaical Hypocrify of the *Banyân*, who, tho' he was

robbing

robbing me openly, yet took care to salve his Reputation. I sent a Letter of Thanks to the *English* Captain, and then set Sail, saluting the Town and Forts as we did at our Entring.

LET.

LETTER V.

The laſt Letter, which gives an Account of what ·paſs'd in our Return, from the Time of our Departure from Moka, *to the Arrival of the Ships at St.* Malo.

WE left the Road of *Moka,* Sir, the 20th of *Auguſt,* 1709, and ſoon after the *Streight* of the *Red-Sea*; afterwards we run along the Coaſt of *Africa* as far as Cape *Guardafui,* from whence the Currents carrying us Northwards, we were conſtrain'd to paſs between the Iſle of *Zocotora,* and the Coaſt of *Fartach.*

The 10th of *September,* being to the Weſtward of the *Maldives,* we met a Ship of *Amſterdam* with forty four Guns, going from *Batavia* to *Surat.* We attack'd her, and, after making a pretty good

Defence,

Defence, made ourselves Masters of her. Her Cargo was reckon'd to be worth more than two thousand Crowns. We found in her several Chests of Silver and Gold in Ingots. We carry'd her to the Island of St. *Maurice*, in order to set the Ship's Crew on Shore.

The Island of *Maurice*.

We saw that Isle, and drew near it, sailing at about half a League from the Coast. We observ'd near the Sea-side, a little Building of white Stone, in form of a Chappel, which made us judge it was inhabited thereabouts. Continuing our Course, we saw soon after the Mountains mark'd in our Sea *Miror*, in the Latitude of which, there shou'd be the best Harbour in the Island, call'd the Port of *Peterbothed*. We cast Anchor at the distance of about three quarters of a League, and sent out our Shallops and Boats to discover this Harbour.

New Land.

Our Men, who were well arm'd, landed, and, having found a Herd of wild Oxen, kill'd two, and carry'd them on board Mr. *Champloret*, who sent us Share of them. The Sailors had in the mean time taken a good quantity of very pretty Fish, which were excellent Food, which made

us

us judge the Land in general to be very proper for taking in Provisions. We shot off three Guns from our Ship, to give notice to the Inhabitants to come to us, but none appear'd.

Next Morning we sent the Shallop on shore, to try to find out the Oxen again; but we made a better Discovery, for our Men found a *Dutch* Huntsman with a Pack of Hounds; they brought him on board, his Hounds making a terrible Yelling on the Strand, where they waited two whole Days, crying almost continually after him.

In the mean time, we learn'd by the *Dutchman*, that he and another Huntsman, whom our People did not see, dwelt pretty near the white House, which we took for a Chappel; that they belong'd to the *Dutch* Governour of the Island, who gave them a Piastre for every Dozen of Stags-Skins, which they brought him; that all their Arms was a Knife, which they made use of when the Dogs had run down the Stag, giving them the Flesh, and keeping only the Skins to themselves, which afterwards was made into Shamois Leather. They had been hunting since Sun rise, and had not heard our Gun go off.

K   Upon

Upon this, we thought fit to do two Things, firſt to ſend back that Man next Morning with a Letter to the Governour, by which we demanded Proviſions and Refreſhments paying for them, both for ourſelves and the *Dutch*, whoſe Veſſel we had taken, without which, they muſt needs be great Sufferers, promiſing to deliver him the Priſoners. 'Twas reſolv'd alſo, that this Hunter, whom we kept from having any Communication in the Ship with the *Dutch men* of our Prize, ſhou'd be conducted by ten of our Soldiers to the Place, where he might find his Comrade: That from thence he ſhou'd purſue his Journey to the Governour, ſending up his Comrade as a Hoſtage till his Return; or, if he lik'd it better, to return himſelf to the Ship, and ſend the other Huntſman with the Letter.

Every thing was well executed, for the Boat return'd the ſame Evening, and brought us the ſecond Huntſman to wait the Return of the other, and the Governour's Anſwer. We learn'd by him, that the *Dutch* did not make much Account of the Iſle of *Maurice*, ſince no more Amber-Greaſe was found there, and Ebony went off ſo badly in *Holland*; that, beſides the Rice Har-

vcſt,

veft had fail'd a long time thro' the extreme
Druth; adding, that an infinite multitude
of Apes and Rats deftroy'd it all. They
told us alfo, that, about the Parts where we
were anchor'd, there were abundance of
Stags and Goats; and that, on the other fide
of the Ifle beyond the Mountains, there
were Droves of wild Boars; that, not long
before, a general Hunting had been order'd
to root them out; and that, the Inhabitants
having affembl'd for that purpofe, they
flew above fifteen hundred of them in one
Day. He told us befides, that there were
not remaining in this Ifland above eighty
Dutch; and that one of the Company's
Ships, which pafs'd that way about two
Years before, had carry'd an Order to the
Governour, to fet out with his Family to
Batavia; and that they every Moment expected the Ship, which was to take him on
board.

　The fame Day we put in with two of Peterbo-
our Veffels to the Port of *Peterbothed*; thed Port.
after caufing the fame to be founded, and
fending the Boats belonging to our Prizes
to the Point of the Banks, which we had
to fear. The other Ships enter'd next Morning, and the Day after our Hunter return'd

　　　　K 2　　　　　　　with

with a Letter from the Governour, and a Prefent of the Fruit of the Country, as Oranges, Citrons, Potatoes; and the Letter imported, that in ftrictnefs he cou'd furnifh us
with nothing, becaufe of the War between
the two Nations, and that he was in a
Condition to defend himfelf, if we attempted to infult him; that neverthelefs, in confideration of the Servants of the *Holland*
Company our Prifoners, he wou'd fend us
Hunters, who might fupply us with Deer
and Goats, defiring to be excus'd from
fending Oxen, having only juft enough for
his own Subfiftance; befides, that it was
almoft impracticable to conduct them fo far
acrofs the Woods; that for Pulfe and fuch
like Things, we might find them very eafily ourfelves.

Upon the Receipt of this Anfwer, we
refolv'd to fend him a Prefent. A Lieutenant who underftood *Dutch*, and a Writer
of Mr. *de Champloret* were the Bearers.
They had, from the Place where we were
at Anchor, feven Leagues to go by Land to
the Port and Fortrefs where the Governour
dwelt. They found in the way a little River
which they pafs'd, beyond which, they met
an Efcorte of twenty five Men well arm'd.
Our

(marginal note:) Lieutenant fent
with a
Prefent to
the Go-
vernour.

Our People were receiv'd kindly by them, and regal'd in the same Place with cold Victuals; their Drink was Beer and Punch, which is a Liquor made of two Parts Water, to one of *Aqua Vitæ*, with Citrons, Sugar and Nutmeg.

The Governour carry'd them to the Fort, where he entertain'd them with a handsome Supper, at which the Governess was present. Next Day he dispatch'd them, loading them with Fruits and other Refreshments. At their Return, we assembl'd the *Dutch* Officers, who had wrote themselves to that Governour to inform him, that two or three Stags a Day was much too small an Allowance for the Crew of the four Ships. The Governour sent immediately the Lieutenant of the Garrison, who came to make us his Compliments, and visit the *Dutch* Officers, bringing with him two additional Hunters; after which we had four or five Stags *per diem*. *[Entertain'd civilly.]*

Mr. *de Champloret* and I, with some Officers, all of us good Marksmen, went also a hunting, and we advanc'd a great Way without meeting the Oxen, which was our principal Desire. We divided ourselves into two Troops, with a Design to range *[Captain goes a hunting.]*

K 3   over

over both Sides of the Mountain, which
was very high, and try to kill at leaſt ſome
Stags and Goats; but we were never able
to come at them, having only had the Pleaſure of viewing a great Number of them.
One ſees from the Top of that Mountain
both the Sides, which are cover'd with
Wood.

We came down again into the Plain,
walking always in the Shade, and we rejoin'd our Men, who, having deſcended by
another Part, found a great Pond, the Water of which was very good; a pretty deep
Stream flow'd into it in that Place, and
iſſued out on the ſide towards the Sea, which
thereabouts form'd an Arm, advancing near
the Pond.

Water
keeps
ſweet 5
Months.

This Diſcovery made us an Amends for
our rude and unprofitable Chaſe; for we
made choice of that Place for taking in our
Water, which has ſo excellent a Quality,
that it never tainted all the while we were
at Sea, which was nigh five Months, from
the Iſle of *Maurice* till we came to
France.

All that we got in our Chaſe, were ſome
reddiſh Pigeons which we kill'd, and which
let us come cloſe enough to knock them
down

down with Stones. I kill'd alfo two Bats
of an extraordinary kind; they were of a
Violet Colour, with little yellow Spots,
having a fort of Claws at their Wings,
wherewith that Bird lays hold of the Branches of Trees, and a Bill like a Parrot. The
Dutch fay they are good to eat, and that
at a certain Seafon they are as palatable as our
Woodcocks. In fhort, we faw wild Cats,
which had been brought into the Ifle in
order to deftroy the Rats which are very
numerous there.

As we drew near the Sea Shore, we Tomb
found by the fide of a little Torrent, a very near the
handfome Tomb of Freeftone, cover'd with Shore.
a Marble, with an Infcription, which gave
us to underftand, that it was the Tomb of
the Wife of a *Dutch* General, who dy'd
in this Ifland going to the *Indies*. . Before
we embark'd, we eat upon the Strand excellent Oyfters, which refrefh'd us after our
Fatigue.

I went on board Mr. *de Champloret*,
where we took into Confideration the Ca-
reening of our Ships which ftood in great
need of it; befides the Danger the Sheathing
was in of being damag'd by the Worms.
I was of opinion that the Ifle of St. *Mary*, Ifle St.
which *Mary*.

which was not above a League diftant from *Madagafcar*, and about twenty Leagues in Compafs, wou'd be much more convenient for that Work upon feveral Accounts. Mr. *de Champloret*, on the contrary, thought it beft to careen in the Port where we were, notwithftanding the Scarcity of Provifions and other Inconveniences. I wou'd not oppofe his Advice, and while they were at work, I took a walk to the white Houfe, where I faw a very good Port, and fome Lodgings at the Foot of a little Hill, which feem'd to me to have been made ufe of by Ships, which came there to anchor. We break-faft'd there, with an Intention to go on to fee the Dwellings of our *Dutch* Hunters. We continu'd our Road through the Woods for a full League; they confifted of Ebony and other Trees fit for feveral forts of Tinctures in Dying. In the mean time, we perceiv'd by Intervals a very

Plant with ftrong Smell of Cloves, tho' that Ifle prothe fmell duces none. This happen'd, as they told of Cloves: us, by means of a certain Plant, which grew to the height of two or three Foot, which has the fame Tafte and Smell of the Clove, as I found by Experience on their fhewing it to me.

After

After we had pass'd a great Brook over *Dutch* Habitation very pleasant. huge Marble Stones, we arriv'd at the Dwellings of the *Hollanders*, which is pleasant enough, and surrounded with five other Houses, one of which is set apart for the Management of the Sugar Canes; we saw them press'd there to make what they call Cane-wine, and elsewhere Frangorin, a white Liquor, which is both strong and Cane Wine. sweet; but the Smell of it is disagreeable to those who are not accustom'd to it. We saw without a fine and great Walk of Orange-trees in form of an Arbour, and on the other side a great Garden, very well inclos'd with little Citron Trees, which serv'd for a Hedge against the Apes. The whole is surrounded with plow'd Fields, in which there grew Potatoes: Our *Dutchman* brought us also to see the neighbouring Habitations, order'd much after the same manner; and after all, a fine Ebony Wood. At our Return we eat some of a Stag, and drank Frangorin. Next Day, as I was walking in their Garden, I was diverted with the sight of above four thousand Apes behind the Hedge in the next Field: They were of the smallest sort; in a Moment, they had pluck'd up out of the Ground

Apes destroy the Gardens.

with

their fore Paws, fitting upon their Rumps, great Quantities of Potatoes: As foon as any of them went away, others came and took their Places, falling to the fame fort of Work. They continued a long time at it before the Dogs difcover'd them, at whofe Approach they fcamper'd off to the Wood.

Beautiful Plains and Woods.

I took a Walk afterwards to the little River, where our People met the Gover- nour. I faw there very beautiful Plains, much Wood, and deferted Dwellings. At my Return to our Hunter's Houfe, I was pretty much furpriz'd to fee Fowl upon the Spit; they told me they were a Breed of Cocks and Hens which came from *Europe*, which fometime before were become wild, fo that to kill the Pullets, they were ob- lig'd to go on the Hunt after them. Thefe Animals feed chiefly on a fort of little Grain, of fo ftrong a Tafte, that a fingle Grain of it has more Power in a Ragoo, than bruis'd Pepper. Next Day I caus'd fome very beautiful Wood to be cut, which is very fit for making Furniture of, and I return'd to our Ships, crofling the Woods, with which the Country is almoft quite cover'd as far as the Sea Shore.

In

In the mean time, our Men continu'd fishing, and took much Fish, which was a great Relief to the Ship's Crew, being weary of eating salt Beef and Bacon. The few Stags which we had were reserv'd for the sick Folks and Officers, who were often reduc'd to eat Fish. We caus'd also a great deal of this last to be salted and dry'd for the Voyage, which prov'd of great Service to us.

At length our sick People being recover'd, our Ships well repair'd, and our Water and Wood laid on board, we kept our Word which we had given the Governour of the Isle, sending him all our *Dutch* Prisoners ; and, having taken our Leave of him, we departed from the Port of *Peterbothed* the 16th of *December*, 1709.

We cast Anchor again without the Port, and then set sail for *Mascarin*, or the Isle of *Bourbon*, inhabited by *French*. I was on board Mr. *de Champloret*, who had perswaded me to remain there, my Ship being at too great a distance : And the second Day we arriv'd at the unsafe Road of St. *Denis*, the only one where great Ships can put in to the Isle of *Bourbon*. We went on shore next Day, being the 19th of the same Month.

We

Set sail for Mascaregnas,

We made our Salute with seven Guns, after we had cast Anchor in that Road, where there is a Fort, which return'd the same. A Captain, accompany'd with some of the Inhabitants, came to receive us at Landing, which is not very easy on account of the loose Stones, which all the Shore is full of, and which make a strange Noise occasion'd by the Rowling of the Sea, which beats against the Breach, and is almost continually swell'd. We went from thence to pay our Respects to Mr. *de Charanville*, who receiv'd us very obligingly, and treated us with a Collation, whereat he sacrific'd several Bottles of his best Wine, which began to fail. We lay at his House, and staid there the next Day to make some Provision. We bought Oxen, but the embarking of them was very difficult.

The same Day we saw our other Ships pass by, having had an Order from us to repair to St. *Paul's Creek*, which is not so much expos'd to Winds, and where the Landing is easier; there being nothing there but Sands. Next Day there arose a terrible Wind, which caus'd the Sea to swell very much; nevertheless, we perceiv'd from the top of the House a Shallop, which

Storm.

parted

parted from our Ship, making way to the Place where we put on Shore. We judg'd at firſt, that there was ſomething extraordinary in the Matter; it was, in ſhort, to give us notice that the Ship drove with her Anchors, and that ſhe was no longer in Safety.

A *Frenchman*, whom we had taken on board in *Arabia*, coming from the *Indies*, had put himſelf into that Shallop of his own Accord, with an Intention to jump into the Sea, when he cou'd proceed no further for the Weather, and ſwim on Shore, to inform us of the Condition the Ship was in; and that was what we ſaw from the Shore where we ran to look out. I never ſaw better Swimming than that Man perform'd; but his Attempt was very raſh; for, when he was about to Land, the Sea was ſo furious, and beat with ſuch Violence againſt the Shore, which was full of thoſe great Stones I have ſpoken of, that it was enough to daſh him in pieces. Nevertheleſs, he try'd ſeveral Times to make his Part good, but the Return of the Waves carry'd him back into the Sea in an inſtant; the moſt hardy Seamen which were in that Place came to us, and us'd all their Endeavours

Misfortune of a Frenchman.

vours to help him, but in vain ; that poor
Man, having at length loft all his Strength,
became for fome time the Sport of the
Waves, and then difappear'd from our Eyes,
a fad Spectacle for us, and an Accident
which gave us all a fenfible Concern.

We fent back the Shallop which ftood off
at Sea, by making a Sign to thofe who were
in it, and, as the bad Weather continu'd,
we made another Signal to the Ship to
depart immediately for the Road of St.
Paul, refolving to go thither ourfelves by
Land acrofs the Mountains. We pafs'd
that Night alfo at the Governour's Houfe,
where, Wine quite failing, we drank of a
certain Wine made of Honey, which was
very good, and which, when it is well fin'd,
has a Flavour as delicious as the beft *Ma-
laga* Sack.

Go by
Land to
the Road
ot St.
Paul.

Next Morning, after we had made a
good Breakfaft, we began our March ; the
Governour, had a mind to be of the Par-
ty, and we caufed a Pair of Colours to
be erected, to fignify further to the Officers of the Ships to fet fail immediately,
and that we were departing for the other
Road, which they apprehended very well,
and executed it in our Sight.

We

We had a great deal of Trouble, after four long Rests under the Trees, to get to the top of the Mountain; especially I, who, never thinking of going a foot, had only a sort of Pumps on, such as the Skippers wear, made of a piece of Buck-skin, fasten'd with a strap of Leather, the most improper thing in the World to climb Mountains with. The Governour had given me two or three Blacks with a Hamock to carry me, but I wou'd not venture myself in that sort of Voiture, in so troublesome a Road, full of Precipices, and dangerous Passages.

Beyond that Mountain, we found a very stoney and uneasy Road, and at length another Mountain, which we were oblig'd to descend for the space of a League and a half, without being able to march any otherwise than on Foot, supported by long Poles. In this manner we arriv'd at a Place call'd the *Bark*, which is just half way; we sat down under Trees to eat and rest ourselves, but we cou'd not find a drop of Water there.

Uneasy Road.

Hitherto our Way was over Mountains cover'd with Wood, among which we found some Citrons, and abundance of Palm-trees

trees with the Heads cut off. The remaining part of our Journey led along the Sea Shore, which was very rocky, like the Road of St. *Denis,* there being no other way for us to take : And this Paffage was rendred ftill more difficult by the Waves of the Sea, which came and dafh'd againft the Rocks, and extended themfelves as far as the Mountain, which runs all along that Coaft ; fo that one muft be very nimble and careful in their Paffage, taking the Opportunity of the Return of the Wave to leap from Rock to Rock : Neverthelefs, the Women and young Slaves went all this Road, as well as that of the Mountains, bare-footed with a furprizing Agility. As an Addition to our Pain on quitting the Sea Shore, we found ourfelves oblig'd to afcend

The *Crown* Moun- tain. a third Mountain, call'd the *Crown,* which was very fteep, and put us to the neceffity of making ufe of our Hands as well as Feet.

At length we arriv'd at the top of this Mountain almoft fatigu'd to Death, and without being able to find one drop of Water. I was ready to die with Thirft, but I was oblig'd to take Courage, having but half a League to the Place where we

were

were to lye. Very fortunately, by much searching on one side and the other of this dreadful Road, we at length found Water, which was of great Service to enable us to perform the rest of our Journey. Night overtook us before we cou'd arrive at the Village where we were to rest, to which they have given the Name of *Bien-* venu [that is, welcome]. We found there a pretty good Supper, and had *Frangorin* or Cane Wine to drink.

Village of *Bien-Vena.*

Next Day we had Horses to carry us to St. *Paul,* the Habitation of the *French,* a good League distant from that Village. A League of that Country is equal to two great ones of *France.* The Road, or rather the Creek of St. *Paul,* is at the end of a plain, bounded by the Mountain which we descended last, and form'd partly by a Point which advances into the Sea. This Plain is about two Leagues long, and a Mile broad, having in the middle of it a large and deep Pond of sweet Water, upon which there are to be seen abundance of Geese and Ducks, and on the Banks of it many Sheep and other Cattle. Every thing is good in its kind in those Parts, and especially of the Fowl; but they sell them very dear,

Road of St. *Paul* a *French* Settlement.

L   a3

as they do the Hogs, which are of a very diminutive Breed. Land and Sea Tortoises are very common there : In a word, they have fish in great plenty, tho' they never fish any other way but with a Line, in the Boats of the Country, which are only Trunks of Trees hollow'd, which neither carry much, nor can venture out at Sea.

Blacks venture to crofs the Channel in little Boats. Nevertheless, there have been Blacks of *Madagafcar,* Slaves at *Mafcarin,* or *Mafcaregnas,* who, in order to escape, have attempted with one of those Boats to pass from one Isle to the other, in which some have succeeded, and others perish'd. They told us, that since that time the Company Royal of *France,* which is in possession of *Mafcarin,* had resolv'd to forbid the Inhabitants to buy *Blacks* from *Madagafcar,* besides, those *Blacks* are the most wicked *The most wicked in the World.* in the World. They seiz'd four of them, which they put in Irons, being accus'd with several others of a Plot against the Life of the Governour, the Officers, and the principal Inhabitants. It was to have been put in Execution on *Chriftmas* Night, which was nigh at hand, and Informations were given in of this Conspiracy.

The

The Day of the Solemnity we affifted at the Grand Mafs, where there were much People, and we faw Women as fair, and with as frefh Complexions, as there are in *France.* They wear Bodice and light Petty-Coats, dreffing their Heads after the *French* Fafhion; the Richer fort wear Lace, and moft of them go bare footed. Both Men and Women are perfectly civil and obliging, which they carry fo far as to ftop one paffing by their Doors, to invite him in to take a Refrefhment. *(Women fair as in France. Their Habit.)*

Thefe Cuftoms were very agreeable to our Officers, but in return, one muft make a Prefent of Punch, a Liquor which is very dear in that Country, *Aqua Vitæ* being often fold for a Piaftre and half the Bottle. *(Punch very dear.)*

The Houfes or Habitations of that Road, are not built in ranges, nor form Streets as in a Town; they are all wooden Buildings ftanding by themfelves, and but one Story high, becaufe of the frequent Hurricans which wou'd overthrow them all, if they rais'd them any higher. *(Houfes.)*

The Ifle in general, which is about fixty Leagues in compafs, is very mountanous, and full of Woods. Some Places afford *(Ifle, its extent and Soil.)*

L 2   very

very good Land, where they fow Wheat
and Rice. The Slaves do all the Husband-
man's Work, the Inhabitants labouring
very feldom.

Among the Trees, one fees very handfome Palms, which are not barren. The
Governour told me, there were about two
thoufand Souls in the whole Ifle, and that
it is good and very wholfome to live in.
So that it is with fome reafon that it has
been compar'd to the * terreftrial Paradife;
but it has almoft no Trade, but what it
carries on with the *French* Ships in their
Paffage to the *Indies.*

Captain
prepares
to depart.

In the mean time, the Day after the
Feafts, we caus'd our Beef and all other
Provifions to be embark'd, in order to depart immediately, notwithftanding the Civility of the Governour, and that of the
Inhabitants, who wou'd fain have had us
defer'd it a while longer.

A Me-
moir re-
lating to
*Mafca-
regnas.*

As we did not ftay long at *Mafcarin,* I
cou'd not learn every thing remarkable
concerning it ; but, after my return, a Friend
put into my Hands the Account which I

---

* A certain Author compares it to the terreftrial Paradife. The *French* firft landed there in 1650.

fhall

fhall add to that which I have already given of this Ifle. One cannot expect to be
better inform'd about it, fince the Perfon,
from whom I had it, drew it up from the
Writings, and the Report of Mr. *de Vil-
liers*, who had been Governour of the
Country for the *Eaft India* Company
eight or nine Years, and has gone all over
it fo carefully, examining it very exactly,
in order to make it fit for a good Colony,
as it already is; and it may become ftill
better hereafter, and alfo a confiderable
Staple for our oriental Voyages. Tho' feveral have written Accounts of this Ifland,
none have related the Curiofities which are
to be found in this Memoir, and which
appear to be very extraordinary.

An Account of the Ifle of Bour-bon *or* Mafcaregnas.

THE Ifle of *Bourbon* lies in the Ethi- Situation.
opic or *Indian* Ocean, almoft under
the Tropic of Capricorn, to the Eaft of the
Ifland of *Madagafcar*, from which it is
about eighty Leagues diftant. It does not
appear to have been known to the Anti-
ents, nor were there any Inhabitants upon

it

it when the *Portugals*, after they had doubled the Cape of good Hope, difcover'd it.
They gave it the Name of *Mafcaregnas*,
from that of their Captain, and the Vulgar
ftill retain it, calling the Inhabitants *Mafca-
rins*. It did not properly begin to be inhabited before the Year 1654, when Mr. *de
Flacour*, a *French* Gentleman, and Governour
of what they poffefs'd in the Ifland of *Madagafcar*, being inform'd that the Soil of that
of *Mafcaregnas* was excellent, and the Air
wonderfully healthful, fent thither feven or
eight of his Men, in order to be heal'd of
their Diforders, which they had contracted
at *Madagafcar*. As they were eafily heal'd,
and in a fhort time, they gave others a
Defire to go thither. From that Time it was
nam'd the Ifle of *Bourbon*. But there was
no confiderable Settlement made there, before the Royal Company of the Eaft took
Poffeffion of it, as at length they did about
the Year 1680, and have peopled it principally with *French*, under the Dominion of
the King. Moreover, there is nothing fpoken there but *French*, nor any Religion
profefs'd there but the [*Roman*] Catholic,
which has Priefts to take care of it. This
Ifle which is longer than broad, ftretcheth
from

Sidenotes:

Nam'd *Mafca-regnas* from the Difco-verer.

Poffefs'd by the *French*.

Call'd by them *Bourbon*.

from West to East, and is about sixty five Leagues in Compass.

The Land quite round the Isle and along the Sea Coast is flat, and continues so up to the Mountains which are not far off, and take up the middle of the Isle extending the length of it. They are interspers'd with Valleys, and several Rivers which spring out of them and water the Lands. The flat Country is divided into three Quarters, *viz.* St. *Denis,* St. *Paul,* and St. *Suzana,* in which the Inhabitants have built their Houses and fix'd their Dwellings, which do not yet make either a Town or Borough. They have already clear'd and cultivated a considerable quantity of Land, reaping Corn, Rice, *Spanish* Wheat, Millet and much Pulse.

Land part Mountain and part Plain.

Its Productions.

The Soil of the flat Country is not above two Foot deep before you come to a Rock, which is the reason that it grows soon out of Heart, and must be let alone. One finds greater depth of Soil in the Mountains, which is pretty extraordinary; those who have Courage enough, and are able to clear it, find their Account in it. In 1708, there were about nine hundred Inhabitants in the Isle, reckoning Heads of

Nature of the Soil.

Number of Inhabitants.

L 4   Fami-

Families, Children and Negro Slaves. There
is a Governour, a Regifter, and a Store-
Keeper for the Company of the Eaft. All

Trade. their Trade, excepting what they drive a
mong themfelves, confifts in fending every
Year a Bark to *Ponticheri,* on the Coaft
of *Coromandel,* [*Cori bandel*] and in receiving the Ships going or returning from the
Indies, which furnifh them with what they
have occafion for, at a very dear rate.

Air ex-
ceeding
healthful. The Air of this Ifle is admirable for
Health, neverthelefs the *Crioles,* who are
thofe born in the Place, do not ordinarily
live to be old , but others often reach a
hundred Years. The extraordinary Diftem-

Difeafes. pers of the Country are the Chotic, and an
accidental Cafe, call *Mal de Chien,* or the
Dogs Difeafe, which is cur'd by burning
the Sick Perfons Heel to the quick * with
a red hot Iron. There is no fuch thing as
a venomous Creature to be feen in this Ifle.

Volcano. Towards the Eaft there is a furious *Volcano,* which is a Mountain that vomits Fire,
and makes great Havock on all Sides: It
is continually burning, and the parts about

* This Diftemper is common in the *Indies,* where
it is call'd *Mordefhin.*

it

it are burnt and cover'd with Stones melt-
ed by that Fire, which are as brittle and
sharp as Flints. This Country is desert,
sulphurous, and worth nothing. They call
it the burnt Country. The Soil upon the
Mountains is better than that below. It is
very cold there, nor are they without Ice, Ice.
which is a thing to be admir'd at, consi-
dering it is under the Tropic.

Among those Plains, which are in the Plain of
Mountains, the most remarkable, and of the
which no body hitherto hath taken any Caffres.
notice, is that call'd the Plain of the Caffres; because a Troop of Caffres, the Slaves
of the Inhabitants of the Isle, went and
hid themselves there, after they had run
away from their Masters. From the Sea
Side, one ascends gently for about seven
Leagues to arrive at that Plain; there is
only one Road to it, along the River of
St. *Stephen*, which may also be travel'd on
Horseback. The Soil is good and even,
till a League and half before you come to
the Plain, adorn'd with large and beautiful Trees, the falling Leaves of which afford Nourishment for the Tortoises, which
are very numerous there. We may reckon
the Height of that Plain to be two Leagues
above

above the Horrizon; and it appears from below quite loft in the Clouds. It may be four or five Leagues in compafs. The

Cold is infupportable there, and a continual Fog, which wets as much as Rain, hinders one from feeing ten Paces before him. As Night comes on, one fees clearer than in the Day, but then it freezes terribly; and in the Morning, before Sun rife, the Plain appears all frozen. But the moft ex-

traordinary Thing to be feen there, are certain Elevations of Earth, cut almoft in the Form of Pillars, round and prodigioufly high; for they cannot be lefs than the Towers of *Notre Dame* at *Paris.* They are plac'd like a fet of Nine-pins, and fo like one another, that one may be eafily out in reckoning them: They call them the *Spikes.* If one has a Mind to ftop and reft himfelf near one of them, thofe who go on to fome other Place, muft not advance above two hundred Paces; if they do, they run the rifque of never finding the Place they left. Thefe Spikes, as they call them, are fo numerous, all fo like one another, and difpos'd fo much after the fame manner, that the *Crioles,* who are the Natives of the Country, are deceiv'd themfelves by them.

them. To remedy this Inconvenience, when a Company of Travellers ftop at the Foot of one of thefe Spikes, and fome of them have a mind to feparate themfelves, they leave fomebody there, who makes a Fire or Smoke, which ferves to direct the other the way back again; and if the Fog proves fo thick, as to hinder the Sight of the Fire or the Smoke, they provide certain large Shells, one of which they leave with the Perfon who ftays at the Spike; carrying the other along with them, and when they have a Mind to return, they blow into this Shell with all their Force, as if it was a Trumpet, which makes a very fhrill Sound, and is heard a great way off: In this manner anfwering one another, they avoid loofing themfelves, and eafily meet again. Without this Precaution one might be bewilder'd there.

There are abundance of Afpin Trees in this Plain, which are continually green; the other Trees are troubled with a Mofs above a Fathom long, which covers the Trunk and great Branches of them. They have no Bows with Leaves on, but appear wither'd, and are fo moiften'd with Water, that there is no making a Fire with them.

The Trees all Leaflefs except the Afpin.

them. If, after much Trouble, they get some of the Bránches kindled, you have only a Fire without Flame, with a reddifh Smoke, which fmokes the Victuals inftead of dreffing them. One wou'd be hard fet to find a Place in that Plain to make a Fire in, except he wou'd pitch upon fome ri-fing Ground about thofe Spires, for the Soil

Exceed-ing Moi-fture of the Soil. is fo moift, that the Water fprings out of it every where; and one is always up to the Calf of the Leg in Dirt and Pud-dle. Ones fees there a great number of blue Birds, which build their Nefts in the Grafs and the Water Fern. This Plant was unknown before the flight of the Caffres. To defcend, one muft take the fame way he went up by, unlefs he has a mind to hazard himfelf in another, which is very rugged and dangerous.

The Sa-lafes. One fees from the Plain of the *Caffres,* the Mountain of the three *Salafes,* fo call'd, on account of three Points of that Rock, which is the higheft in the Ifle of *Bourbon.* All its Rivers flow out of it, and it is fo fteep on every fide, that there is no afcending it.

Silaos Plain higher than the former. There is yet in this Ifle another Plain, call'd *Silaos,* which is higher than that of the

the *Caffres*, and not a Jot better; befides, there is no getting to it without great Difficulty.

The Ifle of *Bourbon* is very woody, but the Trees are different from thofe of *Europe*, and of a furprizing Height and Thicknefs. One finds Ebony there, which is only the Heart of the Tree, and which is never above half a Foot thick. There are alfo certain Trees, of which may be made very good Casks. Much Aloes is alfo produc'd there, and a great quantity of excellent Gums, which lie neglected, may be gather'd without all that nicity and care which they generally require. The Tafamaca Tree, and that of the Benjamin, grow to a great height, as well as another call'd Natte. There are Birds there call'd Flamans, which are taller than any Man.

This Ifle has one great Fault, as neither having a Port, nor any Place to make one in. Two Roads, one of St. *Denis*, and the other of St. *Paul*, are the only Anchorage, where Ships that pafs that way may ftop and refrefh themfelves; but are not fecur'd againft the violent Seafon of the Hurricans, thofe horrible Tempefts, which trouble thofe Seas at certain Times. There

is

[margin notes:] Ifle woody. Ebony. Aloes. Choife Gums. Birds. No Port in the Ifle.

is in this Ifle a very remarkable River, for the Bottom of its Channel is cover'd and pav'd, as one may fay, in fuch a manner, with long and very fat Eels, that it takes its Name from thence.

A Tempeft or Hurrican.

The Evening before we embark'd, the Skie, which was ordinarily calm enough in that Place, was obferv'd to be overcaft, and prefently a fmall Fog began to rife, which turn'd into mifling Rain, without the leaft Breath of Wind all the while. This was the firft Sign of a Hurrican, which was brewing. At Night we heard a great Noife, as if it was Thunder, in the Mountains; and fhortly after, fome of the People who liv'd in the Plain arriv'd, who gave us an Account, that they had feen the Brooks overflow their Banks, and the Birds to fly from the Woods, in which there were heard terrible Noifes.

We prepar'd at Day break, to make what hafte we cou'd on board, at which Time it rain'd and lighten'd excefsively, and the Air was very thick. Mr. *de Champloret* and I, having taken Leave of the Governour, we embark'd feparately in our refpective Boats, which carry'd us to our Ships. It was the Boat belonging to the

Captain

Captain of the Port, which did me that piece of Service; for I was oblig'd to leave mine to carry our Officers, who, not regarding the Appearance of a Hurrican, were ſtill on ſhore, propoſing to divert themſelves.

The Wind which began to blow, encreas'd every Moment, and the Waves ſwell'd in like manner. The Merchants Ships drove with their Anchors, and in ſhort, the Hurrican cou'd not well be greater. The Skie was quite cover'd over with thick and heavy Clouds, in the Inſtant that I had got on board. Storms encreaſe.

I arriv'd luckily, time enough to make ready the top Sails; for, as I obſerv'd before, we dragg'd our Anchors; and, to add to our Vexation, the Fluke of our great Anchor broke, and it was to be fear'd, we wou'd daſh ourſelves to Pieces againſt our Merchant Ships; which we ſhou'd have ſunk into the Bargain. I had juſt got the Cable faſten'd to the Cabeſtan, when we ſaw our Merchantman advance after us. I immediately caus'd the Cable to be cut, and the top Sails to be hoiſted, and the main Sail, which was torn, to be put in order.

Mr.

Mr. *de Champloret* was then to the Windward, endeavouring to get on the other side of us; but he cou'd not bring it about without the Rifque of running foul upon us. Very fortunately I flacken'd my Courfe, and our Merchant Ship, which fteer'd perfectly well, efcap'd: But it was at the fame time in another Danger; for we cou'd hardly bring all this to bear, without the hazard of lofing our other Merchant Men, and ourfelves with them.

As foon as I had got quite clear of the Road, I caus'd the top Sails to be taken in, defigning to ftop at the Cape; for the Wind encreas'd more and more, which oblig'd me to come to a Refolution to put out to Sea; for in thefe Hurricans the Wind Shifts every Moment, and whips round one half of the Compafs in a Trice.

Our Officers arriv'd however, after having gone through a great deal of Trouble and Danger; they were wet through and through, the Ship Boat being fo full of Water, that they were forc'd to quit her, and let her go adrift.

Boat let adrift.

We faw our other Ships ftill in the fame Diftrefs we had been ourfelves. Mr. *de Champloret* had lain by, and waited for

his

his Sloop which was gone to recover its Anchor, but could not get to the Windward, and so ran the Risque of losing her. At last she came up with the *Conqueror*, who happily waiting for her, she recover'd it.

The Wind and Rain continu'd with the same Violence, and I was so wet that I was oblig'd to go for a Minute to *change my Clothes*, during which Time our Officers indiscreetly sail'd before the Wind; so that when I came upon Deck, I had lost Sight of our other Ships; and we tack'd about to the Windward, to get sight of 'em, but to no purpose. The next Morning the Wind abated a little, but the Sea continu'd to be disturb'd.

This Hurrican, which without doubt caus'd as much Damage on Land as at Sea, was in a particular Manner vexatious to us; for of all the Oxen we had embark'd, we were able to recover but two, the rest perishing in the Storm: It was to no purpose that we salted the Flesh, which all we could do would not keep. By good Luck they sav'd forty great Land-Tortoises, which had nothing given them to eat, feeding, as they believ'd, upon their own Fat.

M   We

Meet a
Danish
Ship from
Tranque-
bar.

We had ftill a bad Time of it croffing the *Bank of Needles,* and the Wind being then contrary, and the Sea in a Ferment, we ftaid two Days at the *Cape.* We met with a *Danish* Ship, coming from the Coaft of *Caromandel* [*Coro bandel*] where that Nation has a Factory at *Tranquebar:* He was a long time refolving with himfelf, whether he fhould come and fpeak with us, notwithftanding the Shots which we made at him. He fled from us as faft as he could, thinking we ought to be content with feeing his Flag; at length the repeated Shots, which began to maul his Mafts, made him come to a Refolution to fall to the Leeward, demanding whence we came? We carry'd *English* Colours, and oblig'd him to fend out his Shallop, having no Room to excufe himfelf upon account of the Weather, which was very fine, and the Sea calm.

We examin'd his Pafport, which was of four Years ftanding; the Books of the Factory of *Tranquebar,* which the Director was fending to the *Danish* Company, and read a great many Letters. We detain'd all thofe which were for *England* and *Holland,* wherein they made great Complaints

plaints againſt the *French* Privateers, and
againſt us in particular; ſaying, that three
Ships of St. *Malo* diſturb'd all the Trade of
the two Nations in the *Indies,* and that, if a
Remedy was not apply'd, they ſhould in-
cur great Loſſes; adding, that four *Engliſh*
Ships had been oblig'd to retreat into a
Port, and land all their Money, fearing
they ſhould be attack'd and boarded there.
After we had ſent back the Box of Papers
belonging to the Factory, and all the Letters which no way concern'd ourſelves,
we wiſh'd the *Daniſh* Captain a good
Voyage, who was going to take in Refreſhments at the *Cape of Good Hope.*

We paſs'd the *Cape* ourſelves at length,
but at the Diſtance of about ſixty Miles, and
propos'd to ſteer away for the Iſle of *Aſ-* Iſle of *Aſ-*
cenſion, in hopes to meet our Comrades *cenſion.*
there, or at leaſt to hear ſome News of
them; and to catch Tortoiſes, which are
there in great Plenty, but we cou'd never
hit upon it. Thoſe who touch at that Iſle
uſually leave a Bottle there well cork'd,
with a Letter therein, at the Foot of a
Croſs, to give notice of their Paſſage, and
of what elſe they have a mind.

M 2   There

There happen'd nothing extraordinary during the Continuance of our Voyage, till we pass'd the Line, which we did very happily by means of a fair Wind and a little Rain. We did not feel the same Heats which we found coming from *Europe*; but I am of Opinion this Alteration was only with regard to ourselves, who were now accustom'd to the burning Heats of the *Arabian* Coasts, which were so great, that we never found any thing to come up to them.

Pass'd the Line.

In the Latitude of 34 Deg. to the North of the Line, we had sight of a Ship, which we lost again in the Night; it tack'd about as we did, and work'd its Way by contrary Winds, which made us conclude, that it was bound for *Europe* as well as ourselves: Next day we saw her again, and drew near her. I judg'd it might be one of our Company, which we might easily have discover'd, if, during the Time I was taking a little Rest, our Men had not chang'd the Course, so that we saw it no more.

Azores Isles.

We pass'd at a good Distance the Isles of the *Azores*, and we saw great Numbers of those Birds, nam'd *Calculots* and *Dadins*,

Dadins, which made us imagine, that we
were not far from the *Vegies*, three great
Shelves of Rocks off thofe Ifles.

Ten or twelve Days after we faw a
Ship; and as the Captain continu'd his
Courfe without Fear, having an *Englifh*
Pafs, we came up with him prefently: He
carry'd a *Spanifh* Flag, and we an *Englifh*; he put out his Shallop, to acquaint
us, that he belong'd to St. *Sebaftian*, and
fhew'd us his Difpatches from that Place.
They made ufe of his Shallop to go on
board him, and they gave us an Account,
that the whole Ship's Crew were *Biska-
yans*. It was but eight Days fince that
Veffel fet out on the Whale-Fifhery.
They fhew'd us their Journal, according
to which they were forty Leagues to the
Weft of *Waterford:* Whereupon we cor-
rected our Courfe, finding that we had
committed an Error in computing the
Way our Ship had made, which did not
run fo hafty as we imagin'd, becaufe they
were not well able to clear her Bottom intirely from the Shells which ftuck to it.

We had afterwards for eight Days together Eaft Winds, which were fo directly
contrary to the Courfe we had to fteer,

M 3   that

that they prevented our being able to make
Land: And we had already confum'd two
Barrels of Biskets, which the *Spaniard*
before-mention'd had given us; informing us, that they had in *Europe* a
very fevere Winter; and that Corn was
dear every where. At length the Winds
turning about we continu'd our Courfe;
and two Days after we founded, finding
ninety Fathom; by that we found, that
we were upon the Bank which lies off

The *Sor-* the *Sorlings* about fifty Leagues.
lings.

Next Morning, about eight o' Clock,
we difcover'd four Ships, two of which
were to the Leeward, and the other was
before us. They gave me Notice of it,
and I fpy'd them with a Glafs, without
being able to difcern or difcover the Hull
of the Ship. I ftill held on the fame
Courfe, and in a little Time we came
within Cannon - Shot of the Veffel
which was before us. She took in her
Top Sail, and crowded her Main Sails.
In the mean Time I refrefh'd the Ship's
Crew, to prepare them for the Fight;
but that Ship which feem'd to be a
Hollander, feeing the Difpofition of our's,
which was inferior to it in nothing,
hoifted

hoifted his Sails again; and, without putting out his Flag, continu'd his Courfe, as
we did our's, and at length loft Sight of
him and his Companions.

Next Day, which was the 7th of *May,* The Ifle
1710, we had early in the Morning the ot *Ouef-*
agreeable Profpect of the Ifle of *Oueffant,* *fant.*
and we made towards it. Then fome
Officers, who had bought Goods with the
Money which was found in our Prizes,
long'd for nothing more than to get into *Breft*; and they propos'd it to me,
under Pretence of it's being my Intereft.
I anfwer'd, that neither my Health, which
was already much alter'd, nor my private Intereft fhou'd ever make me forget the general Intereft of the Company,
to which they well knew I was firmly
attach'd ; and that, the Wind being fair, I
was of Opinion we ought to make the
beft ufe of it.

'Tis certain it wou'd have been much to
my Advantage to have put in at *Breft*;
but I was incapable of taking that Refolution, even tho' I had forefeen that I
fhou'd be oblig'd to pay exorbitant Duties at St. *Malo,* and that the Company, for whofe Sake I made that Sacri-

M 4 fice

fice of my own Interests, wou'd treat
me afterwards with Rigour enough, forgetting their Promises and my Services.

In our Way to St. *Malo*, we faw a
Ship of thirty Guns, which parted from
Four, and bore directly down upon us:
She prepar'd also to fight us; nevertheless,
when she was about a League off, she
chang'd her Resolution, beginning to
fly the same Course we were steering:
We lost Sight of her about two in the Afternoon.

Arrive at
St. *Malo.*

Next Day, being in Sight of St *Malo*
and by the Side of the *Conchee*, I order'd
a Signal to be made. The Person, who
was principally concern'd, dispatch'd immediately a Boat to his Agent, who gave
me a Letter from him, ordering me to
bring the Ship into the Port, having sent
me a Pilot for that End. I had already
drawn close to the Place, which is call'd
the great Gate, contrary to the evil Design of the Officers I have already spoke
of, who had plotted among themselves;
having at their Head the most mutinous
and resolute Man that can be, and took
an Oath to bring the Ship in Spight of
me under Cape *Frehele*, and anchor
there;

there, with a Defign to land whatever
they cou'd, threatning to knock out any
one's Brains, who fhou'd oppofe them.
But for all their Talk, I refolv'd to bring
the Ship into the Road, and we caft Anchor there the eighth.

The perfon principally concern'd in
Intereft, whom I mention'd before, came
on board my Ship. Complements being
over, I told him plainly, that fuch and
fuch Officers, which he faw before him,
were fo many unfaithful Servants of the
Company. I took him afterwards afide,
to give him a full Account of the whole
Affair; and particularly to let him know,
that one *William Serot*, call'd *la Croix*,
a Man worth nothing, brutifh in his Behaviour, and of very bad Qualities; was
the Author of the Plot, the Execution
of which I had prevented; and had taken a Bar of Gold of the Value of near
twenty thoufand Livres, which he had
lock'd up in his Cheft, where he had
made a Hiding-Place for the Purpofe.
Thereupon the Lieutenant General of
the Admiralty was apply'd to, before
whom they proceeded againft the faid
Serot, who was imprifon'd in the Town,
and

The Cap-
tain accu-
fes fome
of his
Officers
to the
Com-
pany.

and deny'd the Fact for two Days together. But at length two of that Company wrought upon by Menaces, he
then declar'd, that he had only the middle Part of the Bar, the two Ends of it
having been faw'd off; whereupon thofe
two Gentlemen carry'd him with them
on board the Ship, to fearch for that
pretended Piece of a Gold-Bar, in the
Place where he faid he had put it.
They difcover'd indeed the Hiding-Holes,
and found the Bar of Gold perfectly
whole, without being the leaft diminifh'd
or alter'd.

Some Days after the other Ships, which
I had feparated from, happily arriv'd in
the fame Port, and the Company had
all the Reafon in the World to be fatisfy'd with the Succefs of their Undertaking.

AN

A N

ACCOUNT

OF A

VOYAGE,

From Mocha *to the Court of the King of* Yaman, *in the Mountains of* Arabia, *perform'd in the second Expedition, in the Years* 1711, 1712 *and* 1713.

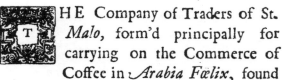

T HE Company of Traders of St. *Malo*, form'd principally for carrying on the Commerce of Coffee in *Arabia Fœlix*, found the firſt Expedition anſwer ſo well, of which we have given ſome Account, that they were not long reſolving upon a ſecond; which has been attended with as good Succeſs, and will no leſs gratify the Curioſity of the Publick, than the former. For this Purpoſe the Company fitted out

two

two of the beſt Ships in that Port, the *Peace* and the *Diligent*, which departed from Saint *Malo* about the Beginning of *January*, 1711, under the Command of Monſieurs *de le Lande* and *Briſelaine*, experienc'd Captains.

These Ships cou'd never make the Straits of the *Red Sea* in the Month of *Auguſt*, the Seaſon in which the Winds were ſtill fair for carrying them thither. They ſaw the Iſle of *Zocotora* very plain, but they cou'd not come near it, no more than the Coaſt of *Aden*, becauſe the *Mouſſon* at

The Cape takes it's Name from the Iſle of *Comar* to the Eaſt of the *Maldives*.

that Time blew from the N. E. To loſe no Time, the Captains agreed to go and cruiſe upon Cape *Comeries*, which with the Iſle of *Ceylon* forms the Strait of that Name, and is one of the moſt famous Paſſages of *Aſia*.

This Courſe was very lucky to them, by throwing in their Way two *Engliſh* Veſſels richly loaden, which they join'd to a *Dutch* Ship taken on this Side the *Cape of Good Hope*; and about a Month after, they return'd to the Coaſt of *Arabia*.

They put in firſt at *Aden*, to take skilful Pilots to conduct them ſafely into the *Red Sea*, but they cou'd get none. 'Tis ſaid
the

the *Arabs* made a Scruple of Religion to embark in our Veffels; neverthelefs they arriv'd happily at *Mocha*, and anchor'd there with the Prizes the 2d of *Dec.* 1711. They found for Governour of *Mocha*, him who was that of *Aden* in their firft Voyage. He had been put in the Room of his Brother *Sheik Saleh*, whom the King of *Yaman* had made *Wazir*, or his principal Minifter. That new Governour receiv'd our Captains perfectly well, and with fome particular Diftinction.

Some Time after, the King of *Yaman* falling ill, his new Minifter extoll'd to him the Skill of the *French* Phyficians, advifing him to fend for one from the Ships arriv'd at *Mocha*. The King thereupon gave his Orders to *Sheik Saleh* himfelf, who immediately fent Deputies to our Captains, with a very courteous Letter, which contain'd the Bufinefs of their Meffage. To fhew that the Voyage was important, the Minifter had made Chief of that Deputation *Sidy Abedil*, principal Secretary to the King, attended by an Officer. He carry'd, as a Mark of his Authority, a little Battle-Ax with a Sil-

ver

ver-Handle, hung at his Girdle, on the Horſe's Saddle.

The Letter from the Miniſter being receiv'd and interpreted, the Captains took the Word, Doctor, which was there often repeated, in ſomewhat too ſtrict a Senſe, and, like true Tars, made Anſwer, that they had no Phyſicians aboard their Ships; but Men that underſtood how to cut off Legs and Arms, and dreſs Wounds, who ſometimes took upon them alſo to manage ſick Folks, and that ſometimes they cur'd them.

The Deputies reply'd, that it was that Sort of Phyſicians the King wanted, being troubled with a dangerous Impoſthume, which he had in his Ear, and that he had great Dependance upon their Skill. Then our Captains conſulted together, and they reſolv'd to make their Advantage of this Conjuncture, to make known the *French* Nation to the King of *Taman*, and to become better acquainted, than any yet had been, with the Country under his Subjection, in Order to draw from thence all the Advantage poſſible for their Commerce.

With

With that View, and to repay the Honour that was done them, they made a formal Deputation to the King of *Ta-man*; the Care of which they laid upon Monſieur *de la Grelaudiere*, Major of the Garriſon of *Pondichery*; who, being deſirous to return to *France*, was come from the *Indies* to *Mocha*, with our Captains, who had given him the Command of the *Holland* Prize. They made choice of him as a Man of Spirit and Conduct, and who underſtood the Language too well to be impos'd upon by a *Portugueze* Interpreter; who was given to him for an *Arab*.

Some Retinue was given to accompany this Deputy, and amongſt the reſt in particular the Sieur *Barbier*, an experienc'd Surgeon of the *Diligent*; but who was only ſecond to the Sieur *des Noyers*, chief Surgeon of the Fleet, whom they judg'd proper to detain for the Occaſion of the Ships. In ſhort, the Captains entruſted the Deputies with ſome Preſents for the King; the principal Piece was, a very fine Glaſs of between five and ſix Foot high; there was among them alſo,

a Pair

a Pair of Piftols curioufly wrought, and fome Pieces of our beft Cloth.

Our Deputies, and thofe of the King of *Yaman*, fet out in Company from *Mocha*, the 14th of *Feb.* 1712, about four in the Afternoon, mounted on very fine Horfes, moft curioufly accoutred. The Cavalcade confifted of about twenty Perfons, conducted by a Troop of Horfe, and follow'd by many Camels, and other Beafts of Burthen; for every one carry'd his neceffary Provifions for the Journey.

Mofa. They march'd all the reft of the Day, and a good Part of the Night, and came at three in the Morning to *Mofa*, a fmall, but pretty handfome country Town, after having travell'd ten Leagues. That Town furnifhes almoft all the Poultry, which is carry'd to *Mocha*, and is the Rendezvous, and Thorough-fare of the Fruits which come from the Mountains.

Manzery. They mounted again at ten in the Forenoon, and came to lye at *Manzery*, where there were but five or fix Houfes. They pafs'd the Night under Palm-Trees and Poplars: This fecond Day's Journey had been fifteen Leagues.

Next Day they parted very early to reach *Tage*, where they arriv'd after marching eight-

eighteen Leagues, but in very good Road, and almoſt always plain. This Town is very famous in the Country; 'tis great and encloſ'd with fair Walls, which are ſaid to be built by the *Turks*, with a good Caſtle upon a Mountain, which commands the Town, and which is ſeen ſix Leagues off. It has thirty great Braſs-Cannons, and 'tis there where the Priſoners of State are or-dinarily confin'd. They have contriv'd ſe-veral Gardens upon the Declivity of that Hill, which makes a very agreeable Pro-ſpect to the Eye, and are of conſiderable Advantage to the Town. The Governour of *Tage* is the Son of the late King, or Predeceſſor to him who now reigns. Our Deputies did not fail to wait upon him in the Caſtle, nor he to receive and regale them very handſomely, chiefly with Coffee of the *Soltana:* He ask'd ſeveral Que-ſtions about the Largeneſs of *France*, and the Power of the King, and was aſto-niſh'd at the Anſwers that were made him. They ſaw afterwards a Part of the Town where there are nine or ten fair *Mosks* [or *Masjeds.*]

From *Tage*, continuing their Journey *Tage.* to reach *Manzuel*, our Travellers had

N   the

the Pleasure to see, about six Leagues from the former, Coffee-Trees for the first Time. They are reckon'd to be the fairest and best cultivated in all *Yaman*; they saw also Abundance of Fruit-Trees.

Manzuel. There is at *Manzuel* nothing but two very old Castles, one of which was heretofore the Habitation of the Kings, in the Time of the Wars with the *Turks*.

From *Manzuel* they undertook to go in two Days to *Yrama*, a Town thirty *Gabala.* Leagues distant, passing thro' *Gabala*, a small Town wall'd on one Side, and whose Mosks have very fair Towers or Menaras. 'Tis a Son of the King now reigning who has the Government; our Envoys went to salute him; that Prince is handsome, and of a good Presence.

They lay upon the Road under Trees, and the next arriv'd at the Town of *Yrama.* *Yrama*, which is large, without Walls, and where also there is a Governour.

Leaving *Yrama*, they found the highest Mountains which are it may be in *Yaman*. The Country, which till then made a Prospect agreeable enough, tho' often interrupted by Mountains, began to appear very dry and barren. They saw no
more

more Trees or Valleys ftor'd with Coffee-
Plantations, as in the preceeding Part of
the Journey; where befides the Land is
water'd by the Streams which fall down
from the Hills, which frequently form
Rills, without making at the fame Time
any River.

From *Trama* they march'd to *Damar*, Damar.
another confiderable Town, diftant from
the former fifteen Leagues of very bad
Way, always thro' very high Mountains,
where reign'd all Day a burning Heat,
without any Wind, or other Coolnefs
till after Sun-Set.

But as foon as they had got to *Da-*
mar, they had no more Fatigue to undergo ; and there they began, as one may fay,
to take Breath; for the Country begins
to open, and extend it felf in very agreeable Plains ; befides, not above three Quarters of a Mile from *Damar*, lies the Town
of *'Muab*, which is the ordinary Abode *Muab*, the
of the King of *Taman*.   Abode of
the K. of

It is fituate on the fouthern Defcent *Taman*.
of a little Mountain, and was built by
the King who reigns at prefent. At a
like Diftance of three Quarters of a Mile,
that Prince has alfo caus'd to be built,

N 2   upon

upon a higher Mountain than the former, a Caftle, which likewife bears the
Name of * *Muab*. 'Tis, as it were, a
Pleafure-Houfe, where the King often goes
to recreate himfelf; fo that, by what has
been obferv'd, *Damar*, *Muab*, and the
Caftle of that Name, form a Kind of a
Triangle, and ftand at equal Diftances
from each other.

Two Leagues and a half from *Muab*,
the King has likewife built upon a little
Mountain a Citadel, where he has plac'd
his beft Soldiers in Garrifon, and a great
Quantity of Artillery.   He retires thither
with the neighbouring Princes in Times
of War, when he apprehends the Approach of his Enemies, and is not ftrong
enough to make head againft them.

The *Arab* Envoys, who had accompany'd our's, feparated from them at a
fmall Diftance from *Muab*, and advanc'd
forward, defiring our's to ftop a little,
that they might have Time to acquaint
the King of their Arrival.   That Prince

---

* I have feen Difpatches dated from that Caftle
which alfo is call'd in *Arabic, Hefn al Mawahib*,
that is to fay, the Caftle, or the Palace, of the
Graces.

refolv'd

refolv'd immediately to fend to meet the *French*, and to give them a remarkable Reception: But our People had not Patience to wait for this Ceremony, on Account of the Extremity of the Heat. They therefore, after a very fhort Halt, march'd forwards, notwithftanding which they found a great Crowd of People, who had flock'd out of *Muab* to fee them, which always happen'd to them wherever they went.

In this Manner our Deputies, after having march'd Day and Night almoft continually, changing Horfes often, arriv'd at *Muab* the eighth Day after their Departure from *Mocha*, having travell'd above a hundred and twenty Leagues in pretty rough Roads, and almoft all along in the Mountains. 'Tis obferv'd in their Memoirs, that their Courfe from *Mocha* was almoft continually towards the North Eaft.

They lighted in the Court of the Palace, after they had pafs'd through five different Gates, where there are Guard-Houfes. They were receiv'd in that Court by an Officer of the King's Chamber, who conducted them by a hand-

N 3   fome

some Stair-Case into the inner Part of the Palace, which is built in two great Wings of three Stories each.

They were defir'd to wait a while at the Door of the King's Apartment, and in the mean Time that Officer difcours'd with them by an Interpreter. This Attendance was not long, and at length Word was brought, that they might enter; which they did, after leaving their Shoes at that Door. The firft they met with was the prime Minifter *Sheikh Saleh*, who after he had made them his Complements, adding that he was a fincere Friend to the *French*, introduc'd them into the King's Chamber.

That Prince, who is an old Man, aged eighty feven Years, well made, of an agreeable Countenance, and moderately fwarthy, was feated upon his Bed, or rather an Eftrade, cover'd with Carpets, and plac'd at the lower End of the Chamber, facing the Door. He was fupported by Cufhions, having next his Perfon the two Princes, his Sons; and a little further off his principal Officers. From the Foot of the Eftrade there ran two Ranks of his Domefticks, which left

a large

a large Paſſage between them, for thoſe to advance who came to have Audience of the King.

The Chief of our Deputation preſented himſelf firſt, made the King a low Bow, and was going to begin the little Speech which he had prepar'd; but the King, in all likelihood mov'd by his Diſtemper, interrupted him, to ask which of them was the Doctor? As ſoon as they had ſhew'd him to the Prince, he immediately roſe up, two of his Officers aſſiſted him to deſcend from the *Sopha*, and conducted him near a great Window; there, taking off his Turban, he ſhew'd the *French* Surgeon the Diſtemper he was afflicted with. The Surgeon diſcover'd immediately both the Impoſthume which was gather'd in his Ear, and the Ignorance of thoſe who had taken in hand the Dreſſing of it; becauſe the Humour run a little, they had thought it ſufficient to apply to it a Sort of yellowiſh Earth, thinking to heal the Diſtemper by drying the ailing Part; but it happen'd quite otherwiſe; for that Remedy, inſtead of drying, had already caus'd an Inflammation; ſo that the poor Prince ſuffer'd continual Pains, which had thrown

N 4   him

him into a Fever, and took away his Reft. Our Surgeon, at the firft Sight of it, af-fur'd the King, that he wou'd cure him; and, in order to hearten and give him Eafe, he apply'd off-hand the Oil of Ro-fes to moiften the Part, and take off all that yellow Earth. After that, he did no more but apply a proper Plaifter, to draw off gently the impofthumated Matter. The King then fhew'd him a Swelling which he had upon his Hand, which the Sur-geon perceiv'd to be of the fame Kind with the Diftemper in his Ear, and that they had alfo treated it in an imprudent Manner; he made the fame Application to it as he had done to the Impofthume, and gave the King Hopes, that he fhou'd foon be deliver'd from the Indifpofition which he labour'd under.

That Prince afterwards went back again to his Seat, and faid feveral obliging Things to our Deputies; he ask'd them many Queftions concerning their Voyage, and receiv'd, with a great deal of Pleafure, the Prefent which they made him in behalf of our Captains; the Looking-Glafs was what attracted his Attention moft, he look'd himfelf feveral Times in it, as did all the

Grandees

Grandees of his Court : And thus the firſt Audience ended.

The *French* did not leave the Palace, for the King was pleas'd that they ſhould be lodg'd there, and be ſupply'd with all Neceſſaries. He appointed them three Apartments, one of which was to ſerve for their Kitchen ; but thoſe Apartments were very bare, being in a Manner without all other Moveables, beſides Foot-Carpets and Cuſhions for the Eſtrades or Sophas, which were to ſerve them inſtead of Tables, Chairs and Beds. This is the Faſhion of almoſt all the Orientals.

As with Regard to the King, the principal Occaſion of this Deputation was his Cure ; the Sieur *Barbier* was very aſſiduous about that Prince : He purg'd him, and gave him ſeveral cooling Medicines, without forgetting outward Applications ; ſo that by Degrees the Diſtemper decreas'd, and his Sleep and Appetite return'd, to the great Satisfaction of every Body.

In the mean Time, Mr. *De la Grelandier* made his Advantage of theſe Opportunities, and had frequent Audiences of the Prince, in which he forgot nothing which might whet and ſatisfy his Curioſity, with regard

gard to the State of *France*, the Power
of the King, the Magnificence of his
Court and his Palace; and in particular,
concerning the Qualifications and perfo-
nal Vertues of that great Prince. The
Account pleas'd the King of *Yaman* much,
who never ceas'd admiring what he heard,
and to difcover his Satisfaction feveral
Ways.

The Care which the King took, that
the *French* fhou'd be well entertain'd at
his Court, is not to be exprefs'd; he
often fent them Difhes from his own Table, and gave exprefs Orders for all the
reft; but our People cou'd not always
conform themfelves to the Victuals which
they fet before them, wherein all Sorts
of Spice, and efpecially Cinnamon prevail d to Excefs. Thefe Meats were commonly Kid, Veal and Mutton, cut into
fmall Pieces and boil'd together, with Rice
and a certain Quantity of Raifins They
were alfo ferv d up with Beef as ftrangely
drefs'd, and fometimes with Fowl, which
the *Arabs* skin as foon as they have kill'd
them, and fry them out of hand. They
deal the fame Way by all their other Sorts
of Victuals, which they drefs without
giving

giving them Time to mortify or grow
tender. As for wild Fowl, they never eat
any. Their Bread, which is infipid enough,
is made much like the Calettes or thin
Cakes, which they eat in *Bretaign* and
Normandy. They do not ufe Wine,
tho' there are Vineyards about *Muab,*
and offer no other Drink but Water and
Coffee.

Our People, as I have already obferv'd,
being not able to take up with this Manner of Living, defir'd that they would
furnifh them only with what Provifions
were neceffary, and leave the Dreffing it
to themfelves; whereupon they fupply'd
them to their Satisfaction, and with a
furprizing Exactnefs.

They ftaid at *Muab* three whole Years, Defcrip-
for it requir'd no lefs Time to reftore the tion of
Muab.
King to his perfect Health. They often
walk'd out of the Palace to fee the Town
and the Places about it. This Town is
confiderable only upon Account of the
Refidence of the Prince; for it is not
large, the Walls are of Earth, as are moft
Part of the Houfes. One of the Suburbs
of *Muab* is entirely inhabited by *Jews,*
who are oblig'd to quit it every Evening,
not

not being fuffer'd to lye in the Town. The
Air of *Muab* is very good ; 'tis cold in
the Morning before Sun-Rife, and after
Sun-Set ; but from 9 a Clock in the Morning till 4 in the Afternoon, the Heat there
is very great.

The King's Officers often bore our People Company in their Travels, which they
took on Horfeback in the Parts about the
Town, where generally the Land appear'd
to be very good. All the Plain Country
was then ferv'd with Rice and Wheat, and
almoft all the Hilly and Valley Part was
planted with very fair Coffee-Trees, not
to mention many Vineyards and abundance
of other Fruit-Trees.

The King, in a private Difcourfe which
he had with our Deputies, had boafted
much of a Garden, which he had actually caus'd to be planted near *Muab*, where
he faid, he had none but choice Coffee-Trees, which they call the King's Coffee-Trees. Our People did not fail going to
fee that Garden, where they found nothing
extraordinary, except it be, that the King
has taken a great deal of Care, to caufe
thofe Trees, which are too common in
his Kingdom, to be plac'd in an Inclofure,
and in a particular Arrangement.

Mr

Mr. *De la Grelandier*, after having prais'd the new Garden to the King, took the Liberty to tell him his Thoughts thereupon, and in what Manner the greatest Princes in *Europe* make use of Trees with Regard to their Gardens, where they put none but for Ornament, and for their Shade; adding, that if there happens to be found any Fruit among them, the Princes take a Pleasure in letting their Courtiers make use of them.

The King of *Yaman* took the Hint very readily, and answer'd, that he did not pique himself less upon a good Taste and Generosity, than the *European* Princes; that indeed, the Coffee-Trees were very common in his Country, but that it was nothing the less dear and agreeable to him upon that Score, because of its continual Verdure, and the Singularity of its Production, which perhaps is the only Instance of the Kind in Nature, and no where else to be found; that it was a perfect Pleasure to him, to see that Sort of Trees grow, which were planted, as it were, with his own Hand, in order to confer his Bounties from them; and that, in a Word, he

knew

knew no Plants or Fruits which in reality exceeded Coffee.

Here might naturally be inferted, as in its proper Place, a particular Defcription of the Palace of that Prince. Our People had all the Opportunity imaginable to fee and examine it; but being more curious to tell nothing but the exact Truth, than to adorn their Narration with chimerical Magnificence; they have declared, that tho' this Palace be large and commodious, after the Manner of the Country, yet nothing is more plain and out of the Way, than its Structure; as nothing furprizes alfo more, than the Simplicity of the Furniture, and the other Ornaments within Side. One may judge by thofe of the King's Chamber, where nothing is to be feen but the Eftrade or Sopha, of which I have already fpoken; and all the Decoration, which belongs to it, is a plain *Indian* Skreen, which goes round the Chamber, of about 5 or 6 Foot high only; this Skreen begins, takes its Sweep from each End of the Eftrade, which ferves for a Bed, and which is thought to be fufficiently adorn'd by Carpets and Cufhions, which are not over magnificent.

The

The Perſon even of the King favours alſo of this Air of Simplicity. They never ſaw him in any other but a little Habit of pretty fine green or yellow Cloath, without any Sort of Ornament, going with his Legs and Feet bare, and wearing Slippers after rhe *Turkiſh* Faſhion; all that he wears for Diſtinction Sake, is a Sort of Vail of white Silk over his Turban, which covers all his Head, falls down before, and is tyed under the Chin, much after the Manner that the Women among us wear their Mode-Hoods.

I know not whether, in ſo great Plainneſs as is obſerv'd in the Houſe, and even in the Perſon of a ſomewhat powerful King, there be not ſome Affectation, or that it may not proceed from ſome Principle of the *Mahammedan* Religion. I have remark'd elſewhere, that this Prince aſſumes the Quality of *Imam;* that is to ſay, of Prieſt or Pontiff of the Law of *Mahammed.* He might be of Opinion, that Pride and Oſtentation are not compatible with that Dignity, as generally wherever Mahammediſm prevails. We ſee the Mufti's, the learned Doctors, the ordinary Mams, the

Cadis alfo, and the Minifters of Juftice, affect an extraordinary Modefty in their Habits, and in every Thing which relates to them.

The King's Way of living.

With regard to the King of *Taman's* Way of Living, it is very uniform, that Prince rifes as foon as Day appears; he dines at 9 a Clock in the Morning, in order to lye down again at 11; and precifely at 2 in the Afternoon the Drums beat, and the Hautboys play up. He who is call'd the Chief of the Drummers, or the Drum-Major, is the only one who has the Priviledge of entring into the Prince's Apartment, fleeping or waking. He is by Nation a *Turk*, and drefs'd very comically, wearing a fwinging Belt, all overlaid with great Plates and Hooks of Silver, with the Figure of a Palm-Tree, embroider'd upon the fore Part of his Turban; not to fpeak of a Silver-Chain which goes round it feveral Times in a very whimfical Manner. As foon as it is publifh'd by this Officer, that the King is awake, he is vifited by the Princes and the Grandees, who entertain him till the Time fet apart for Prayer, or ftate Affairs. As to the Reft, they never approach

him

him, except it be to take him by the
right Hand, which he lays upon his
Knee for them to kifs, which they do
with the moft profound Refpect: He
has alfo his fet Times for Walking, and
Vifiting the Women. In fhort, this Prince
concludes the Day by going to Reft regularly, at eleven a Clock at Night, after
he has fupp'd at five.

But if any thing is capable of fetting
off the Plainnefs, which has been obferv'd,
and of making the Majefty of a King appear in him, it is, without doubt, the
March which this Prince makes, when he
goes every *Friday*, at two a Clock in the
Afternoon, to the Place appointed for
publick Prayer; every one knows, that
among the *Moflemans*, *Friday* is their
Day of Devotion, or their Day of Affembly (as they call it themfelves) which
anfwers to the *Saturday* of the *Jews*, and
to the *Sunday* of the *Chriftians*.

That March begins by a thoufand
Foot-Soldiers, who proceed in good Order, after they have fir'd a Volley at their
fetting out from the Palace. There are
two Ranks of thofe Soldiers which carry Colours, to which they give the Name

O   of

of Enfign of *Mohammed* and *Aly*. Immediately after the Soldiers follow 200 Troopers of the King's Guard, mounted on very beautiful Horfes, and compleatly accouter'd: Thefe Horfemen befides the ordinary Arms, *viz.* the Sabre and the Carabine, carry Half-Pikes, the Iron-Points of which are adorn'd with Fringes. The Officers of the King's Horfe and his Women, nobly mounted, follow this Troop; and at a certain Diftance the King appears, mounted on a very fine white Horfe, which is a very gentle Creature, and which for a long time has carry'd no boby but the King. He has at his Side the two Princes, his Sons, mounted on very coftly Horfes, with rich Furniture. An Officer, very ftately mounted, carries over the King a large Umbrello, or rather a Sort of Canopy, under which he marches cover'd from the Sun. This Canopy is of green Damask, with a Kind of Falbala of red Stuff about eight Inches deep, which goes quite round it, and is enrich'd with a Gold-Fringe. On the Top of the Canopy ftands a Globe of Silver gilt, and underneath the Globe a fmall Pyramid gilded alfo.

Imme-

Immediately before the King, one of his Officers on Horſeback carries the Coran, inclos'd in a Bag of red Cloth: Beſides that Officer, there rides another who carries a Standard of green Damask; the Piece is ſquare, and it is call'd the Standard of the King. There is no Figure upon it, as on the others, but only ſome *Arabic* Characters, which are embroider'd. This Standard is ornamented round the Edges with a Gold-Fringe. Laſt of all an Officer on Horſeback behind the King, carry'd his Sabre, the Handle and Scabbard of which are very rich; the Scabbard is cover'd with a falſe one of Scarlet. So long as the March continues, the Drums never ceaſe beating, no more than the Timbrels to ſound, and the Hautboys to play.

All this Preparation is for no more than to go to the neighbouring Plain, about three quarters of a Mile from *Muab*, where there is a Pavilion ſet up to receive the King, which alſo ſerves him for an Oratory, or a Maſged.

While that Prince is on his March, he finds on his Way 50 of his beſt Horſes which are led, and have Houſings and Caparifons richly embroider'd, with Birdles ftudded with Gold and Silver. They carry on one Side of their Saddles a beautiful Sabre, and on the other a Battle-Ax. Thefe Horfes come from *Damar*, where the King has his principal Stables. They are follow'd by a like Number of Camels, no lefs compleatly equipp'd, with Packfaddles, each of which has a great Silver-Pummel to it. The Camels carry on their Heads a great Plume of black Oftriches Feathers. All thefe are led forth only for Parade, and to adorn the Feftival; for the Horfes and Camels ferve for no Ufe, after they have pafs'd before the King, but to go feveral times round the Tent, or Pavilion, I have already fpoke of.

The King only enters into that Tent, and continues there a whole Hour, to difcharge the Functions of his Miniftry, and his Quality of *Imam*, which confifts in beginging or finging the publick Prayer, and afterwards in making the *Khothab*, a Kind of Homily or Sermon, in which, after giving Praife to God, they celebrate the Memory of *Mohammed*, and pray for the reigning Prince. The Princes and all thofe who have accompany'd the King,

fay

fay their Prayers at the fame Time with him, following him in every Thing with regard to the requifite Ceremonies; for that Tent is very open, and almoft every Body can fee the *Imam*.

After the Prayer is over, the King remounts his Horfe at the Sound of Timbrels, Drums, and Hautboys, and fets forwards on the March to return in the fame Manner as he went; the Soldiers making feveral Difcharges upon his paffing out of the Tent, and the People fending up Vows and Acclamations.

On his Arrival at *Muab*, one Part of that Cavalry enters into the Court of the Palace, and the other Part ftays without; and when the King has made his Re-entry, he takes feveral Turns, and performs divers Exercifes on Horfeback, the Troopers running a-tilt at each other, and making regular Attacks, which gives the People, who are affembled, a Reprefentation of a Battle. That Day all thofe, who wait upon the Road to fee the King pafs by, have the Privilege of approaching and kiffing his Hand, which he never refufes any Body when he travels.

For

For the reft, it is not eafy to comprehend, how that Prince having built a new
Town with a Palace, in order to make it
his ordinary Refidence, not to mention
the Caftle which is not far off, fhou'd yet
never have built fo much as one Mafged;
infomuch, that he is oblig'd to fay Prayers in the open Field, in the Manner we
have already related. 'Tis a Myftery which
our Deputies have not div'd into, and
which perhaps turns only upon the Diftruft of the *Arab* Prince, who not content with having fecur'd and cover'd his
Perfon by a long Tract of Mountains, dare
not fhut himfelf up in a Temple where
he might run the Hazard of being furpriz'd by his Enemies, or betray'd by his
own Subjects. Accidents of this Kind
are not without Example, fince the famous *Aly*, Son in Law of *Mohammed*,
was affaffinated in a Mafged, on the Day
of Affembly, or publick Prayer of the
Moflemans.

And to fay the Truth, the Memoirs inform us, that the Kingdom is not hereditary, and that the Prince who makes
moft Friends, and is moft powerful, or
underftands Intrigues beft, ordinarily carries

ries it from his Competitors, whom he
fometimes either puts to Death, or impri-
fons : But it muft be underftood however,
that tho' this Kingdom has continu'd for a
long Time paft in the fame Houfe, it does
not regularly follow the natural Succeffi-
on of the Branches which compofe it;
fo that often the eldeft are excluded from
the Crown, when the youngeft Sons, or
the Princes who are further off related,
have Power or Conduct enough to obtain
it. 'Tis in this Manner, that the reigning
King has fucceeded the King, his Brother,
to the Prejudice of the Son of that Brother, who is no more, as we have already
obferv'd, than Governour of the Town
of *Tage.* Neverthelefs, the King of *Ya-*
man takes Meafures to fecure the Crown,
during his Life-time, to the Prince, his
eldeft Son, whom every Body confiders
already as his Succeffor; and 'tis in all
Likelihood with this View, that he has
fortify'd himfelf in the higheft Mountains, and obferves the Precautions which
we have taken notice of.

If our Travellers had had more Curiofity, and the Knowledge of the Language
of the Country, one might have found

O 4 here

here fome certain Account of the Family
of the King of *Taman*; for the great Families are always well known among
the *Mohammedans*, and there are to be
found among them Hiftories and Genea-
logies, which may be depended on.

Family of   I was at firft of Opinion, that this
the pre- Prince might have been of the illuftrious
fentKing. Houfe of *Thabatheba*, in which fome
trace the fovereign Power in *Arabia* as
far back as the Time of *Charlemayn.*
That Houfe has form'd a Dynafty of Princes, who are Defcendants of *Aly*, and it
is certain, thofe Princes have reign'd in
Taman in *Egypt* fince the tenth Age. Neverthelefs, I rather believe, that the King,
we are now fpeaking of, derives his Original from the Family of *Ayub*, fo call'd
from the Name of *Ayub*, or *Job*, the Head
of another great Family, which gave Birth
to the famous *Saladin* [*Salah Aldin*] and
his Pofterity. One Branch of this Family of *Ayub* reign'd indeed in this fame
Country of *Taman*, in the 13th Century,
and he who was then Head of it, affum'd
the Quality of *Chalifa*, and that of *Imam*,
which is infeparable from it; which the
King

King of *Yaman* does at prefent, as I have already obferv'd.

Another mark of Grandeur and royal Magnificence with that Prince, which he has in common with all the Princes of the Eaft, is the great Number of Women which he maintains at his Court, and which amount to 6 or 700 : Their Seraglio is in the Caftle of *Muab* ; thefe Women are of divers Nations, and they affirm particularly, that there are *Georgian* Women of an extraordinary Beauty, and even *Arab* Women, which are very fair. They go and come from the Caftle to the Palace, where there are at leaft 30 lodging Rooms in one private Apartment ; their ordinary Carriage is a Camel, a crofs which they put a Sort of Cradel cover'd with Scarlet, and well furnifh'd with Cufhions, upon which thefe Ladies either lye down or fit. They pafs out of them by a little Opening, which is in the fore Part, having their Faces cover'd with painted Linnen very fine and clear.

Moft of the Women of this Country wear a large Gold-Ring at the End of their Nofes, which are bor'd to receive that Ornament ; and, befides that, they

wear

wear on their Arms, on their Wrifts, and above their Ancles, certain Circles or Bracelets of *Silver*; the richer Sort have them of Gold. They moreover always carry about them abundance of Odours, and the ftrongeft Perfumes. We fhall fay nothing concerning the Cuftom which they have of blackening themfelves under the Eyes, and of rubbing their Hands and Feet with a certain Drug, which gives a lively Colour to thofe Parts, and makes the Nails very red; this paffes in *Arabia*, and in other Parts of the Eaft, for a Kind of Beauty.

Our People obferv'd, that at *Muab*, as at *Moka*, the Ladies vifit one another in the Evening, but that the Jealoufly of the Men makes them more ftrict and morofe than elfewhere; infomuch that their Women dare hardly appear in the Terrafes to take the Air. The Sieur *Barbier* was the only one of all the *French*, who had the Privilege of coming nigh the Ladies of *Muab*, and that only by vertue of his Profeffion, on account of a Rheumatifm with which one of the Wives of the prime Minifter, and another belonging to one of the King's Officers, were

attack'd ;

attack'd; the *French* Doctor was defir'd
to come to fee and take care of them;
the Diforder had particularly feiz'd one
Arm and Leg, which he was under a
Neceffity of handling: He found thefe
two Perfons very fair, confidering they
were *Arabs*, and he apply'd Remedies to
them which perfectly recover'd them.
The Sieur *Barbier* affirms, that notwithftanding the Confidence which thofe
Women, and their Husbands had in him,
he was never able to get a Sight of their
Faces.

During the ftay of our Deputies, there
arriv'd at the Court a *Turkifh* Ambaffador, who came from *Conftantinople*, by
the Way of *Egypt*, from the Grand
Signior to the King of *Yaman*; which is
a further Mark of his Sovereignty and In-
dependance. 'Tis well known that the
Otoman Court is very referv'd in the
Matter of Embaffies: This Ambaffador
appear'd with a great deal of Pomp, and
a large Retinue; he was lodg'd and maintain'd, as well as all his Attendants, at
the King's Expence : He brought feveral
Prefents to that Prince, and among others
a Clock

a CLOCK of great Value and fine Work-
manſhip.

With regard to the Subject of his Embaſſy, our People underſtood, that in Appearance, it was an Embaſſy of Honour and
Ceremony, to keep up Friendſhip and a
good Underſtanding between the two
Moſleman Monarchs; but that in reality
his Buſineſs was to tranſact Matter relating to Trade, and particularly that of
Coffee. They complain'd at the Port, that
Coffee was become ſcarcer and dearer in
Egypt, and the reſt of *Turky,* ſince the
Europeans made it their Buſineſs to trade
directly to the *Red-Sea,* in order to load
great Ships with it, to the Prejudice of
the Subjects and Cuſtoms of the Grand
Signior ; upon which Points the Ambaſſa-
dor was to inſiſt very earneſtly with the
King : But it was ſaid alſo, that the King
was not pleas'd with thoſe Inſtances, which
ſeem'd, in ſome meaſure, to attack the ſo-
vereign Authority, and, there is room to
believe, he had no manner of Regard
to them ; ſeeing we bought up as much
Coffee as our Ships were able to hold, and
almoſt at the ſame Price, as in our firſt
Voyage. They obſerv'd, in ſhort, that the
King

King made it his Bufinefs to difpatch that *Turkifh* Minifter, with all the Diligence imaginable; either that, being a good Manager, he found the Expence a little too heavy; or that, being naturally diftruftful, he had taken Umbrage at his Prefence, and the Abode of fo many *Turks.*

There happen'd alfo, much about the fame Time, an Infurrection of fome Malecontents, who had taken Arms towards *Giddah,* or *Gedda,* the Port of *Mecca,* about 60 Leagues from *Muab;* the King fent thither at firft a Body of 3000 Men of his beft Troops, who defeated the Rebels, and kill'd many among them: They brought the News to the King with five Heads, which were expos'd in the Streets of *Muab;* the reft of the Rebels were difpers'd, retiring into the Woods. There were Rejoicings upon this Occafion at the Court, and in the Town, by way of Bonefires, the Principal of which was lighted in the great Court of the Palace.

[marginal note: Infurrection towards Giddah.]

When the King was thoroughly cur'd, the *French* defir'd Leave of him to return; which the King at firft was loath to confent to, giving them to underftand, that he wou'd willingly detain them longer at his Court.

But

But at length he appointed them a Day
for Audience of Leave ; and in the mean
time our People learn'd, that the King,
as old as we have obferv'd he was, marry'd a young *Turkish* Woman, who was
but 18 Years of Age.

After the Ceremony of that Marriage,
which had nothing extraordinary in it,
the Deputies were conducted to their laft
Audience, which was very long and agreeable, the King being accompany'd by the
Princes, and a Court more numerous than
ordinary : After fome obliging Expreffions from the King, which fignify'd his
Efteem and Acknowledgment, and after
the refpectful Thanks which our Deputies
return'd him for the good Treatment, and
the Prefents with which he had honour'd
them ; the King turn'd the Converfation
upon what had been told him of *France*,
and of the great Prince, whom he ftil'd
Emperor, who reigned there with fo much
Glory.

They were oblig'd to renew their Difcourfe upon that Subject, to fpeak of his
Armies both by Sea and Land, of his Re-
venue, of Matters relating to the Navy,
and of Commerce, of his Court, the
State

State of his Family, and of his principal
Officers: To defcribe to him the Grandeur and Magnificence of his Royal Pa-
laces, and efpecially of the ftately Caftle
where the King ordinarily refides, at fome
Diftance from the capital City, of which
they did not forget to give him alfo an
Account, as of one of the Wonders of
Europe, withou- reckoning' the fortify'd
Places, and the Frontiers of his Kingdom.
The *Arab* King never ceas'd asking
Queftions and admiring; at length, full
of thefe Ideas, he told our Deputies, that
he fhou'd efteem himfelf happy to make
an Alliance, or at leaft, to hold a Correfpondence with fo powerful a Prince;
and he defir'd them to order it fo, that when
the Captains return'd to *Europe*, he might
have fent an Abridgment of the Hiftory of
the Empire of *France*, a Profpect of his
principal Palace, and, in fhort, if it was
poffible, his Picture *, and thofe of the
Princes of his Family.

He ask'd, at the End, if our Emperor
had any Efteem for Coffee? It is that (fays
he)

---

* All the *Mohammedan* are not alike fcrupulous
about Pictures, *&c.* the Phyficians and the other Fol-
lowers of *Aly* make no Difficulty to ufe them.

he) which we have moſt valuable here,
and which divine Providence has granted
us, withholding it from all the other Climates of the Univerſe ; 'tis alſo all that
I am able to offer him, if your Captains
will take care of 500 Bales of the beſt
which is in my Kingdom, as a Preſent
to him from me, I will order them to be
carry'd to their Ships.

The Deputies anſwer'd every thing that
was proper to the Demands of the King,
promiſing to make known in *France* his E-
ſteem for our Emperor, and the Things
which he deſir'd to have ; as well on account of that Eſteem, as out of Curioſity.
As to the Propoſal about the Coffee, they
excus'd the Captains from accepting of it,
pretending that the Ships had receiv'd too
much of their Loadings to ſpare room for
ſuch a Quantity ; but in reality they did
not believe that the Captains dar'd of their
own Heads, and without acquainting the
Court with it, to receive ſuch a Preſent.
The Audience ended, by the King's wiſhing
Proſperity and a happy Return to the
French ; and the Deputies paid their Complements, by making new Proteſtations of
their Reſpects, and a perfect Acknowledgment

kdgment towards fo human and beneficent a King.

The Prefents, which the King fent them
the Evening before, confifted in two Habits after the Fafhion of the Country,
one of fine Scarlet, and the fecond of
another beautiful Cloth of a Rofe Colour ; with two Vefts, one of an *Indian*
Stuff with Gold and Silver-Flowers on it,
and the other of Cloath·Serge, trim'd with
Gold Lace; thefe were all for M. *De la
Grelaudiere.* There was as much fent
for the Sieur *Barbier.* And befides that,
he gave them each a very fine Horfe moft
neatly equip'd. He fent them alfo Habits,
and very fine Horfes for the Captains.

Our People, after having took Leave Return to *Mokha.*
of the prime Minifter, and principal Officer of the Court, departed at length
from *Muab,* about the End of our *Lent,*
accompany'd by an Officer and a Con-
voy, as before, and our Charges borne
in like Manner all the Way. They took
the fame Route, but, as they were not
in fuch Hafte, they did not take fo great
Journeys. They came almoft every Night
to pretty good Lodgings, and efpecially
at the Beginning, where they found all
P   requifite

requifite Conveniences, and even Stables to hold 500 Horfes.

We have already faid, that this long Journey lies almoft all the Way thro high Mountains, feparated by fome Plains. Our People have obferv'd, that in thofe Mountains, many of which are barren, and burnt by the Heat of the Sun, there are no Woods of tall Trees to be feen; but there are Groves and Grafs enough, particularly upon the little Hills. They have feen Patridges with red Legs, which are bigger than our Quails, and Turtle-Doves in abundance, which the *Arabs* never fhoot; Foxes fo bold that they let one come as near them as one will; and, in fhort, Apes without Number, and of the largeft Kind, which are no wilder than the Foxes.

Fowl.

But what our Travellers were moft curious to obferve, was that which regards the Plantations of Coffee, which they met with on their Way, to examine nearly the Tree of that Name, and to get from the *Arabs* all the Inftruction necef-fary, that they might be ignorant of no-thing that related to the Purpofe. All thofe Things have appear'd very curious

to

to me, and fo little known amongft us *to* this Day, that I thought it requifite *to* draw up a feparate Memoir, *to* put at *the* End of this Relation, to avoid Inter-ruptions.   Befides, while our Deputies were at *Muab*, the Sieur *de Noïers*, head Surgeon of the Fleet, a curious and inge-nious Man, apply'd himfelf to ftudy the Nature, and to inform himfelf chiefly in every Thing that related to the Coffee-Tree on the Side of *Betelfaguy*.   I fhall then put together what each of thefe Travellers have told me in particular, to make but one Work of the whole.

Befides the Coffee-Trees, our Travellers faw, in the Plantations themfelves, feveral Fruit-Trees of divers Kinds, Peach, Abri-cot, Almond, Citron, Orange, Pome-granate, Plum-Trees, Fig-Trees alfo, the Fruit of which is four, and a few Apple-Trees ; in fhort, a great Number of Quince-Trees, of which they make the ex-cellent Quince-Pafte, which is had in the remarkable Towns, and bears a great Rate. They have alfo feen Vineyard-Plots in cer-tain Places, and affirm, that they have eaten in *Arabia* as good Raifons as any in *Spain*.

Fruit-Trees of feveral Kinds.

P 2   In

In the mean Time our Envoys arriv'd at *Mokha*, the 27th of *March*, which was the Day of *Easter* Devotions. They were as one may judge, very well receiv'd by the Captains, to whom they gave an Account of their Commission, and who soon perceiv'd this Journey had done them no small Service, by gaining a Reputation to the Nation, and making the Governour more ready to do whatever might befriend the Commerce of Coffee, and the quick Dispatch of the *French* Ships; not to mention the abolishing of a new Tax, which the Governor of *Betelfaguy* had exacted.

Those who have made the Voyage of *Muab* all agree, that the Country there differs very much from that where *Mokha* is situated; for, as we have observ'd elsewhere, for fifteen Leagues round about that Town, they saw nothing of any Thing they found in the other Parts of *Taman*; all the Land scorch'd and dry'd, and, besides that, impregnated with Nitre, produces nothing but Palm-Trees very common; insomuch, that if it were not for the Goodness of the Port of *Mokha*, where they bring Commodities from all Parts, and

espe-

efpecially of Corn and Rice, the Town
and the Country about it would be fa-
mifh'd.

Our People learn'd, that, befides the
Town they had feen, there were alfo other
confiderable ones in the Kingdom, the
chief of which is called *Sanaa,* fifteen
Leaugues from *Muab,* and a hundred and
forty from *Mokha.* 'Tis a pity Curiofity,
or fome other Caufe, had not engag'd
them to fee that Town, which no *European* Traveller has yet vifited *; it muft
needs have feveral curious remains of Antiquity ; for, long before *Mohammedifm*
had a Being, it was the Capital of *Arabia
Fœlix,* and under the Dominion of the
Tobbais, powerful Kings, who there kept
their Court. The Palace of thefe Princes
was ftately, and built upon a little Hill in
the City. In Procefs of Time, and ftill
before *Mohammed,* the Emperor of *Ethiopia,* mov'd by the *Chriftians,* which
groan'd under the Tyranny of the *Arabs,*
having conquer'd *Arabia Fœlix,* caus'd

P 3   to

---

* The *French* Editor, it feems, was unacquainted
with Sir *Henry Middleton*'s Journey there in 1611,
which follows this Relation.

to be built in *Sanaa*, and upon the fame
Hill, a magnificent Temple in Oppofition
to that at *Mecca*, in order to draw off
the *Arabs* from the fuperftitious Worfhip
and Idolatry which they practis'd; but the
Ethiopians did not maintain their Conqueft
long. The oriental Authors, where thefe
Circumftances are found, which we relate
by the way, fay farther, that *Sanaa* is a
very antient, rich, and populous Town;
and that there is a greater Trade there for
Silver, than Merchandizes. The Walls
are fo broad, that eight Horfes may march
there on a Breaft. *Abulfeda*, a famous
Geographer, adds, that *Sanaa* altogether
refembles *Damafcus*, for the Abundance
of its Waters, and delicious Gardens. I
know not, if with this View we may not
refer to this Part, that kind of terreftrial
Paradife, nam'd *Iram*, and planted in the
Happy Arabia, by an antient King, which
Mohammed himfelf calls impious in his
Koran; a famous Paradife amongft the
Mohammedans, and of which almoft all
the Works of the *Mufulman* Poets make
mention: However it be, the Air in and
about *Sanaa* is very temperate, and the
Days and Nights much of a Length.

Our

Our Travellers were inform'd likewise, Roads that there are several great Roads, some *there.* *Yaman.* of which also were pav'd, above a hundred Leagues long each, that lead into divers Parts of the Kingdom, which is of a great Extent, altho' it contains but a Part of *Arabia Fœlix.* The rest of the Country which bears that Name, and is divided into other Kingdoms, produces the Gums, the Myrrh, and the Spices, of which they met with never a Tree in their Journey to *Muab:* But in the other Countries of the same Kingdom, there is Incense in abundance. We shall speak nothing of the Balm-Trees, because they grow out of the *Happy Arabia,* and about *Mecca.*

Our Ships remain'd yet above three Months in the Port of *Mokha.* In the mean Time, our People saw an Execution, according to the Manners and Customs of the *Arabs,* which is worth relating. An Inhabitant of *Mokha* having kill'd a Man in a Quarrel, he was condemn'd to dye by the Governour, without any Ceremony: The Criminal was led to one of the Gates of the City; there the nearest Relation, to him that he had kill'd, cut open the

P 4   Bot-

Bottom of his Belly with a common Knife; the Prisoner immediately fell upon his Knees, and then the same Executioner rais'd his Head, and cut it off instantly; as soon as he had done his Work, he shelter'd himself in a neighbouring House, assisted by some Horse of the Governour's Guard, who are sent to back the Execution; for the People of *Mokha* are ready enough to Mutiny, and don't see with a good Will such Sort of Spectacles.

All Things being at length ready for their Departure, the *French* Ships put to Sail the 10th of *July*, 1712. They made several Stops by the Way, and staid some Time at *Mascarin*, on the Isle of *Bourbon*; and as Prizes are commonly bad Sailors, these Ships cou'd not arrive at St. *Malo*, the one till the 11th of *June*, 1713, and the other, which was oblig'd to put in upon the Coast of *England* with one of the Prizes, Provisions failing, and their Tackling being out of Order, before the — of *July* following.

A few Days after, the Company and Captains of the Fleet, engag'd Monsieur *De la Grelaudiere* to come to Court, to give an Account of his Journey to that

of

of the King of *Taman*; upon which Occasion he acquitted himself perfectly well. 'Tis from him, that, during near three Months Stay at *Paris*, I have gather'd, in divers Discourses, the Materials of this Relation. The Sieurs *Des Noïers* and *Barbier* have also communicated to me their particular Memoirs, by Means of Monsieur *De la Merveille*, who brought them me himself to *Paris*; so that any one may reasonably depend upon the Truth of what it relates.

A TREA-

A

TREATISE

Concerning the Tree and Fruit of Coffee, *drawn up from the Observations of those* Frenchmen, *that made the last Voyage to* Arabia Fœlix, *in* 1709.

Descrip-
tion of
the Cof-
fee-Tree.

 HE Tree, which produces the Coffee, grows from six to twelve Foot high ; the Body of it is from ten to fifteen Inches Circum-
ference. When it comes to Perfection, it resembles very much, in Figure, one of our Apple-Trees of eight or ten Years growth. The lower Branches ordinarily bend,
when

when the Tree comes to have a little
Age, and form themſelves round, making
a Kind of an Umbrello. The Wood is
very ſoft, and ſo pliant, that the End of
the longeſt Branches may be brought
down within two or three Foot of the
Ground. The Bark of the Coffee-Tree
is whitiſh, and a little rugged. Its Leaf
comes very near that of the Lemon-
Tree, tho' neither altogether ſo pointed,
nor ſo thick ; the Colour is alſo of a
deeper Green. The Coffee-Tree is continually green, and never ſheds all its
Leaves at a Time, which grow on both
Sides the Bows at a moderate Diſtance,
and almoſt oppoſite one to another.

For the reſt, nothing is more ſingular in its Kind, than its Productions; for,
in almoſt all Seaſons of the Year, the
ſame Tree is ſeen to bear Bloſſoms and
Fruit, ſome of which are ſtill green, and
others ripe, or near their Maturity.

Theſe Bloſſoms are white, and reſem-
ble very much thoſe of the Jeſſamin, having, in like Manner, five ſmall Leaves
pretty ſhort; the Smell is agreeable, and
has ſomething of the balſamick, tho'
the Taſte be bitter. They grow out of

that

that Part where the Stalks of the Leaves joyn the Branches.

When the Bloſſoms fall, there remains, or rather there comes in the Room of each, a ſmall Fruit, very green at firſt, but which becomes red as it ripens, and is not altogether unlike a Cherry; 'tis very good to eat, nouriſhes, and is very cooling. Under the Pulp of that Cherry lies, inſtead of a Stone, the Bean, or Berry, which we call Coffee, cover'd with a very thin Skin. This Berry is as yet extreme tender, and its Taſte diſagreeable: But, as the Cherry ripens, the Berry within by degrees grows hard, and the Sun having at laſt entirely dry'd up this red Fruit, the Pulp, which was eaten before, becomes a Husk or Clove, of a very brown Colour, which makes the firſt, or outward Shell of Coffee, and the Berry is then ſolid, of a very clear Green. It abounds with a kind of thick Liquor, brown colour'd and extremely bitter. The Clove, which is faſten'd to the Tree by a little ſhort Stalk, is ſomething bigger than a Lawrel-Berry, and each Clove contains no more than a ſingle

gle Bean, which ordinarily is cleft in two Halves.

This Bean is immediately cover'd, as we have faid, with a very thin Skin, which may be call'd the fecond or inward Shell. The *Arabs* make great Account of both the one and the other, for compofing that which they call their Coffee of the *Soltána*, of which we fhall fpeak hereafter.

Our Voyagers affure us, that the Coffee-Tree has its Original from a Seed (and not from a Slip broke off a Bough, as fome fay) by putting a Berry, come to Perfection, in the Ground, which afterwards fhoots up its Plants in the Nurfery, in order to be replanted where one will.

The Foots of the Mountains, and little Hills, in the more fhady and moift Parts, are the Places which Coffee requires for its Plantation. The greateft Piece of Husbandry, that belongs to them, confifts in turning the Courfe of the Rivulets and Springs, that defcend from the Mountains, into their Nurferies, conveying the Waters by little Canals, to the Foot of the Trees; for it is neceffary, to the bringing the Fruit to Perfection, that they fhould be water'd and well moiften'd.

'Tis

'Tis for this Purpofe, that, in Replanting the Coffee, the *Arabs* make a Ditch of three Foot broad, and five deep, which they line with Stone, to the End that the Water may the more eafily foak deep into the Earth, with which it is fill'd, and retain the Coolnefs requifite. Neverthelefs, when they fee much ripe Coffee on the Tree, they drain off the Water from the Foot of it, to let the Fruit dry a little on the Branches, which too much Moifture wou'd hinder.

If our People had not made the Jour to *Muab*, we might have been a long Time ignorant of a Particular with regard to the Coffee-Tree, of which no one has hitherto fpoken, *viz.* that in the Places facing the South, or which are much expos'd to the Weather, thefe Trees are found planted under other Trees, faid to be a Kind of Popiar, which ferve to fhade and fhelter them from the exceffive Heat of the Sun. 'Tis probable, that without this Shelter, which keeps it cool underneath, the Flower of the Coffee wou'd be quickly burnt, and never produce any Fruit, as appears by fome fituated in the fame Place, which want thofe bene-

beneficial Neighbours. In Effect, thofe Poplars extend their Branches prodigioufly, and form, by their Difpofition, a perfect Umbrello, which covers all below.

It was at a certain Diftance from the Town of * *Tage*, as we have obferv'd, that the *French* faw the Coffee-Trees the firft Time, difpos'd in this fingular Manner, becaufe the Country thereabouts is found to be more open and expos'd than others, to the intenfe Heat of the Sun. They obferv'd throughout the whole Plantation, that each Poplar cover'd with its Shade a certain Number of Coffee-Trees, and that the latter are planted regularly, as it were by a Line, like as the Apple-Trees in *Normandy* : In fhort, the Curiofity of one of our Travellers, who was qualify'd for the Bufinefs, led him to take a Draught of the Coffee-Tree upon the Place, with all the Exactnefs he was capable of, having chofen one that feem'd to him moft proper to exprefs the Beauty and Nature of this Production ; 'tis the fame Draught we have given here, which will be without doubt acceptable to the Curious.

In

* 'Tis call'd *Tage* in *H. Middleton*'s Journal.

In the Places lefs hot, one fees none of thofe great Trees which ferve to fhelter them. The Coffee-Trees are there alone in the open Air, and, without their Affi. ftance, bring forth Fruit to a Miracle. The Sieur *De Noiers* has feen abundance of thefe laft in the Voyage, which he made on purpofe to *Redia* or *Zedia*, a fmall Village in the Mountains, twelve Leagues from *Betelfaguy*; this, as he was inform'd by the Governour of *Redia*, is one of the beft Diftricts in the whole Country; for befides the Coffee-Trees, which are the beft to be feen any where, there are other Fruit-Trees in great abundance. There is one excellent kind of Wheat, and other Corn : There are alfo found Store of Melons and Cucumbers. In this Place too, like as in the Road to *Muab*, the Coffee-Trees are planted in order, as it were laid out by a Line, at a moderate Diftance from one another.

The Sieur *De Noiers*, by the way, feems to me the moft judicious and exact of our Travellors, from whofe Obfervations it is that I have given the Defcription of the Coffee-Tree, which is at the Beginning of this Memoir; and as he had the

Curi-

Curiofity to bring from the Place an entire Bough, with the Fruit on it, which
by his Care is perfectly preferv'd ; it was
not difficult to take an exact Draught of
it. The Curious in obferving this Bough,
the Leaves and the Fruit of which are
drawn of the natural Size, will eafily perceive how very different this is from all
thofe, which we have feen in many Books,
where the Authors have pretended to reprefent the Boughs of the Coffee-Tree.

With regard to the Harveft, or Gathering
of Coffee, as the Tree which bears it is
all the Year round full of Flowers, and of
ripe and unripe Fruit, there is a Neceffity
for making it at three different Times ; and
on this account it may be faid, that there
are three Seafons in the Year proper for
gathering of Coffee ; but thefe Times are
not very fixt and regular, infomuch that
the *Arabs* allow no Harveft properly, but
that of the Month of *May*, becaufe it is
the greateft of the whole Year.

When they have a Mind to gather the
Coffee, they lay fome Pieces of Cloth under the Trees, which they afterwards fhake,
and all the ripe Coffee falls down eafily;
thefe are put in Sacks to be carry'd elfe-
Q   where,

where, and laid in Heaps upon Mats, in order to dry them, for some Time, in the Sun; and that the Husks, which contain the Bean, might afterwards open, by Means of the great Stone, or wooden Rollers very weighty, which pass over them.

When by this Means the Coffee is squeez'd out of its Husk, and separated, as we see, into two little Beans, or rather into two Parts, which made but one before, 'tis put over again to dry in the Sun, because it is still pretty green; and that the Coffee which is too new, and not thoroughly dry, runs a Risk of spoiling at Sea: Afterwards it is winnow'd to cleanse it, that it may go off the better; for those, that don't take care to clean and dry their Coffee sufficiently, sell it at a much lower Rate.

'Tis Time to say something with regard to the Preparation and Drinking of Coffee among the *Arabs* in general; their Manner is just the same as that all over the *Levant*, which we imitate daily in *France*, with this Difference, that the *Arabs* take it the Moment it is boil'd, without letting it stand to settle, always without Sugar, and in very small Cups. There are some

among

among them who, in drawing the Coffee-Pot from the Fire, wrap a wet Cloth about it; this caufes the Grounds to fall immediately to the Bottom, and clears the Liquor; by this Means alfo there rifes a Sort of Cream a-top, and, when 'tis pour'd into the Cups, it fteams a great deal more, diffufing a Kind of oily Vapour, which they take a Delight in fmelling to, becaufe of the good Quantities they attribute to it.

People of Fafhion have another Cuftom particular to themfelves; they don't make ufe of the Coffee-Berries, but only of the Husks or Pods which invelope them, mingling therewith a Quantity of the thin Skin, which immediately covers the Bean * in fuch wife, that when the whole is rightly

Q 2   pre-

---

* They take the Husk or Bark of the Coffee perfectly ripe, grind and put it in a little Skillet, or earthen Pan, over a Charcole-fire, keeping it conftantly ftirring, that it might not burn like the Coffee, but only get a Colour; in the mean Time they have a Coffee-Pot of Water boiling, and when the Husk is ready, throw it in with a fourth Part, at leaft, of the outer Skin, letting it boil like ordinary Coffee. The Colour of this Liquor is like that of the better fort of *Englifh* Beer. Thefe Husks are kept in Places very dry, and clofe fhut up, for the Moifture gives them an ill Tafte.

prepar'd, they think no drink comparable to it. Our *Frenchmen,* who at the Court of the King of *Yaman,* and where they were treated by the Governour and Men of Quality, draw no other Sort of Coffee, declare that there is fomething in it very palatable and delicious; adding, that there is no need to ufe Sugar, becaufe it has no Bitternefs to correct; but that, on the contrary, one is fenfible of a moderate Sweetnefs, which is very agreable. This Liquor is called Coffee of the *Soltana,* which is in great Efteem all over the Country. For the reft 'tis reafonable to believe, that it is not to be made to Perfection but upon the Place; becaufe thefe Coffee-Husks, which, at beft, have not much Subftance, when they become too dry, and tranfported or kept, lofe a great deal of their Quality, which confifts chiefly in the Frefhnefs.

Our People have often asked, as well the better as common Sort of the Country, the Reafon why they drink fo much Coffee? What Benefit they find by it? If ufing it is a Remedy againft any Diftemper? And, in fhort, where was the Good of it? The Anfwer has been general, that

Coffee

Coffee nourishes, and does good in several Respects; besides, it is to them a sweet
Amusement, and an agreeable Custom.
I know not if, to this great Use of Coffee
among the *Arabs*, we may not apply that
Remark of our Voyagers, which is, that
the Natives are very frugal, and for the
most part lean, and of a dry Constitution,
tho' of a Stature good enough.

I shall conclude this Memoir with two
Observations; the first is, that the *Ara-
bians* of *Yaman*, as indeed all the Orientals
also, are of strong Persuasion, that the
Coffee grows in no other Part of the
World but their own Country: They believe, notwithstanding, that it came originally from *Ethiopia*, from whence it
has been transplanted into *Arabia Fœlix*:
This Opinion is in some measure confirm'd by the Relation * of a Voyage,
which *Charles James Poucel* made into
Ethiopia, in the Years 1698, 1699 and
1700. This Traveller informs us, that there
are still to be seen Coffee-Trees in that
Country; that none plant them, but for

Q 3   Curi-

* This Relation is incerted in the fourth Collection
of Letters of foreign Missions, printed at *Paris*, 1704.
Tis also publish'd in *English*.

Curiofity. He alfo defcribes the Plant, with
out affirming that he had feen it; bu‾
that Defcription, where the Plant in Que
ftion is compar'd to the Myrtle, is fo dif.
ferent from the Coffee-Tree, which our
People have feen in *Arabia*, that there muft
neceffarily be fome Miftake in the Matter:
Befides, the beft Relations we have of *Ethiopia*, of which the moft efteem'd, is * that
of Father *Tellez*, a *Portugueze* Jefuit, and
the Hiftory of M. *Ludolfus* fo curious and
fo exact, make no mention at all of the
Coffee-Tree.

However, fince Coffee has come fo much
all over *Europe*, they have not fail'd to
encreafe its Species, which they do more
and more every Day, in Proportion to
the Confumption and Profit of it; infomuch that, at prefent, there are Coffee-
Trees in many of the Mountains and other
Places of *Yaman*, which, till of late, had
never borne any.

The laft Obfervation is with Regard to
a Notion which has almoft generally obtain'd

* If it be true that the *Abyffins* came originally
from *Arabia* into *Ethiopia*, as M. *Ludolfus* writes, they
might bring the Coffee-Tree thither, which, it feems,
has not throve very well, fince it is very uncertain,
whether it be found at prefent in *Ethiopia*.

tain'd in *Europe*, tho' it begins by degrees
to lofe Ground, *viz.* that the *Arabs*,
jealous of a Benefit which is found only
among themfelves, fuffer no Coffee-Beans
to be carry'd out of their Country, which
have not firft pafs'd thro' the Fire, or boiling
Water, to caufe the Bud, as they fay, to
dye; to the End that, if any fhould think
to fow it elfewhere, it might be to no
Purpofe.

John Ray, an *Englifh* Phyfician, one
of the moft famous Botanifts of our Time,
has, like others, given into this Error; for,
after having fpoken of the Virtues of Coffee, he tells us very ferioufly, * *that the*
Coffee-Tree growing only in Arabia Fœlix,
he is aftonifh'd that fo little a Corner
fhould furnifh fo much, and that thofe
who are Mafters of fo efteemed a Fruit,
have' fo much Wit as to prevent its being
in any one's Power to have, in any other
Place, a fingle Grain capable of growing,
and thereby diminifh their Profit, &c. An
Error which can no longer fubfift after the
Teftimony of our Voyagers, and by the
Return of our Veffel, which have tranf-

Q 4   ported

---

* *John Ray*, in his univerfal Hiftory of Plants. *Lon-
den*, 1686.

sported several Sacks of the entire Coffee, that is to say, with the Clove and its double Rind or Bark, without having suffer'd the pretended Alteration.

Besides, 'tis known, that the *Hollanders*, whose Sagacity and Genius for Commerce cannot be too much commended, have carry'd Coffee from *Arabia* to *Batavia*, which they have sow'd there, replanted, and happily rear'd about that famous City; but without much Success, since they continue to send from thence their Vessels into the *Red-Sea*, and their Money to the *Arabs* to trade for Coffee. 'Tis said that the excessive Heat of the Climate brings forth almost all the Fruit of the Trees before the Time, which, as we have observ'd, require a temperate Heat, as well as a shady and cool Situation. The *English* have yet planted Coffee-Trees at *Madraspatan* *, which thrive much worse than those of *Batavia*, and which are, at present, in a Manner neglected.

I understand also, while I am writing this Treatise, that there is some Coffee sown in the Plant-Garden, belonging to *Amsterdam*, and that, at last, they have

made

* * Fort St. George.*

made a fhift to rear the Coffee-Plants, fome
of which have already borne Fruit of three
Years ftanding; and that there is actually
one of thefe very young Plants in the
Garden Royal at *Paris*; to which we may
add, that *Meffieurs*, the Magiftrates of
Amfterdam, fent to the King a Coffee-
Tree at perfect Growth, loaded with its
Fruit, and in the Perfection we have juft
now obferv'd, which ferves to prove, that
the *Arabs* underftand no fuch Management * of the Coffee, and that it is not
impoffible to have in Time this Tree in the
moft famous Gardens of *Europe*. I fay,
in the moft famous Gardens; for fhould
the Coffee Trees thrive there, yet will they
always pafs among us for rare and curious Plants, in which Art in fome meafure forces Nature; and it is to be believ'd,
that they will never be of Confequence,
with regard to making Coffee plenty, in
Climates fo different from that which
Providence has deftin'd for the Production
of this Plant.

* This Fiction feems rather to have been contriv'd
by the Merchants, to prevent any from making an
Experiment, which might fpoil no inconfiderable Article in their Trade.

An

An Account of the

CAPTIVITY

OF

Sir *Henry Middleton*

By the TURKS *at* Moka, *or* Mokha; *and of his Journey from thence, with thirty four* Englifhmen *more, to the* Bafha *at* Zenan, *or* Sanaa: *With a Defcription of the Country, and a Journal of their Travels to that City, and back again.*

T is not our Bufinefs here to give a Detail of Sir *Henry Middleton's* Voyage from *England* to *Mokha*, of which the Reader will find a particular Account elfewhere *: But

it

---

* See *Purchas's* Pilgrims, Vol. I. Pag. 247.

it will be proper to recite in brief the Circumstances of his Captivity, by the *Turks* in that Port, in order to explain the Occasion of the Journey from thence to *Zenan* or *Sanaa*.

Sir *Henry Middleton* came to Anchor before *Mokha*, *November* 13, 1610, with three Ships of the *East India* Company under his Command, *viz.* the *Trades-Increases* of 1000 Tons, in which was the General, Sir *Henry* himself Admiral; the *Pepper Corn* of 250 Tons, Captain *Nicholas Dorinton*, Vice-Admiral; and the *Darling* of 90 Tons, attended by the *Bark, Samuel*, of 180 Tons, as a Victualler: Upon his Arrival the Governour of the Town call'd *Rejib Aga*, sent the *Emier-bahare* *, [*Anûr al Bahr*] or Lord of the Sea, to know who he was, and to offer him a free Trade; next Day the *Aga* sent Sir *Henry* a Letter full of Complements, offering himself, and the whole Country, at his Service. A few

Days

* There is some Confusion in Sir *Henry's* Relation about the Names of the Governour of *Mokha*, and the *Basha* of *Sanaa*; the first of whom was called *Rejib*; the latter *Jaffer*. See Captain *Dowtan's* Voyage in *Purchas*, ibid. p. 285.

Days after the Interpreter came from the
Governour, to intreat him to come on
Shore, if he was a Friend of the *Turks,*
and intended to trade.

According to the Governour's Invita-
tion, on the 20th of the fame Month, Sir
Henry Middleton went on Shore. He was
receiv'd at the Water Side by feveral of the
principal Inhabitants, and with Mufick
conducted to the *Aga*'s Houfe, where he
was treated with a great deal of feeming
Kindnefs and Ceremony, he alone fitting
with the *Aga*, while all the reft ftood.
After the firft Complements were over, Sir
Henry deliver'd King *James* the Ift's Letter
with a Prefent to the *Basha*, whofe Name
was *Jaffar* ; he alfo made another to the
Aga, who caus'd a Veft of crimfon Silk
and Silver to be put on him : After taking
Leave he was mounted on a fine Horfe
with rich Furniture, and conducted to the
English Houfe, his Horfe led by a great
Man, and the Mufick playing as before.

There did not a Day pafs, but Sir *Henry*
had fome Prefent from the *Aga*. At length,
on the 28th of *November*, about 8 in the
Evening, the Houfe was befet with Soldiers, who, upon Sir *Henry*'s being ftruck
down,

down, fell upon the reft of the *Engliſh*, eight of whom were ſlain, and fourteen grevioufly wounded; they were all put in Irons: Sir *Henry* and ſeven more were chained together by the Neck, others by the Feet, ſome by their Hands. Their next Attempt was on the Ships; an hundred and fifty *Turks* in three Boats, with the *Ancir al Bahr* at the Head of them, boarded the *Darling* all at once, and killed three Men; but they were at length all killed or drowned by the *Darling*'s Men, except one who hid himſelf.

Soon after the *Aga* ſent for Sir *Henry*, and with a ſtern Countenance ask'd him, How he, being a *Chriſtian*, durft come ſo near their holy City? of which he pretended *Mokha* was the Door. Then he was inquiſitive to know, what Store of Money and Proviſions there was on board the Ships; and ſpoke to Sir *Henry* to write to them to ſurrender, threatening otherwiſe to cut his Head off. To all which Sir *Henry* made proper and reſolute Anſwers, upbraiding the Governor with his Treachery, and peremptorily refuſing to write to the Ships to the Purport the *Aga* wou'd have him; letting him know, at
the

the fame Time, that if he did, they wou'd not be fuch Fools to put themfelves in his Power.

Then Sir *Henry's* Chain and Collar being taken off, both his Hands and Feet were fetter'd, and he thruft into a Dog-kennel under a Pair of Stairs ; whence however he was releas'd at Night, by the Intreaty of the Conful of the *Banians,* and put into a Room with one of his Men. The Governor often vifited him, to endeavour, by fair and foul Means, to get him to write to the Ships.

Sir *Henry* and the reft expected nothing every Hour but Death or Slavery, when, on the 20th of *December,* there came an *Aga* of the *Chaufes* from *Zenan,* with Orders to bring them all up. At his firft Lighting, he was defirous of feeing the Prifoners, and after fome Difcourfe to the Purport mentioned, the *Aga,* whofe Name was *Ifhmael,* advis'd him to fend on board for warm Cloaths, for that they fhould find it very Cold in the Mountain-Country. Sir *Henry* made a Requeft, that he fhould go attended only by a few of his Men, and the reft be fent to the Ships ; but *Ifhmael Aga* told him, thé *Bafha's*
Order

Order was, that they fhould all go up.
Having premis'd thus much concerning
the Occafion of the Journey, we fhall
give an Account of it in the Words of
Sir *Henry* himfelf, only abridging fome
Things here and there for Brevity's fake.

The 22d of *December*, our Irons were
knock'd off all our Legs, except thofe of
fome fick Men who could not travel, and
of the Carpenters and Smiths, who were
kept at *Mokha* to build up the Pinnace.
About 4 o'Clock we fet out 35 in Number, all mounted on Affes, except Mr.
Femel and I, who were on Horfe-back.
I found a great Friend of one *Hamed
Aga*, who fent me divers Prefents, and
will'd me to be of good Comfort, for my
Caufe was good : He fent me and my People Provifion of Bread for our Journey,
and withal, his Letters to *Abdallah Chal-
larby*, or perhaps, rather *Chellabi*, the *Bafha's Kayha*, or Lieutenant, who is a very
difcreet Man, and governs the Kingdom.
The Conful of the *Banians* likewife came
every Day to fee me, and never empty
handed ; and *Tookehar* was our great
Friend all the while we were their Prifoners ;

foners; he fent to each Man every Day being fifty one in Number, (including perhaps thofe who came up from *Aden*) two Cakes of white Bread, and a Quantity of Dates. He departed two Days before us from *Zenan*, promifing me at his Departure to do all he cou'd with the *Bafha* for our Good; and at *Zenan* I was told by feveral, that he labour'd hard in our Bufinefs both with the *Bafha* and his *Kayha*.

About 10 at night Mr. *Pemberton* flip'd away. We faw it, but faid nothing. He was tempted to that defperate Attempt, concluding, as we all did, that we cou'd be carry'd up menacled and guarded at that rate, to no other End but to be put to death, or made Slaves of. About one in the Morning we eame to our Inn at a Town called *Moreffi*, they number'd us at our Arrival, but mifs'd none; but in the Morning, on numbering of us again, they mifs'd one; the *Aga* queftion'd me about it, but I pretended Ignorance.

On *Chriftmas* Day we arriv'd at *Tayes*, four Days Journey from *Mokha*, where we were marfhall'd into the City, two and two in a Rank, as they do at *Conftanti-*
nop'e

nople with Captives taken in the Wars, our *Aga* riding in Triumph as a great Conqueror, being met a Mile or two out of Town by the chief Men of the City on Horfe-back, Multitudes of People ftanding all the way gazing and wondring at us: Thus were we us'd in all Cities and Towns we pafs'd through.

I kept no Journal from this Time forward, but I remember we found it very cold from *Tayes* to *Zenan*, our Lodging being the bare Ground. I bought moft of our Men, who were flenderly clad, furr'd Gowns to keep out the Cold, otherwife I think they would have ftarv'd. I would not believe at *Mokha*, when I was told of the Cold we fhould have upwards, and that made me go but thinly cloath'd myfelf; but Experience taught me otherwife, wifhing, when it was to late, I had come better provided. Every Morning the Ground was cover'd with hoar Froft; and in *Zenan* we had Ice a Finger-thick in one Night, which I could hardly have believ'd had I not feen it.

We were fifteen Days between *Mokha* and *Zenan*, the Diftance an hundred and eighty Miles, or thereabouts, as I judge

R   North

North North Eaſt.   The 5th of *January*, two Hours before Day, we came within two Miles of the City, where we lay upon the Ground till it was Day, being ſo pinch'd and benum'd with Cold, that we were ſcarce able to ſtand.   About a Mile from the Town we were met by the *Sub-Baſha* or *Sherif*, with, at leaſt, two hundred Shot, Drummers and Trumpets. We were caus'd to go one by one in order, a pretty Diſtance from each other, to make the better Show.   Our Men had their Gowns taken from them, and were made to march a-foot in their thin ragged Cloaths, the Soldiers leading the Way; Our Trumpets were placed next before me, and commanded by the *Aga* to ſound, but I forbad them : After the Trumpets came Mr. *Femel* and myſelf on Horſe-back, and laſtly came our *Aga* riding in Triumph, with a ſpare Horſe richly furniſh'd led before him.

In this Order we were led through the Heart of the City till we came to the Caſtle, all the Way being ſo full of People, we cou'd hardly paſs for them : At the firſt Gate there was a good Guard of arm'd Soldiers, the ſecond Gate had two great
                                              Pieces

It is in the Original North North West, *but it muſt be a Miſtake.*

Pieces of Ordnance ready mounted at the Entrance thereof. After we had pafs'd this Gate, we came to a fpacious Yard, twice the Length of the *Exchange* in *London.* The Soldiers, at the Entry of the Gate, difcharg'd their Shot, and plac'd themfelves among many others that were there before them, fome on the one fide and fome on the other, and a Lane left in the midft.

At my firft coming in I alighted, and was plac'd on one fide with my Men; we had not ftay'd long there before Mr. *Femel* and I were brought before the *Bafha:* It was their *Diwân,* or Council-Day. At the upper end of the Yard we mounted a Pair of Stairs, fome twelve Steps high, at the Head of which two great Men came and took me by the Wrifts, holding me very hard, and fo led me to the *Bafha.* The Place was a long fpacious Gallery, lined on each fide, all the Length of it, by Men of Figure, which made a good Show; at the upper end the *Bafha* was feated alone, many other great Men ftanding on each fide. The Floor was cover'd all over with *Turky* Carpets.

We ftopp'd within two Yards of the *Bafha,* who, with a frowning and angry

Countenance, demanded of what Country
I was, and what Bufinefs I had in thofe
Parts? He faid, it. was not lawful for any
Chriftian to come into that Country, and
that he had given Warning to Captain
Sharpeigh (who had been at *Mokha* fix
teen Months before in the *Afcenfion*) that
no more of our Nation fhou'd come thither. I anfwer'd, that Captain *Sharpeigh*
was caft away upon the Coaft of *India*,
and came not to *England* to give us fuch
Notice, which, if he had done, would have
prevented all our Troubles; that *Rejib
Aga* was the Perfon who had abus'd us,
having firft invited us on Shore, with
many fair Promifes, and then affaulted us,
murdering feveral of my Men, and taking
me and the reft Prifoners. He faid, *Rejib Aga* was but his Slave, and had no
fuch Power to pafs his Word to us without his Leave; that what was befallen to
us, was by his Order to *Rejib Aga*, and that
he himfelf likewife had fuch Order from
the Grand Seignior, to chaftife all *Chriftians*
who come into thofe Parts. I told him,
we had fuffer'd much Harm, and that if
he would let us return to our Ships, it
would be a fufficient Warning to our Nation,

tion, for ever coming into thofe Parts again. He faid, no, he could not let us depart fo, but that I fhould remain there and write to the Ambaffador at *Stambola* ; *Conftanti-* and he would likewife write to the Grand *nople.* Seignior, to know his Pleafure, how we fhould be difpos'd of, or whether he would permit us trade or not. He then difmift me for that Time, bidding me go to the Lodging appointed for me, and take with me four or five more, fuch as I thought fit. We were convey'd to the Keeper of the Prifon's Houfe, and the reft carry'd to the common Prifon, where they were clapt in weighty Irons. One of our Youth's, at fuch Time as I was brought before the *Bafha*, thinking I was fo led to have my Head ftroke off, fell in a Swoon for fear, concluding his Turn would not be long after ; and, falling Sick upon it, fhortly after dy'd,

The 6th of *January*, I was fent for the *Bafha's Kayha*, or Lieutenant-General of the Kingdom, to breakfaft with him ; and the next Day he feafted me and Mr *Femel* at his Garden, telling me that we fhould foon have our Liberty, and be fent to *Mokha*, where all my Wrongs fhou'd be

R 3   redrefs d,

redrefs'd; promifing to be my Friend, and,
before many *Turks* and *Arabs* of Quality, faid, what Kindnefs he did me was
only for God's Sake, but I well knew it
was in hopes of fome great Reward from
me. *Shermal,* the *Bannian* of *Mokha,* had
made this Man our Friend, and *Hamed*
Aga's Letter did us no fmall Good.

This Day came to Town a *Moor* of
Cairo, an old Acquaintance of the *Bafha's,*
and one that had fent him great Sums of
Money, at his Departure from *Conftanti-*
nople, when he was but Poor. He was
our next Neighbour at *Mokha* before,
and when we were betray'd, had a Ship in
the Road bound for *India,* which he
fear'd our Ships wou'd have taken, by way
of Reprifal; but letting her depart, contrary to his Expectation, he became our
great Friend. He wrote to the *Bafha* in
our Behalf, blaming him for his Conduct,
and faid he went about to deftroy the
Trade of the Country, by taking fuch
Courfes with us. At his coming before
the *Bafha,* he fpoke to the fame Effect,
and advis'd him to return me all my Goods,
and fend us away contented. None in
the Country durft fpeak fo boldly as he.

It

It was his Letter that faved my Life: For, when the *Basha* fent for us up, it was his Intention to have put me to Death, and to have made Slaves of all the reft. All which Intelligence I had from *Shermal*, and *Hamed Waddy*, a very rich *Arab* Merchant of *Zenan*. He is call'd the *Basha*'s Merchant, and fpoke much in our Behalf.

The 11th, the *Kayha* fent for me, and told me all Things were ended, and that we only waited for the reft of my Company which were coming from *Aden*. The 17th, Mr. *Fowler* and eighteen more with him arriv'd. He and two others were fent to me, the reft were put in Irons, and would have died with Hunger, if I had not reliev'd them better than the *Basha*, whofe Allowance was brown Bread and Water.

The 25th, a Bargain being ftruck, after four Days Chaffering, betwixt *Shermal* and me to pay the *Kayha*, who wou'd not appear in it himfelf, 1500 Venetiano's after my Deliverance. Mr. *Femel* follow'd that Minifter from his Garden, where we had fome previous Difcourfe about our Affair, to that of the *Basha*. We waited an Hour

at the Garden-Door, before we were admitted : We found him feated in a Summer Houfe, in a Chair, with half a dozen
Perfons at the Back of it, his *Kayha* ftanding at his right Hand.   I was led by two
Men, who held me by the Cloak tilhel
came within two Paces of the *Bafhay* and
there they ftopp'd me, Mr. *Femel* following
behind me without his Leaders.   He askd
how I did, bid me be of good Cheer,
for that fhortly I and all my People
fhou'd have their Liberty, and be fent to
Mokha, where I and twenty nine more
fhould remain (the reft being fent on board)
till all the Ships of *India* were came
into *Mokha,* and the Winds fettled We-
fterly ; after which we fhould be permitted
to go to our Ships, and proceed on our
Voyage.   He refusd to furrender our
Goods which he had taken, or the Pinnace,
all which, he pretended, were put to the
Grand Seignior's Account ; but he promisd
all the Tackle belonging to the Ships,
which were afhore, fhould be deliverd to
me punctually.   And that the aforefaid
Time being expir'd, not a Man of us
fhould be ftay'd, had I a *Turk* to my Slave;
for which Kindnefs I gave him Thanks.
                                                      Then

Then he began to excuse himself, praising his own mild Nature, and our good Luck in falling into his Hands ; for that, had it been in the Time of any of his Predeceffors, we had all fuffer'd Death for our Prefumption, in approaching fo near their holy City. He fignify d alfo, what had befallen us was by Order from the Grand Seignior, to whom the *Bafha's* of *Cairo* and *Swakhen*, and the *Sharif* of *Mecca*, had certify'd, that the *Afcenfion* and her Pinnace, at the Time of her being at *Mokha*, had bought all the choice Wares of *India*, to the great Diminution of his Cuftoms ; and that if a Stop was not put to fuch Practices, it would be the Overthrow of the Trade of thofe Seas. Whereupon the Grand Seignior by his Letters commanded him, that if any more *Englifh*, or other *Chriftian* came into thofe Parts, he fhould confifcate their Ships and Goods, and kill or captivate all the Men they could get into their Power.

The 1ft of *February*, Mr. *Femel* and I, by the Direction of the *Kayha*, went to compliment the *Bafha* upon his being made a *Wazir*, which he took very kindly. In the mean Time many of our People

fell

fell sick and weak, through Grief, Cold, bad Air, Diet and Lodging, with weighty Irons, but, by my constant solliciting of the *Kayba*, they were on the 11th all freed from their Prison and Irons, being allowed a House in Town, and Liberty to walk abroad and take the fresh Air. Also the next Day, the *Kayba* sent me half a Dozen of Beeves, to bestow amongst my Men, so that in a few Days all of them recover'd their former Health and Strength.

The 17th, the *Kayba* sent for me, Mr. *Femel* and others, and told me, we shou'd depart for *Mokha* the next Morning. *Rejib Aga* had written earnestly to the *Basha*, that we might be sent to *Aden*, and there taken into our Ships, but the *Kayba* had prevail'd to have it otherwise. After Breakfast he brought us to the *Basha* to take our Leaves. He began to extol his own Clemency, the Power of the Grand Seignior, saying, he had a long Sword, and charg'd me to come no more into those Seas. He refus'd me an Answer to his Majesty's Letter, or to write to *Rejib Aga* to perform what he had promis'd me, answering haughtily, Is not my sole Word suffifufficient to turn a whole City upfide down? If *Rejib Aga* wrong you, I will pull his Skin over his Ears, and give you his Head. Is not he my Slave? And there-upon appointed the *Kayha* to write my Difpatch.

The *Kayha* this Morning gave me an hundred Pieces of Gold, worth forty Madines each. He had given me fifty not many Days before. I told him I had never a Weapon, and defir'd I might have Leave to buy a Sword, and not ride down, as I came up, like a Prifoner: He acquainted the *Bafha* therewith, who fent me one of his caft one's.

The 18th, I paid all Duties of the Prifon, and went to the *Kayha's* Garden, where we break our Faft, receiv'd my Difpatch, and a Letter to the Governour of *Aden*, for reftoring the *Pepper-Corn* Boat, with another to the Governour of *Tayes*, for the Delivery of a Youth of Mr. *Pemberton's*, who was left fick there, and had been forced, as I was inform'd, to turn *Mohammedan*. I then took my Leave and departed.

The City of *Zenan* [*Sanaa*] is in the Latitude of 16 Degrees 15 Minutes, as I obferv'd

Defcription of *Zenan* or *Sanaa*.

obferv'd by an Inftrument which I made there. It is fomewhat bigger than *Briftol*, confifting of good Houfes built with Stone and Lime: There are alfo Churches or Masjeds. It is enclos'd with a Mud-Wall full of Battlements and Turrets: Within which on the Weft Side is a great deal of fpare Ground, where they have their Gardens, Orchards and Gardens of Pleafure. It ftands in a barren and ftony Valley, furrounded at a fmall Diftance with high Hills, one of which overlooks the Town to the Northward. On this Hill is built a fmall Caftle, to keep off the Mountain-People, who are accuftom'd to offend the City. It hath no Water, but what comes out of Wells, which they dig deep to come at any. Wood is fetch'd from far, which makes it very dear. On the Eaft Side is the Caftle compafs'd with Mud-Walls full of Turrets, in which every Night they place their Watch, which keep fuch a hollowing one to another all Night long, that a Man, who is not acquainted with it, can hardly fleep. The *Bafha*, and fome other principal Men. dwell within this Caftle Wall; to which the Keeper's Houfe, wherein I was impri-

fon d,

fon'd, adjoins; and at the Foot of the
Wall is a fpacious Yard, wherein a great
Number of People, for the moft part
Women and Children, are kept Prifoners
or Pledges, to prevent their Parents, Huf-
bands and Kindred from rebelling. Thofe
Women and Children live in little Cottages made of purpofe. The Children
go for the moft part naked, except it
be very cold, and then they have Sheep-
skin Coats to keep them warm. They
are, as wild and rude as if they were
brought up in the Mountains. The Boys,
while they are little, are fuffer'd to go at
liberty about the Yard; but when grown
big, they are clapt in Irons, and carry'd
to a ftrong Tower, where they remain
during the *Bafha*'s Pleafure.

Mr. *Femel*, *Fowler* and I were mounted
on Horfes, all the reft of our Company
on Affes and Camels. We had two
Chawfes on foot, and one Horfe-man to
conduct us. This Night we arriv'd at
Siam, diftant from *Zenan* 16 Miles: It
is a fmall Town, with a Caftle, upon the
Side of a Hill; the Place and Country
about is very barren, and yieldeth fmall
Relief to Travellers.

About

About Midnight we departed from *Siam*, and the next Day being the 19th, we came to *Surage*, about 10 in the Forenoon: It is a small Village, about 18 Miles from *Siam*. The Country is barren, and the People poor, going almost naked, save a Cloth about their Wastes reaching down to their Knees.

Damar, a good City.

We departed about Midnight, and the 20th in the Morning, towards 8 a Clock, arriv'd at *Damâr*. It is a City built with Lime and Stone, but separated into five Parts, one a pretty Distance from the other, so that it seemeth to be so many Villages. Tis seated in a spacious Valley or Plain, having plenty of Water, and all Kind of Grain; with all other Provision for Sustenance both for themselves and their poor Neighbours, who live in great Penury and Want. It is distant from *Surage* 20 Miles. We staid here two Days, by Order of the *Basha's Kayha*, who is Governour of this Province.

The 22d, we left *Damâr* about 2 a Clock after Midnight, and came to *Ermin* betimes, it being a small Village, some 15 Miles distant.

The

The 23d, we arriv'd at *Naqual Samâr*, being a common Inn for all Travellers, fome fourteen Miles from *Ermin:* The *Turks* call them Cenfors, which are built at the Expence of the Grand Seignior, for the Relief of Travellers. There be many of thefe Cenfors between *Mokha* and *Zenan:* This Cenfor is fcated in the midft of a very fteep Hill, call'd *Nakkel Samar*, and fome few fcattering poor Houfes about it. Upon the Top of this Hill is a great Caftle, wherein the Governour of the Province, who is an *Arabian*, dwells.

Thefe craggy Mountain-Countries are for the moft part govern'd by *Arabs*; for the People of thefe Mountains cannot brook the proud infolent Government of the *Turks*. No *Turk* may pafs this Way, neither upwards nor downwards, without a Paffport of the Governour of the Province from whence they came.

The 24th, we came to *Mohader*, a little Village at the Foot of the great Hill, diftant from *Nakkel Samâr* about 13 Miles. Our *Chawfes* had a Warrant from the *Bafha*, to take up Affes on the Road for our Men to ride on, which accordingly they perform'd overnight; but the next
Morn-

Morning the *Arabs*, way-laying us, took
back their Affes, neither of our Guardians daring to give them an ill Word

The 25th, we arriv'd at *Rabaltamain*,
a Cenfor with fome Cottages and Shops
adjoining thereunto; it is feated on the
Side of a Hill, 16 Miles from *Mohader*.
Thereabouts grows Poppy, of which they
make their Opium, but it is not good.

The 26th, we refted at a *Cough-Houfe*,
[or Coffee-Houfe] in the midft of a Plain.
It is call'd *Merfaddin*, and diftant from
Rabaltamain 16 Miles.

The 27th, we arriv'd at *Tayes*, a City
half as big as *Zenan*, and encompafs'd with
a Mud-Wall. It ftands in a Valley under
very high Hills; on the Top of one of
the higheft, is a fair and ftrong Caftle:
All kinds of Provifions are very cheap here.
In the Country about it is made Indico,
but in what Quantity, or of what Quality,
I could not learn. The City is very po
pulous, and fo indeed is all the Country
and Towns we travell'd through.

Here we ftaid all this Day and the next,
in which Time I did my beft to recover
the Youth of Mr. *Pemberton's*, before
mention'd. The Governour *Hamed Aga*,
who

who had forc'd him to turn *Turk*, would
by no means part with him : But *Walter
Talbot*, who fpoke *Turkifh*, was permitted
to fpeak with him, in a Chamber among
other Boys and Youths. He wept, and
faid he was deluded by them; that they
told him, at firft, I and all the reft were
flain, and promis'd to fave his Life if he
would turn; but finding they could not
prevail on him that Way, fome of the
Governour's Servants carry'd him to a hot
Bath, and when they had him naked, cir-
cumcis'd him by Force. My own Endeavours failing, I deliver'd the *Kayha's* Letter, which when the *Aga* had read, he
faid, it was Warrant fufficient for keeping
the Youth, as ordering him to be reftor'd
in cafe he was not turn'd. I fufpected the
Letter was to that Effect, and that made
me not deliver it at firft.

The 1ft of *March*, we departed and
came to *Eufras* about Noon, being 16
Miles from *Tayes*, thro' a mountainous and
ftony Country. The Town is little, fituate
on the Side of a Hill. About the 5th of
January, great Multitudes of People refort
hither from far, where they do fome foolifh
Ceremonies to one of their Saints, and holy

Men, who is interr'd there. After which they go in Company to *Mecca* on Pilgrimage. The Governour of this Town. is a *Turk*, and us'd us very kindly, both going and coming, fending one 6 Miles to a Place, where two Ways met, to bring us on our Return to his Town.

The 2d, we went from thence and lodg'd at a Cenfor, call'd *Affambin*, fome 11 Miles from *Eufras*. Here is no Town, but a few poor Cottages.

The 3d, we left *Affambin*, and came to *Accomoth*, another Cenfor, fome 13 Miles off. It ftands in a barren Common with a few Cottages by it.

The 4th in the Morning, we departed thence and came to *Moufa*, [It is call'd before *Mowffi*.] 17 Miles from *Accomoth*, thro' a plain and barren Country, very thinly inhabited; but the Town is very populous, tho' not great, and unwall'd. It ftands in a Plain indifferently fruitful. Hereabouts likewife is made fome Indico

We quitted *Moufa* about Midnight, and the 5th in the Morning, about 8 - Clock, came to *Mokha*, where we had arriv'd before Day, if we had not refted two or three Hours by the Way, at a Chutch,

at

or Cough-Houfe, call'd *Dabully*, built by
a *Dabul* Merchant. A Mile without Town
we were met by our Carpenters, Smiths,
and fuch others as were detain'd there,
their Irons having been knock'd off the
Day before, and Liberty given them to
walk abroad. They told me Mr. *Pemberton* lighted on a Cannon, and got a-
board. At the Town's End, and all the
Way to the *Aga*'s Houfe, the People ftood
very thick, and, as we pafs'd by, bid us
welcome back; for it was nothing pleafing
to the People of the Country, to hear
how treacheroufly the *Turks* had us'd us.

We rid till we came to the *Aga*'s Houfe,
where we allighted: Mr. *Femel*, Mr.
Fowler, and myfelf were brought before
him, where I deliver'd my Letters from *Zenan*. He receiv'd me in his wonted dif-
fembling Way, with a Shew of Love and
Kindnefs; bidding us welcome, and faying he was glad of our fafe Return, and
forry, and afhamed of what was paft.
He pray'd me to pardon him, and to affure
myfelf, that, for the future, he would be
my Friend; declaring he did nothing but
what his Mafter commanded him. I
footh'd him up, but believ'd nothing he

faid.

faid. He read the *Basha's* Order, and faid all Things fhould be perform'd accordingly : Thereupon he call'd in for Breakfaft, and caus'd us to fit down with him, bidding me eat and be merry ; for now he had eaten Bread and Salt with me, I need not fear any harm. After Breakfaft he went to feek for a Houfe for me. We had a fair large Houfe appointed us near the Sea-fide, where we continu'd two Days ; after which, for fear we fhould attempt an Efcape from thence, we were remov'd to a great ftrong Houfe, ftanding all alone in a fpacious Church Yard, in the middle of the Town, with a Captain and his Company to guard us in the Day, and at Night our Houfe was befet with arm'd Soldiers.

Defcription of *Mokha.*

Moha (or rather *Mokha*) is one third Jefs than *Tayes* ; unwall'd, very populous, and feated by the Sea, in a falt, fandy, barren Soil. The Governour's Houfe is clofe by the Water-fide ; and near it the Key, or Bridge, which fhoots a pretty Diftance into the Sea: To which Key, all Boats, belonging to any Shipping, are enjoyn'd to land, for fear of ftealing of Cuftom. And clofe adjoyning to the Key

is

is a Platform, whereon are planted fome Dozen of Brafs-Pieces. At the weftern End of the Town, there is a Fort, wherein is the like Quantity of Ordnance. This Fort was in Ruins at our firft coming thither, but fince it hath been pull'd down, and rebuilt.

Sir *Henry Middleton*'s Journey, between *Mokha* and *Sanaa*, ending here, we fhall go on briefly to give an Account of his Efcape from the *Turks*, in the fame Manner as at the Beginning we have related his Captivity. On the 6th and 7th he was invited to Feafts made for the *Dabullian* Merchants by the *Aga*, who, in Prefence of them all, kifs'd the *Korân*, and voluntarily fwore he had no ill Will to Sir *Henry*, but wou'd do him all the Good in his Power, and was forry for what was paft. Next Day they were all fent for before the *Aga*, who fingling out the Merchants, Carpenters, Smiths and others, with Sir *Henry*, to the Number of thirty, to ftay on Land; the reft, who were thirty fix, were fent, the 9th, on board the *Darling*, which repair'd to the reft of their Ships on the Coaft of *Habafh*, where they had found out an excellent

Road

Road, call'd *Assab*-Road, safe against all Winds. Sir *Henry* might have made his Escape that Day, if he had not been more careful about others than himself.

April 1, 16:1, the *Darling* departed from *Assab*, with Leave to return every ten Days to see how Sir *Henry* did, which gave him Hopes by that Means to compass his Freedom; as the daily Arrival of Ships from *India* seem'd to promise him ample Satisfaction for the Troubles and Damages he and his People had sustain'd.

The 10th, the *Darling* came in again, and the next Day the *Aga*, with all the chief Men of the Town, having rid abroad in great State to his Garden to be merry, which gave Sir *Henry* an Opportunity of executing his long meditated Escape. He immediately wrote to Mr. *Pemberton*, to send the Boat ashore well mann'd, for that he intended to convey himself into an empty Butt, and so be carry d down to the Boat as an empty Cask. He directed Mr. *Femel* and others to a certain Place, where he promis'd to take them into his Boat; and appointed the Carpenters and some more to repair to the Southward of the Town, where lay a Boat, hard by the
Shore,

Shore, ready to receive them; but charg'd them not to embark themselves till such Time as they saw the Ship's Boat put off from the Key.

It must be observ'd, that all Sir *Henry's* Company had free Liberty to walk abroad any where in the Day-time without Suspicion. The Eyes of his Guards were solely upon him. He never went out of the Doors without two or three Soldiers attending him : This made it the more difficult to contrive his Escape. However, all Things succeeded according to his Wishes ; for while the *Sub-Basha* (who was their Ward, and left in Town only to look after him) fell to drinking hard at an Arrack-House, Sir *Henry* was fuddling the Soldiers with Aqua Vitæ and Wine.

The Boat being come, the Guards all drunk, and every Thing ready, about 12 a Clock at Noon the *Sub-Basha* returns, and being in one End of the House, where his Lodging was, (there being only a Wall between him and the *English*, the better to guard them) Sir *Henry* was convey'd into his Tub, (as he calls it) and safely set aboard the Boat ; which being done, he forc'd out the Head of the Cask and came

S 4   forth.

forth.   Then he caus'd them to bear up
to the leeward Point, where he took in
Mr. *Fowler* and ten more.   Mr. *Femel*
and others, being too flow, were taken before they could reach the Boat.   The
Town being alarm'd, partly by the indifcreet Running of fome of the Men, and
partly by feeing the Boat fteer contrary
to its wonted Courfe.   However, the Carpenters efcap'd alfo in their Boat, only one
Man, ftaying too long behind, and at-
tempting to get on board by Swimming,
was drown'd.

Sir *Henry*'s Efcape caus'd no fmall Confufion in the Town; the Keepers knew
not how to anfwer it to the *Aga*, nor
the *Aga* to the *Bafha*.   The Governour
at the Sight of Mr. *Femel*, and the reft
look'd pale : He threaten'd them with the
Lofs of their Heads, and order'd them all
to be chain'd by the Necks ; but they were
quickly free'd at the Intreaty of the *No-
huda*'s, or Captains, *Malec Ambar* and
Mohammed of *Cananor*, more out of Fear
than Love ; for their Ships were then under Sir *Henry*'s Command.

As foon as Sir *Henry* got aboard
his Ship, he laid all the Veffels in the
Road

Road under an Embargo, and sent to the *Aga* to demand his Men, the Ship's Tackle, the Youth which they detain'd, the Pinnace, and 70,000 Rials of Eight, to make good the Damages he had sustain'd, threatening otherwise to burn all the Ships, and do his best to batter the Town about his Ears. After many Negotiations carry'd on by the *India* Merchants between Sir *Henry* and the *Aga*, and several Expresses backwards and forwards between the *Aga* and the *Basha*, at length, on the 19th of *June*, an Agreement was made, whereby Sir *Henry* had all his Demands granted, except in the last Article, which on Account of the Restitution of some of his Goods, was reduc'd to 18,000 Rials of Eight in Money, payable in 15 Days.

The 3d of *June*, Sir *Henry* with the rest of the Ships went over to *Assab*-Road. From whence on the 24th they set sail for the Island of *Camaran*, there to wait for the great Ship, which came yearly about this Time richly laden from *Sues* to *Mokha*, but she escap'd them in the Night. However, Sir *Henry* returning the next Year into the *Red-Sea*, made up all Deficiencies at the Expence of

of the *India* Ships which traded at *Mokha.*
After having oblig'd them to exchange the
beft of their Commodities for his, he got
from them about 30,000 Rials of Eight,
for the Liberty of remaining in the *Red-
Sea*; Sir *Henry* intending to have taken
them back again with him to *India*, in
order to revenge himfelf on the *Turks,*
by the Lofs he fhould caufe them to fuftain
thereby in their Cuftoms *.

Notwithftanding all this Oppofition and
ill Treatment, given to Sir *Henry Middleton*, by the *Turks* at *Mokha*, in 1611, the
Settling of a Trade in 1613 was attempted
by Captain *Saris*, who in all Probability
wou'd have effected it, *Rejib Aga* being
difplac'd, if Sir *Henry's* Return into the
Red-Sea had not broken his Meafures †.
However, in 1618, the *Royal Ann*, commanded by Captain *Andrew Shilling*, being fent for that Purpofe from *Surat*, by
the Directions of Sir *Thomas Roe*, a Trade
was fettled at *Mokha* the fame Year with
the fame *Rejib Aga*, who was reftor'd
while the *Englifh* were there. He laid
the Fault of the ill Ufage towards Sir
Henry

---

* See *Purchas*, ubi fupra, p. 309.   † Ibid. p. 341,
345.

Henry Middleton, on the diforderly Behaviour of the Sailors, and bad Difpofition of the then *Bafha* of *Sanaa* * ; one
named *Mohammed* being *Bafha* at this
Time. As it was neceffary to have the
Bafha's Grant alfo, *Jofeph Salbank,* one
of the three Merchants which made the
Voyage upon this Occafion, was fent to
Sinan, (or *Sanaa*) in order to obtain it † :
that this is the fecond Time the *Englifh*
had been at that Capital of *Yaman,* which
the *French* have not yet feen.

   Mr. *Salbank* carry'd with him a Prefent
for the *Bafha,* and fome Merchandize.
The *Scrivano* lent him his Mule to ride
on. He was furnifh'd with two Camels,
one Cook, one to attend the Horfes, three
Servants of the Governour's, whofe Wa-
ges he had compounded to pay, and an
Interpreter. He had alfo Letters of the
Governour. He left *Mokha* the 23d of
June about fix in the Evening, the Nights
being the accuftom'd Time of travelling,
and return'd the 27th of *July,* before Day,
with his *Firmans.* We find only a few
Particulars relating to this Journey, which
                                    is

* See *Heynes's* Journal. Ibid. p. 624, 627. † Ibid.
p. 628.

is obferv'd to have been a hard one. But
to make amends for the Fatigue of the
Road, he was treated with Refpect where-
ever he came, being always met before
he enter'd any Town of note, with Horfe
and Foot to guard him to the Governour's-
Houfe, by whom he was well receiv'd.
His Provifions were provided by their Officers, but at his own Charge ; the Governour of *Mokha*'s Servant commanding
every Thing in the Name of the *Bafha.*
Before he came to *Sinan*, he was met a
Mile without the City by 40 or 50 *Turks*
well hors'd, fent by the *Bafha*, by whom
he was convey'd to a Houfe ready and
richly furnifh'd againft his coming. He
receiv'd friendly Entertainment of the
principal *Xeriffe (Sharif)* and the *Bafha*'s
chief Treafurer, who were appointed to
welcome him. And two Days after the
Bafha himfelf gave him an Audience, entertain'd him courteoufly, and gave him two
Firmans, both of the fame Tenour ; but
one written in a fairer Character than the
other, to fhew to the Grand Seignior, if
Occafion requir'd.

He obferv'd that thefe Parts about *Sinan* are cold for three Quarters of the
Year

Year: Nay, that in the Summer, when he was there, a Man might well have endur'd a Fur-Gown. About 40 or 50,000 *Turks* belong to the *Basha*'s Court, moft of them cloath'd with *Venetian* Cloths of great Prices. Alfo not far from the City, there lay a Leskar (or Camp) of 30,000 Soldiers, who were continually in the Field againft an *Arab* King, as yet unconquer'd, inhabiting the Mountains adjoining. Which Soldiers were reported to wear Coats quilted of Cotton, made of *India* Pintadoes (a Wear which is dear and little ferviceable) for want of Cloth to keep them from the Cold, which is there extreme. There is a Leskar alfo at the City *Tyeis* (*Tayes*) of 30 or 40,000 Soldiers, commanded by a Renegado *German*, and fubject to the *Basha* of *Sinan*, where much Cloth is worn. For it is very Cold there, tho' not above five Days Journey from *Mokha*. From which Circumftances, the Perfon who hath written the Account from the verbal Relation of Mr. *Salbank*, concludes that fome Quantity of *Englifh* Cloth may be fold every Year in that Country *

It

* See *Heynes*'s Journal, p. 628, 629.

It is obfervable, that tho' Sir *Henry Middleton* was curious enough to be at the Pains to make an Inftrument for taking the Latitude of *Sanaa*; yet neither he, nor any of the *Englifh* who made the Voyage after him to *Mokha*, nay, nor the *French* themfelves in their late Voyages, have given us the Latitude of this laft City. In regard to the Name of which, fome may be apt to tax thofe, our firft Navigators, with bringing in a Corruption, calling it *Moha* inftead of *Mokha*, which is the *Arabic* Orthography; but it muft be confider'd, that they took the Name from the *Turks*, who then were Mafters of the Town, and who, not ufing the Gutturals, pronounce the *Arabic Kha* like the *Ha*.

I fhall conclude with one Remark concerning Coffee. That tho' we read of Cough Houfes in Sir *Henry Middleton's* Journal, yet he no where mentions the drinking of Coffee; tho it was doubtlefs as much in Ufe at *Mokha* and *Sanaa*, when he was there, as in the Time of Captain *Saris* and *Heynes*, who found it at all Entertainments; but neither of them feems to have taken much Notice of it. The
firft

firſt mentions it only occaſionally, ſpeaking of their Drink at Feaſts, which, he ſays, was Water ſimply, or elſe Water boil'd with an Herb call'd *Cauhaw* *, which comes pretty near the Pronunciation of the true Name, *Kahwah*. The latter calls it *Cohoh*, but gives no Account of what ſort of Liquor it is ; and, what is ſtranger, he ſuppoſes it to have been brought from *Diu* by the *Portugals* † : By which one would be apt to conclude, the *Arabs* had not yet begun to export Coffee into other Countries, if we had not very good Proofs to the contrary, and were not ſenſible now negligent and incurious thoſe generally are, who go into foreign Parts on Account of Trade.

* *Purchas,* ubi ſupra, p. 341, 345.　† Ibid. p. 628.

AN

Hiſtorical Treatiſe

*Concerning the Original and Pro-
greſs of* Coffee, *as well in* Aſia
as Europe; *of its Introduction into* France, *and the Eſta-
bliſhment of the Uſe of it at*
Paris.

T ſeems ſtrange at firſt, that
Coffee, being the Thing moſt
in Uſe all over *Turky*, and
the *French* having *ever* made
Voyages either for Trade or
Curioſity to *Egypt*, the neareſt Province
to the Country from whence the Coffee
comes, that there ſhould be no Tidings
of it till of late, not only in *France*, but
alſo the other Nations of *Europe*. It may
be doubted therefore, whether the Cuſtom
of drinking of Coffee, even in the *Levant* itſelf, be ſo antient as ſome Authors
would

would infinuate, for thofe who have writ of the Liquors of the *Eaftern* People, about the middle of the 16th Age : And among others *Peter Belon*, who travell'd in thofe Countries from the Year 1546 till 1549, and has carefully defcrib'd the moft curious Plants of *Egypt* and *Arabia*; thefe Authors, I fay, make no manner of Mention of Coffee. {General Silence of *European* Authors upon the Subject of Coffee, till the Time of *Profper Alpinus*,}

The firft *European*, that brought Tidings of it, was *Profper Alpinus*, a famous Phyfician of *Padua*, and great Botanift, who, in the Year 1580, follow'd a Conful of the Republick of *Venice* into *Egypt*, and during a Refidence of 3 or 4 Years, became fo thoroughly acquainted with all the Plants of that Country, that he wrote a particular Book upon them *. {who fpeaks the firft of it about the End of the 16th Age, after having feen one of the Trees in *Egypt*, &c.}

' I have feen at *Cairo* this Tree, fays *Profper Alpinus*, Cap. 16. ' in the Garden ' of a *Turk*, nam'd *Aly Bey*, and I have ' given here the Figure of one of its

T   ' Boughs;

---

* *Profper Alpinus* has alfo writ a Tract about the Phyfick of the *Egyptians*, where he fpeaks alfo of Coffee; a Treatife of Baume, and another of exotick Plants. He was profeffor at *Padua*, and Director of the Garden of Plants, which is the moft antient in *Europe*, having been founded by the Republick in 1540, at the Sollicitation of *Damal Barbaro*, Patriarch of *Aquileia*.

‘ Boughs; ’tis that fame which produces
‘ the Fruit so common in *Egypt*, which
‘ they call *Bon*, or *Ban*. There is made
‘ with it, among the *Arabs* and *Egyptians*,
‘ a Kind of Decoction, very much in Use,
‘ and which they drink instead of Wine.
‘ The same is publickly sold as Wine
‘ amongst us. This Drink is call’d *Coava*.
‘ The Fruit we speak of comes from *Ara-*
‘ *bia Fœlix ;* as to the rest, the Tree which
‘ I have seen seems to me to resemble the
‘ Evonyme *, having the Leaves notwith-
‘ standing thicker, harder and greener;
‘ moreover, it never sheds all its Leaves.

’Tis after this Manner that *Alpinus* expresses himself, with regard to the Tree
and Drink of Coffee. Nor does he forget, as a Physician, to relate the Qualities
attributed by the Orientals to this Liquor.
which are much the same as have been
since discover’d, and admitted by our best
Physicians.

In the Year 1640, a new Edition was
publish’d of *Prosper Alpinus*’s Treatise of
Egyptian Plants, with the additional
Notes of *Veslingius*, another famous *Ita-*
lian

* That is the Tree which the *French* call Fuzain,
and the *English* the Spindle-Tree, or Prickwood.

lian Phyſician upon it. They are both dedicated to *Nicholas Contarini,* and printed ſeparately alſo in 1638, at *Padua.*

Veſlingius informs us in his Obſervations, that he alſo made the Voyage of
Egypt after *Proſper Alpinus*; but could
never find the Tree in Queſtion, which he
look'd for in all the Gardens he had the Opportunity of ſeeing. This Tree 'tis likely
was periſh'd either by Age or Accident,
for *Egypt* propuces no Coffee-Trees, and
that had been rear'd out of pure Curioſity.
Veſlingius adds, that at the Time of his
Abode at *Cairo,* there were in that great Great
City 2 or 3000 Coffee-Houſes. That Number
of Cof-
ſome began to put Sugar in it to correct the fee Hou-
Bitterneſs, and that others made Comfits of ſes at *Cairo.*
the Coffee-Beans. In fine, the Commen-
tator upon *Alpinus* alſo, as a Phyſician,
makes his Remarks upon the Qualities of
Coffee, diſtinguiſhing thoſe which are proper to the Husk or Pod, which cover the
Bean, from thoſe which belong to the
Bean itſelf, which he calls the Kernel of
the Fruit of Coffee: Not forgetting to obſerve, that the Uſe of Coffee is ſo common,
not only in *Egypt,* but throughout the
whole *Turkiſh* Empire, 'That from thence

‘ it comes, fays he, that Coffee is dear even
‘ in the *Levant* itfelf, and that 'tis a Rari-
‘ ty among *Europeans*, who are depriv'd
‘ thereby of a very wholfome Remedy.

It may be judg'd by this Expreffion, that, at the Time *Veflingius* wrote, Coffee was not altogether unknown in *Europe*, at leaft at *Venice*, whereto, there is Reafon to believe, Coffee firft was brought out of *Afia*, by Means of the *Venetian* Traffick.

Chancellor *Bacon*, who dy'd in the Year 1626, makes mention of Coffee in his Works, but fo fuperficially, that he feems to have been not well inform'd; and that the Thing, of which he fpeaks, was not known in *England*.

But fince that Time, Coffee having con-ftantly been brought from the *Levant* in-to *Italy* by the *Venetians*, *Fauftus Nai-ron*, a Maronite, Profeffor of the Oriental Languages at *Rome*, publifh'd there a fmall Treatife in *Latin* * concerning Coffee. 'Tis properly the firft Work written parti-cularly

---

* De faluberrima potione Cahue, feu Cafe nuncu-pata, Difcurfus *Faufti Naironi* Banefii Maronite, Lin-guæ *Chaldaicæ* feu *Syriacæ* in almo Urbis Archigym-nafio Lectoris. Ad Eminentiff. & Reverendiff. Prin-cipem D. *Jo. Nicolaus*, S. R. E Card. de Comitibus, *Romæ*, 1671.

cularly upon the Bufinefs, the Extract of which is found in an *Italian* Journal of the Year 1671. That Author was capable of informing us to the Purpofe, being originally a *Syrian*, and, befides that, curious and learned. Neverthelefs 'tis fuppos'd, that he has not fucceeded accordingly, and that he was deceiv'd in fome effential Points, as we fhall obferve in its proper Place.

It feems as if the Performance of fome thing more finifh'd and elaborate upon this Subject was referv'd for the *French*. Nothing perhaps is to be found more methodical and particular than *Philip-Silvefter Dufour*'s Treatife upon Coffee. He was originally of *Manofque* in *Provence*, and only a Merchant of *Lyons*, but learn'd, curious, and judicious, efpecially in natural Pholofophy. *Philip-Silvefter Dufour, a Frenchman, Author of a Treatife upon this Subject.*

At firft he publifh'd only a *French* Tranflation of a *Latin* Manufcript, that fell into his Hands, which treated of Coffee, of Tea, and of Chocolate * An Extract

T 3 of

* This Tranflation was printed at *Lyons* the firft Time, *Ann.* 1671, under the Title of the Ufe of Coffee, Tea, and Chocolate, and dedicated to *R. P. John de Buffieres*, of the Society of Jefus.

of this Tranflation may be found in the Journal *des Savans*, of *January* 28, 1675; in which it was faid, that there were then at *Paris* feveral Shops wherein Coffee was fold. The Author of the Journal adds of himfelf, that Coffee was known to the *Englifh* above 20 Years fooner than us, but that wants to be made out. As to the reft, that Manufcript Memoir was not very exact, efpecially touching the true Country wherein the Coffee grows, which it remarks to be about *Mecca*, contrary to what it really is.

Since then, Coffee becoming every-Day more and more in Ufe in *France*, chiefly at *Paris*, *Lyons* and *Marfeille*, as we fhall obferve hereafter: Monfieur *Dufour* undertook a Work of his own upon this Matter, none having done the like before in the Kingdom. He conceiv'd that his Profeffion of a Merchant was no way incompatible with that of an Author's, efpecially in treating of a Subject, the Knowledge of which comes by Merchants, and in which a Merchant may be better inform'd than a Philofopher.

Thefe are the Author's own Words, who tells us, that not fatisfy'd with confulting

fulting a great Number of learned Men, both in and without the Kingdom, with which he kept a Correfpondence, he has even carry'd his Enquiries to the further End of the Eaft, where he trades: 'Tis with thefe Advantages, that he gave us at laft, in 1684, the faid Treatife. The Journal *des Savans* gave the Publick an Account of it, *January* 28, 1685. This Treatife was never printed at *Paris*, but it has been twice at *Lyons*, in 1684, and in 1688, and at the *Hague* in 1685. Monfieur *Bayle* makes it a curious Article in his *Nouvelles de la Republique des Lettres*, and treats the Author very honourably, ' Who knew, fays he, how to reconcile Learning with ' Traffick, skill'd in Languages and Books, ' writing well, and having always carry'd ' on an ingenious Correfpondence with ' Men of Rank and Merit.' The learned Journalifts of *Lipfick* do the fame Honour to the Treatife of Monfieur *Dufour* in their Month of *March*, 1686, adding that the foregoing Year it was publifh'd in *Latin*, and in *Dutch*, printed at *Budiffen* * ;

T 4   the

---

* *Budiffen*, a Town of *Lufaw*, in the Electorate of *Saxony*, commonly *Bautzen*.

the *Latin* Tranſlation is Monſieur *Spon's*, according to Monſieur *Bayle*, whom we have already cited.

This Treatiſe is divided into three Chapters, which contain all that could be ſaid, and all that was then known, touching Coffee. However, there may be diſcover'd ſome Miſtakes in it, which are not ſo much the Author's Fault, as thoſe that pretended to inform him. This appears eſpecially in the Deſcription of the Coffee-Tree, and more ſtill in the Draught which he has given of it in a Copper-Plate before the Book, which reſembles nothing leſs than it does the Tree itſelf.

The Derivation of the Name of Coffee, tho' given by Monſieur the Chevalier *d'Arvieux*, Conſul of *Aleppo*, and skill'd in the *Arabic*, is not right, as we ſhall prove hereafter. In ſhort, the little Hiſtory of the Diſcovery of Coffee, aſcrib'd by *Fauſtus Nairon* to an Abbot of a Monaſtery, who was inform'd, by one who kept Camels and Goats, that ſometimes his Cattle never reſted, but skipp'd about all Night, after having browz'd on the Coffee-Tree, or eaten of its Fruit; which gave the Abbot the Hint, to make the Monks take it to

prevent

prevent their sleeping during the Offices
of the Night.   That History, I say, receiv'd by Monsieur *Dufour*, upon the Credit of *F. Nairon*, and follow'd by other
French Authors, is look'd upon as fictitious
by those who examine Things closely, as
we shall shew by and by.

I shall wave entring upon a Detail of
the rest of this Work, where the Author
argues the Matter pro and con by himself, in which his Sagacity and Exact-
ness is not to be sufficiently prais'd ; for
he examines, like a good natural Philo-
sopher, all the Qualities of Coffee ; he has
likewise given the chymical Analysis, after
having had the Operation made before
himself and the celebrated Monsieur *Spon*,
a great Artist, in order to give, as he has
done, a Reason for its Effects, and to remark the several Distempers, which the Use
of Coffee might be instrumental in heal-
ing, helping, or preventing.   All this Account is very curious, and the Author advances nothing which is not founded upon
the Authority of the best Physicians, from
that of the most famous Travellers, and by
choice Examples, which sometimes divert
the Reader.

We

We ſhall paſs by the judicious Arguments againſt the odd Opinion of *Peter Della Valle*, who pretends * that the *Nepenthe* † of *Homer* ||, which that Poet ſays *Helen* had from *Egypt*, and of which ſhe made a Medicine againſt Melancholy, *&c.* is no other Thing but Coffee-Wine ; and againſt that of *Simon Paul*, a *Daniſh* Phyſician, who ſpeaks much to the Diſadvantage of Coffee, upon the Report of *Olearus*, who gives a pleaſant Story enough * *, to prove that it decays Nature in Men, and brings Impotency on them.

The

* Vol. I. Let. iii. from *Conſtantinople.* † Monſieur *Petit*, a Phyſician of *Paris*, who died in 1687, has written a Diſſertation in *Latin* upon the *Nepenthe* of *Homer*, which was publiſh'd by M. *Greaves* in 1689. He does not give into the Sentiment of *Peter Della Valle* ; but Monſieur *Paſch*, in his *Latin* Treatiſe upon the new Diſcoveries made out of Antiquity, printed at *Leipſic* in 1700, pretends that the Coffee is meant by the Preſents which *Abigail* made to *David*, in order to appeaſe him, 1 *Kings* ch. xxv. v. 18.   Odyſſ. 4. *Vilemont*, lib. ii. cap. 30. believes the *Nepenthe* with more Probability to have been Opium.   * * The Story is of a *Perſian* Queen in the laſt Century, who, ſeeing the Grooms about to geld a Horſe, and calling to Mind the Obſervations ſhe had made of the Effects of Coffee on the *Shâb*, her Husband, told them, they need not put the Beaſt to pain, ſince giving him Coffee would effectually take down his Mettle.

The laft Chapter of that Treatife is employ'd to fhew the Conftitutions and Di-
ftempers for which Coffee is not proper.
The Reafoning is very juft. For what remains, Monfieur *Galland*, who is there
cited as an Example of Perfons, who have
never been able to accuftom themfelves
to Coffee, does not agree to this pretended
Antipathy. He only calls to mind that,
being at **Conftantinople** troubled with a
Spitting of Blood, he was thereupon oblig'd
to abftain from Coffee, which aggravated
his Diftemper, which has, without doubt
been mifunderftood by thofe who have
fpoken of him to Monfieur *Dufour*.

But we muft not finifh the Article relating to Coffee, without making two Remarks: The firft is, that, according to
Monfieur *Dufour*, Coffee was not known
in *France* till about the Year* 1645; and
that, when he writ this Treatife, it was
little more than 25 Years fince it began
to come in Ufe. ‘ Before that Time, fays
he, ‘ People knew fo little what it was,
‘ that one of thofe, that have fpoke of it,
‘ had fo far miftaken the Matter, as to call
                                          it

---

* Thefe Facts are better made out and adjufted at
the End of this Treatife.

' it the Mulberry-Tree, in a Pamphlet
' which he put out at *Paris* *, when firft
' Coffee began to bedrank.'

The laft Remark is, that, in Monfieur
Dufour's Time, there were Phyficians
that did not approve of the Ufe of Coffee: This appears by the Attestation of
Mr. *Falconet* the Son, given at *Lyons*,
May 10, 1683, to the Treatife we are
fpeaking of: ' A Difcourfe, fays that learn'd
Phyfician, ' capable of undeceiving the
' moft prepoffefs'd, and of informing thofe
' who continue to enquire, whether Cof-
' fee animates or refrefhes.   All thofe
' Things, continues he, are clear'd up in
' this Book, where nothing appears which
' is not ufeful, very curious and proper to
' convince every Body, that he was better
' acquainted with the Subject than any
' one befides.

Not-

---

* This Pamphlet is inferted in the Tranflation already
mention'd, made by Mr. *Dufour*, and publifh'd at *Ly-*
ons, 1671, entitl'd, *the moft excellent Vertue of the Mul-*
berry, call'd COFFEE. The Fruit of *Coffee* was not
altogether unknown to this Author; his Miftake lay
in calling it a Sort of Mulberry. See the Defcription
of this Fruit in the Memoirs, &c.

Notwithstanding this Encomium, and the judicious Reflection that concludes it, there appear'd at the Beginning of the Year 1687, another Treatise upon the same Subject, under the Title, *Du Bon usage du The, du Cafe, & du Chocolat*, compos'd by *Nicholas de Blegny*. This Work, printed by *Michallet*, may be look'd upon as the Effect of an indiscreet Emulation, or the Desire of Writing, (for Monsieur *Dufour* had also handled these three Subjects) rather than of a sincere Desire to serve the Publick, and benefit it by new Discoveries. In short, all that is worth any Thing in that Treatise, is to be found in that of Monsieur *Dufour*; and 'tis observable, that when the Author, in order to appear the Original, speaks his own Sense, he never fails to go beside the Mark. We leave to the Expert in true Chymistry, the Judgment of the medicinal Preparations of Coffee; to wit, the Salts, its fixt Oyl, distill'd Water, and its Syrup, which Monsieur *de Blegny* pretends to have found out, and to put in Practice with a great deal of Success. I shall only hear observe, that the Fact which he reports upon Hearsay, of a Coffee-Tree, *sow'd and*

Another Discourse upon Coffee, by Nicholas de Blegny.

and cultivated with Succeſs by a Gentleman near Dijon, *many Years ſince, which came up in the ſame Form as that of* Arabia, *&c.* this Fact, I ſay, is like a great many more of the ſame Kind *, whoſe Error will appear upon Examination.

But tho' the Author of the firſt Treatiſe has carry'd his Reſearches very far, yet the Subject was not quite exhauſted under his Hand. For that which was moſt curious and difficult to be known, with regard to Coffee, remain'd ſtill. in the Dark, when it pleas'd Monſieur *Galland,* who has travell'd into the *Levant,* and is very well vers'd in the oriental Languages, to give us another Piece upon that Subject. He writ it near 20 Years ago, at the Intreaty of a Perſon of Merit and Diſtinction, to whom he preſented it in Form of a Letter†, upon the Occaſion of a Diſcourſe which the Coffee had rais'd.

The

---

* Theſe Matters are treated as a Dream, in a Theſis pleaſant enough, upon *Coffee,* maintain'd at *Paris,* in *March,* 1715, uti ſomniaverunt creduli, qui pro illo cicer arietinum jam gaudio in hortis vegitaſſe mirabantur.   † The Letter is dated at *Paris,* the 15 of *December,* 1696, under the Title, of the Original and Progreſs of Coffee, out of an *Arabick* Manuſcript in the King's Library. Printed at *Caen,* and ſold at *Paris* by *Florentin* and *Peter de Laune,* 1699.

The Foundation is entirely built upon two Hiftorians, the one an *Arab,* and the other a *Turk.* The Work of the former is inthe King's Library, N°. 944. M. *Galland* does not forget, upon this Occafion, his Acknowledgments to Monfieur, the Abot of *Louvois,* who, doing himfelf a Pleafure to oblige the World, and particularly the Learn'd, has had the Goodnefs to communicate to him the *Arabick* Manufcript. Twas a pitty that our Author, when he printed this Treatife, had no more than a fmall Number wrought off to diftribute among his Friends; infomuch, that it is hardly to be met with; but the Value of it may be judg'd by the Account we are going to give of it, which may very well pafs for a Supplement to that of M. *Dufour.*

In the firft Place, to afcertain the Etymology and Signification of the Word Coffee, miftaken by former Authors, we are told, that this Word comes from *Kahveh,* as the *Turks* pronounce it with a *v* Confonant, and is the fame Thing as *Cahwah* among the *Arabs,* who don't ufe the *v* Confonant : Thus, by the changing of a Letter, and pronouncing it a little different
ferent

ferent from the Orientals, we have made
the Word *Caufe*, (and in the *Englifh*
Coffee) of the *Turkifh* Word *Kahveb*,
deriv'd from *Kahwah*, originally an *Arabick* Term.

Kahwah is the Infinitive of a Verb, and
fignifies to loath eating, to have no Appetite ; and is alfo one of the different
Names the *Arabs* give to Wine, according to the Copioufnefs of their Language :
In fhort, Wine drank to excefs diforders
the Stomach, and takes away the Appetite, contrary to the Opinion of *Golius*,
but according to that of a *Mahometon*
Doctor, cited by the *Arabian* Author, of
which we are going prefently to fpeak.

Of *Kahwah*, fignifying originally Wine
in particular, the *Arabs* have fince made
a general Term to fignify all Sorts of Drink.
Thus the Word fignifies neither the Tree,
nor the Beans, or the Fruit of the Tree,
which we call improperly Coffee, but only the Drink made of the fame.

Upon this Principle, the Orientals diftinguifh three Sorts or Kinds of Coffee, *viz.*
Wine and all intoxicating Liquors ; that
which is made of the Husks or Pods that in-
clofe the Bean, call'd by us Coffee ; and that
                                                    which

which is made with the fame Bean, fuch as is in Ufe with us.

The *Arabs* call that Bean, *Bon,* and the Tree which bears it, the *Bon*-Tree, which gives room to M. *Galland* to obferve a Miftake of *Fauftus Nairon,* who, in his Treatife of Coffee, has taken the *Bonk,* a Root of which * *Avicenna,* and other *Arab* Authors fpeak of the *Bon,* or Coffee; and who moreover has ill ex-prefs'd in *Arabick,* tho' his Mother-Tongue, the Plant known to the Bota-nifts by the Name of *Spina Egyptica.* In fhort, *Fauftus Nairon* is again found fault with, upon the pretended different Pronunciations of the *Arabick* Word, *Bon, Ban,* and *Ben,* as if it was but one and the fame Thing. Whereas M. *Galland* maintains by the Principles of Gram-mar, and the Authority of the *Moham-*

U   *medan*

---

* M. *Galland* obferves elfewhere, that *Avicen* has alfo fpoken of *Bon,* or Coffee; 'tis the Opinion of *Profper Alpinus, Veflingius,* &c. which is difputed by other Authors. *Ben Jazlab,* a great Phyfician, almoft contemporary with *Avicen,* alfo makes mention of it; whence it is eafy to perceive, fays M. *Galland,* that we are beholden for Coffee to Phyfick, as well as for Sugar, Tea, and Chocolate, and all that goes to its Compofition.

medan Doctor already quoted, that they are two Plants altogether different.

But if *Fauſtus Nairon*, a skilful Profeſſor, has been deceiv'd in ſpeaking his own Language, we have all the Reaſon in the World, to excuſe Monſieur the Chevalier *d'Arvieux*, who, in the Treatiſe of M. *Dufour*, pretends, that *Kahweh* is the *Arabick* Name for Coffee, tho' that Pronunciation be rather *Turkiſh* than *Arabick ;* the *Arabs* not having the *e* in their Alphabet *, and calling, as we have obſerv'd, Coffee, *Kahwah*. M. *d'Arvieux* has beſides inadvertantly confounded the *Arabick* Term *Cawa*, [rather *Kowwah*] which indeed ſignifies Force and Vigour, with that of *Kahwah*, ſignifying the Coffee, written and pronounc'd after quite another Manner.

After this ſhort grammatical Explanation, which is not unneceſſary for underſtanding the Subject, let us ſpeak of the *Arabick* Manuſcript belonging to the Royal Library, and its Author, whoſe Name

* This is a trifling Criticiſm, and it may as well be ſaid they have no *a* in their Alphabet ; for, properly ſpeaking, they have no Characters to expreſs any of the Vowels, which they apply upon occaſion in Writing by Points.

Name is *Abdalcader Mohammed Alan
zari, al Geziri, al Hanbali.* That is to
fay, the Servant of God, the Son of *Mohammed,* originally of *Medina,* Native
of *Geziri,* of the Seat of *Hanibal.* 'Tis
the Manner of the Eaſtern People thus
to expreſs their Names. The Title of this
Work runs in theſe Words:

*That which one ought moſt particularly
and ſincerely to believe touching Coffeĕ,*
viz. *if it be permitted to Moſulmam* *
[rather *Moſlem*] *to uſe it.*

This Piece is divided into ſeven Chapters, the firſt of which ſpeaks of the Etymology, and Signification of the Word
Kahwah, ſuch as we have already obſerv'd; of the Nature and Properties of
Coffee; of the Countries where it began
to be in Faſhion, and of the Deſign with
which it was firſt taken. The other Chapters run chiefly upon a religious Diſpute,
which was ſtarted at *Mecca* on the Subject of Coffee, and ends with a Collection
of *Arabick* Verſes, compos'd in the Praiſe
of

* i. e. True Believers, a Name the *Mahometans*
aſſume, to diſtinguiſh themſelves from thoſe of other
Religions, which they reckon Infidels.

of that Drink, by the moſt famous Poets in the Time of that Diſpute.

The Author writ in *Egypt,* in the Year 996 of the *Hegirah,* which anſwers to the Year 1587 of the Chriſtian Era.

M. *Galland* did not undertake the Tranſlation of this Manuſcript, becauſe it contains many Things very tedious to read, with Regard to the ſcrupulous Rites and Precautions of the *Mohammedan* Religion; contenting himſelf to extract what ſeem'd to him moſt curious, and fit for his Purpoſe.

For the reſt, that which *Abdalcader,* the Author of the Manuſcript, has written about the Original and Progreſs of the Drink of Coffee, is taken, according to his own Confeſſion, from *Shabebaddin Ben Abduljaffar Almaleki,* another Author, who wrote long before him upon the Subject; an Author ſo much the more credible and authentick, as living near the *Epocha* of Coffee, whereof we are going to ſpeak.

Jem al Addin Abu Abdallah, Mohammed Benſaid, ſirnam'd *Al Dhabhani,* (becauſe he was a Native of *Dhabhan,* a ſmall Town of *Arabia Fœlix*) being *Mufti* * *ti* * of *Aden,* a famous Town, and Part of the fame Country, about the Middle of the 9th Age of the *Hegirah,* and of the 15th of our Lord, had occafion to make a Voyage to *Perfia.* During his Stay there, he found fome of his Countrymen who took Coffee, which, at firft, he took no great notice of; but at his Return to *Aden,* his Health being impair'd, and calling to mind the Coffee, which he had feen taken in *Perfia,* he took fome, in Hopes it might do him good. Not only the *Mufti's* Health was reftor'd by the Ufe of it, but he foon became fenfible of the other Properties of Coffee; particularly, that it diffipates Heavinefs in the Head, exhilarates the Spirits, and hinders Sleep without indifpofing one.

Coffee firft in ufe at Aden, the capital City of Arabia Fælix.

He made particularly his Account of this laft Quality, taking Coffee with the *Derwifhes,* or religious *Mohammedans,* when Night came on, for performing Prayers, and other Exercifes of his Religion, with the greater Vivacity.

The Example and Authority of the *Mufti* giving a Reputation to Coffee, one

U 3   might

---

* An Order of Priefts amongft the *Mahometans,* which may be call'd their Bifhops.

might prefently fee the Lawyers, Students, afterwards the Artificers, who were oblig'd to work by Night; Travellers, who would avoid the Heats of the Day ; and, in fhort, the whole Town of *Aden* taking Coffee; not only at Night by thofe who would fit up, but alfo by-Numbers in the Day-time, for the Benefit of its other good Qualities.

The *Arabian* Author adds, that they found Coffee fo good, that they entirely left off the Ufe of another Liquor, which was in Vogue at *Aden*, made of the Leaves of a Plant, call'd *Cat*, which cannot be fuppos'd to be the *The*, becaufe this Writer fays nothing which might favour that Opinion.

Such was the Original of the great Ufe of Coffee, the Author of which was *Mufti Jemaleddin*, a Man of Parts and Authority, who knew the Vertues of it, and undertook to bring it in Requeft, in Conjunction with another reputable Doctor, named *Mohammed al Hadhrami*, born or educated at *Hadramaut*, the capital City of a Country of the fame Name in *Arabia Fœlix*.

Before

Before that Time it might be ſaid, that Liquor was in Obſcurity, and very little in Uſe, either in *Arabia* which produces the Fruit of which it is made, or in *Perſia* where it was a little known : But this Obſervation does not reach *Ethiopia*, where, according to our *Arabian*, Coffee was common from immemorial Times.

M. *Galland* leaves his Author here a Moment, to charge with Falſhood the pretended Original of Coffee, as reported by *Fauſtus Nairon*, without any Authority : But at the ſame Time he treats it as a Story, and vulgar Notion. He acknowledges that this Story is grounded, in ſome meaſure, upon the Hiſtory of the true Original of Coffee, to which the oriental *Chriſtians* have been pleas'd to do honour ; for, ſays he, the Prior or Abbot of the Convent and his Companion, are no other than the *Mufti Jemaleddin*, and *Mohammed al Hadhrami*; and the Monks are the *Derwiſhes*, who ſpent the Night in Prayer with them. In ſhort, the Maronite Profeſſor is confuted by the Circumſtances of Hiſtory and Chronology, ſo well choſen, and accompany'd with ſuch rational Reflections, that one cannot but

U 4 　　　　allow

allow that to be the true *Epocha*, for the frequent Ufe of Coffee, which the Author of the Manufcript in the Royal Library informs us of, from an original Author, and almoft a Contemporary. In order to confirm and always adjuft that *Epocha*, to the Time which he has obferv'd, 'tis neceffary to add that the *Mufti Jemaleddin* dy'd in the Year 875 of the *Hegirah*, which was in the Year of our Lord 1470.

Coffee thus receiv'd at *Aden*, where it has continued ever fince without Interruption, pafs'd by Degrees into many other neighbouring Places, and it arriv'd at *Mecca* about the End of the 9th Age of the *Hegirah*. The Ufe of it began there at *Aden* by the *Derwifhes*, who took it in the famous Temple of this City, with the fame Intention as mov'd the faid *Mufti*, to enable them the better to perform in the Night the Exercifes of their Religion. That Coffee was not made of the Berry, but of the Husk of the *Bon*-Tree, which was brought to *Mecca* from *Arabia Fœlix*. For according to the exact Remark of M. *Galland*, *Mecca* is not comprehended within the Country of that Name, but in a particular Province of *Arabia*,

bia, (taken in general) call'd by some *Te-hamah,* and by others *Hejaz.*

The Inhabitants of *Mecca* found this Drink so agreeable to their Taste, that, without troubling themselves about the Intention of the Devout and Learned, who may be said to have been the first Institutors of it, they made its Use so common, that it was sold publickly in Coffee-Houses, where they flock'd together, under that Pretence to pass away the Time more agreeably; there they play at Chess, and at *Mancalah* *, even for Money. There they sing, play on Instruments and dance; Things which the more rigid *Mahometans* cannot endure; which did not fail to bring Trouble in the End.

In the mean while Coffee spread from *Mecca* into divers other Towns of *Arabia,* and particularly *Medina;* whence, passing at length the first Time out of *Arabia,* After-wards to *Medina,* and other Places of *Arabia,* and at last into *Egypt.*

* *Mancalah* is much in Use among the Orientals. Only two Persons play at a Time, as at *Chess,* with 72 little Shells, or other like Things, putting them first by 6 in a Parcel in 12 small round Holes, made upon two Lines in a Piece of Wood about a Foot long, and 5 Inches broad. This Play has nothing in it extraordinary. M. *Galland* describes it at length.

bia, it came into *Egypt*, to *Grand Cairo*.
There it was introduc'd by the *Derwishes*
of *Yaman*, who, having a particular Quarter in that City, took Coffee in their
Mosks the Nights they defign'd to continue longer than ordinary at their Devotions. It was contain'd in a great Veffel
of red Earth, and they receiv'd it very
refpectfully at the Hands of their Superior, who pour'd it out for them himfelf
into the Cups.

This fell out about the Beginning of the
10th Age of the *Hegirah*, and 16th of
our Lord, and was prefently imitated by
many Devouts of *Cairo*, whofe Example
was follow'd by the Studious, and after by
fo many People, that at length Coffee became as common in that great City as at
Aden, *Medina*, *Mecca*, and other Places
of *Arabia*.

The great Ufe of Coffee, owing, as has
been faid, to the Sagacity and Devotion
of *Jemaleddin*, encreas'd ever fince without Oppofition, till the Year of the *Hegirah* 917, and of *Chrift* 1511, a Year
fatal to this Liquor, by the Condemnation pafs'd upon it for the firft Time; the
Occa-

Occasion and Manner of which are briefly as follow.

Khair Beg, Governour of *Mecca* for the *Soltan* * of *Egypt,* who had not yet heard speak of Coffee, nor the Manner of taking it, going out from the Mosk one Day after Evening-Prayer, he was offended to see, in one Corner of it, a Company of Coffee-Takers, who propos'd to pass the Night in Prayer. At first he believ'd it was Wine they were drinking, nor did his Surprize lessen, upon being told the Use and Qualities of that Liquor; on the contrary, learning by these Devouts how common it was grown at *Mecca,* and of all the Merriment that pass'd in the publick Houses where it was sold, he imagin'd that the Coffee intoxicated, at least, that it made them commit Things forbidden by the Law.

Wherefore, after having order'd those People to retire from the Mosk, with a Prohibition from assembling there upon the like Occasion; the next Day he call'd together a great Assembly of Officers of Justice,

Coffee condemn'd at Mecca, as contrary to the Musulmans Religion.

* *Mecca* had then been a long Time under the Dominion of the *Soltans* of *Egypt,* of the *Dynasty* to the *Cirassian Mamlucs,* who had dethron'd the Successors of *Salahaddin.*

Juftice, Doctors of the Law, Devotees, and Chiefs of the City of *Mecca*, to whom he divulg'd what he had feen the Evening before in the Mosk, and what pafs'd in the Town with regard to Coffee ; adding, that he was refolv'd to rectify that Abufe, upon which Accoun the was pleas'd to confult them.

The Doctors were fenfible what pafs'd in the Coffee-Houfes needed a Reform, as contrary to ftrict *Mohammedanifm* ; and faid, that, with Regard to Coffee, it was neceffary at leaft to examine, whether it were hurtful either to the Body or Mind ; and if it was the Occafion of the faid Diforders ; for, if it was not, it would fuffice to put down the publick Places where it was fold. The Refult was, that it was neceffary to confult the Phyficians.

The Governour upon this had two fent for to the Affembly, who were Brothers, *Perfians* by Nation, and were efteem'd the chief Phyficians in *Mecca*, tho' but indifferently qualify'd, and better vers'd in Logick than Phyfick. One of thefe two had writ a Pamphlet againft the Ufe of Coffee ; jealous, it may be, fays our Author, that it might prejudice their Practice. Thus
they

they did not fail to avouch, that the *Bon,*
of whofe Husks they made their Coffee,
was cold and dry, and confequently that
it was moft prejudicial to Health.

A Doctor of the Affembly made anfwer, that *Ebu Jazlah**, an old honoura-
ble Phyfician, in his Treatife of *fimple
Medicines* and *Ailments,* affirms, that the
Bon digefts and confumes Flegm, and that
it could not have the Quality which they
afcribe to it. The Remark was judicious,
for, upon the Occafion of this Difpute, all
the Phyficians of that Time agreed, that
the *Bon,* or Coffee, was hot and dry, and
not cold and dry.

The two *Perfian* Phyficians, to fupport
what they had afferted, reply'd, that the
Bon, the Doctor fpoke of, was not the
Plant in Queftion, but another of the
fame Name, which caus'd different Effects;
and after that, without putting themfelves
to the Trouble of proving, pretending to
be Cafuifts, advanc'd, that tho' the *Bon*
might be reckon'd in the Number of in
different Things, of which it was lawful
for

* *Ebu Jazlah,* a celebrated Phyfician of *Bagdat,*
liv'd about the fame Time with *Avicen.* He dy'd in
Year of the *Hegirah* 49.

for every body to make Uſe; but ſince it led to forbidden Things, the ſafeſt Way for Moſlemans was to hold it unlawful.

All approve of this Deciſion ; many alſo thro' Prejudice, or counterfeit Zeal, affirm'd, that Coffee had diſturb'd their Brains. One of the Standers by went ſo far as to aſſert, that it inebriated like Wine, which made the whole Aſſembly laugh; becauſe, to be able to be a Judge of that, he muſt have drank Wine, contrary to their Religion, which prohibits it. He was ask'd, if he had drank any? and had no more Wiſdom than to anſwer in the Affirmative ; ſo condemning himſelf to the Baſtinado, a Puniſhment inflicted on the Tranſgreſſors of the *Mohammedan* Law.

The *Mufti* of *Mecca*, a Divine and Lawyer by Profeſſion, undertook ſingly with ſome Warmth the Defence of Coffee, againſt the Determination of the Aſ-ſembly ; and, maugre the Reſolution of the Governour, who was inſtigated by his *Imam*, a very ſcrupulous Man ; but all the Courage of the *Mufti*, and his beſt Argu-ments, ſerv'd but to draw upon him the Affronts of the Zealous.

Coffee

Coffee was then condemn'd in a folemn Manner, as a Thing forbidden by the Law, and the Sentence of this Condemnation was drefs'd up in very affected and emphatical Terms, to exprefs a Kind of Triumph upon the pretended Abufe being extirpated: Several Doctors fign'd it with the Governour, who fent it as a Difpatch of Importance, to his Mafter the *Soltan* of *Egypt*.

At the fame Time he publifh'd an Exprefs and folemn Prohibition, with Refpect to Selling and Drinking Coffee, either in publick or private, under the Penalty incurr'd by thofe who offend againft the Injunctions of that Religion; a Prohibition which was attended with an exact and rigorous Search by the Officers of Juftice, who caus'd all the publick Coffee-Houfes in *Mecca* to be fhut up, and all the Coffee they could find there to be burnt, not exempting even what was in the Merchants Warehoufes.

The Lovers of Coffee, who were very numerous, could never be brought to fubmit to that Prohibition, but continu'd to drink it in their Houfes; perfuaded moreover, that the Affembly had determin'd wrong,

wrong, and the Condemnation was unjuft, fince it had pafs'd againft the Confent of the *Mufti* : Notwithftanding, a certain Perfons having been furpriz'd at home in the Fact, was feverely punifh'd, and afterwards led upon an Afs through the publick Streets.

But this Rigour did not continue long, for the *Soltan* of *Egypt*, far from approving the indifcreet Zeal of his Governour of *Mecca*, was quite aftonifh'd that he fhould dare to condemn a Thing which was fo well approv'd of at *Cairo*, the Capital of his Dominions, where there were Doctors of greater Account than thofe of *Mecca*, and who found nothing in the Ufe of Coffee contrary to the Law.

Coffee re-eftablifh'd at *Mecca* by Order of the *Soltan* of *Egypt*. The *Soltan* then order'd him to revoke his Prohibition, and to employ his Authority only in hindering Diforders, if any happen'd in the Coffee-Houfes; adding, that becaufe the beft Things might be abus'd, even the Waters of the Fountain of *Zemzem* *, in fuch Veneration with all *Mahomme-*

* The Fountain or Pits o' *Zemzem*, according to the *Moflemans*, is that which God caus'd to appear in favour of *Agar*, and her Son *Ifhmael*, in the Defert, after *Abraham* had oblig'd her to depart. 'Tis within the Temple

hammetans, that was no plaufible Reafon
fot abfolutely forbidding them.

The Governour was oblig'd to obey in
fpight of him, nor was that the only Sa‑
tisfaction which the *Soltan* gave to the
People of *Mecca ;* for that fame Gover‑
nour fo fcrupulous in Appearance, that
Mohammedan Pharifee, was a mere Extor‑
tioner and publick Robber ; in fhort, his
Succeffour, after having receiv'd Orders to
call him to an Account for his Conduct,
put him to a tormenting Death the Year
after. His Brother laid violent Hands up‑
on himfelf to prevent the like Fate.

The *Arab* Author adds, that the two
Perfian Phyficians, who had fo great a
Hand in the Prohibition of Coffee, came
likewife to an ill End. Grown into Con‑
tempt at *Mecca,* after the Re-eftablifhment
of that Liquor, they remov'd to *Cairo,*
where, being convicted of curfing *Selim,*
the firft of that Name, Emperor of the
Turks, who had conquer'd * *Egypt,* they
were executed by his Order.

X   Since

Temple of *Mecca,* which the *Mohammedans* drink out
of Devotion, attributing to it extraordinary Virtues.

* *Selim* I. conquer'd *Egypt* from *Canfon Gaurus,*
[*Kânfu al Ghauri*] the laft of the *Soltans,* and the fame
who

Since the Reſtoration or Coffee at *Mecca* till the Year 1524, it met with no Oppoſition; but that Year the *Cadi*, or chief Judge of the Town, caus'd all the Coffee-Houſes to be ſhut up, on account of the Diſorders which were committed in them, without hindring the Uſe of it in private Houſes; neverthele(s his Succeſſour permitted them to be open'd again, and ever ſince there has been ſuch Order found in them, that there has been no occaſion for the Magiſtrate to exerciſe his Authority.

A. D. 1542. *Soliman* forbids the Uſe of Coffee to no purpoſe.

'Tis true, that in the Year 950 of the *Hegirah*, there arriv'd at *Mecca*, by the Caravan of *Damaſcus*, an Order from *Soliman* the Magnificent, to drink no more Coffee; but that Order was ſcarce put in Execution, becauſe it appear'd to have been given unadviſedly upon a Surpriſe, at the Intreaty of one of the Lady's of the Court, a little too preciſe with reſpeƈt to this Liquor.

For what remains, the *Soltan* of *Egypt*, who had caus'd the indiſcreet Prohibition of Drinking Coffee to be revok'd by his Governour of *Mecca*, had the Doƈtors of the

who had re-eſtabliſh'd Coffee at *Mecca*. This Conqueſt was made in the Year of our Lord 1516.

the Law confulted thereupon, who gave
their Opinion in Writing ; and prov'd from
very good Reafons the Injuftice of that
Condemnation, and the Ignorance of thofe
who occafion'd it ; which ferv'd to give
a Sanction more than ever to the Ufe of
Coffee at *Cairo*. But in Procefs of Time,
that great City faw Difturbances rife. upon
that Subject.

This happen'd in the Year of our Lord
1523, and 930 of the *Hegirah*, occafion'd by a precife Doctor. It came into his
Head to form a Queftion in thefe Terms,
and fend it to other Doctors : ' What is
your Opinion touching the Drink call'd
Coffee, which People take upon a Sup-
pofition, that it is in the Number of thofe
Things which are lawful to ufe, tho' it
is the Occafion of great Diforders, flies
into the Head, and affects Health ? Is that
lawful or forbidden ?' At the End of the
Queftion propounded, was his own Opinion fign'd by himfelf, ' That the Ufe of
Coffee is unlawful. ' None of his Fra-
ernity were of his Mind, becaufe it was
evident that Coffee had not thofe bad Qua-
ities which he afcrib'd to it, infomuch,

X 2   that

that it had no Effect upon so universally receiv'd a Custom.

But about 10 Years after, a Preacher exclaim'd so furiously against Coffee, affirming that it was forbidden by the Law, and that those who took it were not true *Moslemans*, that a Crowd of the Auditors from the Mosque rush'd into the first Coffee-Houses in their Way, demolish'd the Coffee-Pots, and Dishes, and abus'd those they found there.

This gave Rise to two Parties in the Town, the one of which maintain'd that Coffee was forbidden by the Law, and the other that it was not; but the chief Judge having summon'd a Consultation of Doctors, they unanimously declar'd, that the Question was already absolutely decided by their Predecessours in favour of Coffee, that they were of their Opinion, and that it was necessary only to prohibit the extravagant Zeal of Devotees, and the Indiscretion of ignorant Preachers. The Judge who presided, and was of the same Sentiment, order'd Coffee forthwith to be serv'd to the whole Assembly, and took it himself; an Example which presently made them unanimous,

nimous, and gave a Vogue to Coffee more than ever.

Notwithftanding 4 Years after, the Officer of Policy, having found People affembled at Night in a publick Coffee-Houfe, in the Time of *Ramadan*, or *Mohammedan* Lent, he fent them to Prifon, and order'd each of them to be baftinado'd upon the Soles of their Feet, only for having taken it publickly in a Time of Devotion, and at an unfeafonable Hour.

After all that has pafs'd with Relation Coffee, the moft Scrupulous have but a forry Reafon to alledge, which is, that Coffee ought to be rejected, becaufe it is taken in Company, and after the fame Manner as one drinks Wine; but their Argument may be refuted by the Example of *Mohammed* himfelf, who drank Wine among his Friends, in the Manner one drinks Coffee.

The Adventures which happen'd to Coffee in *Arabia* and *Egypt*, thus far related by the Authority of the *Arabian* Author, M. *Galland* finds out, that it fpread from thence into *Syria*, where it was receiv'd without any Obftacle, firft at *Conftantinople*.

Coffee paffes from Egypt into Syria, and at laft is brought to Conftantinople.

X 3

at *Damascus* and *Aleppo*, and afterwards thro' all other Towns of that great Province; adding, that from *Syria*, without passing gradually from Province to Province, it was at length brought directly to *Constantinople*. This we learn from the Testimony of *Belighi*, a *Turkish* Poet, in a Sonnet which he has made on Coffee, and which M. *Galland* has given us with a *French* Translation *.

The *Turkish* Poet calls Coffee seditious, alluding to the Troubles bred at *Mecca* and *Cairo* upon its Account, and since that at *Constantinople*, as we are going to observe, after having intimated, that what follows is extracted from a *Turkish* Historian, nam'd *Pichevili*, from *Pichevi*, a Town of *Hungary*; he was one of the *Defterdars*, or Treasurers-General of the Empire,

---

* This *French* Translation of M. *Galland* is turn'd into Verse by the Editor, which may be thus English'd.

From mighty *Cair* the pretious Fruit which makes
That charming Drink, which so diffusely takes,
To *Demshak*, and to *Haleb* did resort,
Before it came to triumph at the Court.
   There that seditious Mutineer,
   For Vertues sure without compare,
   Hath, by its sweet enchanting Power,
All Wines supplanted from that happy Hour.

Empire, who writ the Hiſtory of *Soliman*
and his Succeſſours, until the Death of
Amurath IV, who recover'd *Bagdat* from
the *Perſians*.

Before the Year of the *Hegirah* 962,
which began the firſt * of *November*,
1554, there was ſeen at *Conſtantinople*,
neither Coffee, nor any Place where it
was ſold, and, if the Truth was known,
that happen'd by means of the *Soltana*,
who endeavour'd to aboliſh that Faſhion
at *Mecca*, upon the Relation of the Pilgrims, or thoſe who frequented *Syria* and
Egypt.

But this ſame Year, which was about When,
the Hundredth from the Inſtitution of the and by
whom
Uſe of Coffee by the *Mufti* of *Aden*, and were
under the Reign of *Soliman* the Great, Coffee-
Houſes
the Son of *Selim* I, two private Perſons, open'd at
nam'd *Shams* and *Hakem*, the one coming Conſtantinople, &c.
from *Damaſcus*, and the other from *A-*
leppo, open'd each of them a Coffee-
Houſe at *Conſtantinople*, in the Quarter
X 4   call'd

---

* This is a Miſtake, for it began the 25th of *No-*
vember, O. S. The Author ſeems to have taken it out
of *Greaves*'s Tables in his *Epochæ Celebriores*, and to
have miſtaken the Day of the Week, for the Day of
the Month.

call'd *Takhtacalah*, and began to fell it
publickly, People taking it upon Sofas,
or Alcoves, handfomely accommodated
for the Purpofe.

The Men of Study, efpecially Poets,
the Lovers of the Game of Chefs, and of
Tricktrac, were the firft that frequented
the Coffee-Houfes, call'd fince by the
Turks, Cahveh Khaveh, Places very con
venient to divert themfelves in, to make
Acquaintance, and fave Charges; for the
Difh of Coffee coft no more than an
Afper, a very fmall Silver Coin, worth
about an Half-penny.

Thefe Houfes and Affemblies increas'd
infenfibly; there might be feen to come
young Men who had juft finifh'd their
Studies, and were ready to enter into Offices of Judicature; *Cadhis* out of Place,
who were at *Conftantinople* to follicit their
being reftor'd, or to fue for new Employs;
Maderis or Profeffours, who came to refrefh their Spirits, and feveral others. At
length, after the Officers of the Seraglio,
one might fee alfo the *Bafha's*, and principal Lords of the *Port*, go to them,
which very much enhans'd the Reputation and Number of the publick Coffee-
Houfes

Houfes at *Conftantinople,* and it may be too much.

Indeed, at the Time that this Fafhion feem'd to be beft eftablifh'd, the *Imams* and Officers of the Mofques made a great Noife that they faw them empty, at the fame time the Coffee-Houfes were full. The *Derwifhes,* and all the profefs'd Religious, murmur'd at it grievoufly, and at laft the Preachers let themfelves loofe, not only againft Coffee itfelf, maintaining that it was abfolutely forbidden by the Law ; but that it was lefs Sin to go to a Tavern, than a Coffee-Houfe.

After much Noife, and fpending their Lungs to no purpofe, the whole Clergy laid their Heads together, how they might have Coffee condemn'd with Authority. For this· they bethought themfelves to maintain, that roafted Coffee was a Kind of Coal, and that every Thing that was like Coal was forbidden by the Law. Upon this they drew up a Queftion in Form, and prefented it to the *Mufti,* praying him to decide it, as in Duty, by his Office oblig'd.

The Ufe of Coffee authentickly condemn'd, then tolerated, and at laft established.

That Head of the Law, without giving himfelf the Trouble to examine the Difficulty,

ficulty, gave a Refult perfectly conforma-
ble to the Drift of the Churchmen, and
decreed, that Coffee was forbidden according to the Law of *Mahomet*.

The Authority of the *Mufti* is fo highly
reverenc'd, that none is allow'd to call in
Queftion his Decifions.   Thus all the
Coffee-Houfes were of a fudden fhut up,
and the Officers of Policy order'd to fee,
that none took Coffee upon any account
whatever.

Notwithftanding fome Rigour was us'd
in putting this Prohibition in Execution,
yet there was no reftraining thoroughly
the private Ufe of Coffee.   They had
alfo an Opportunity under the Reign of
Amurath III, to refume the Liberty with
Regard to a Thing fo agreeable, which befides they did not believe contrary to Religion, as it did not hinder it to encreafe
more and more, and was continu'd to be
drank in private Houfes.   At laft the Officers of Policy, feeing there was no Remedy, for a Piece of Money tolerated any
one to fell it, provided it was not done
in publick : Infomuch that one might go
and take it in private Houfes, the Door
being

being fhut, or at certain Merchants in their Back-Shops.

There needed nothing more by little and little to re-eftablifh Coffee-Houfes. It happen'd alfo, that a new *Mufti* lefs fcrupulous, or more knowing than his Predeceffours, declar'd peremptorily, that Coffee ought not be confider'd as a Coal, and that the Drink made of it was not forbid by the Law. After this Declaration, the Zealots, and the Preachers, the *Mufti* himfelf and the Lawyers, far from running down Coffee, took it themfelves; and their Example was univerfally follow'd at Court, and in the Town.

Coffee-Houfes after this became more numerous than before, which in the End tempted the Avarice of the Grand *Vizir*'s, who made a good Penny of this Occafion, by affuming a particular Authority over thefe Houfes, and exacting from each a Tax of one or two *Chekins* a Day; and for that Reafon they encreas'd them extreamly, without permitting any to take more than an *Afper*, for each Difh of Coffee: From whence we may guefs, the great Quantity that was fold of it. This
Price

Price of an *Asper* continues till this Day at *Constantinople*.

These are the Particulars found in the *Turkish* Historian, touching the Establishment of Coffee in the imperial City, and its Progress till the Time he wrote. What M. *Galland* informs us afterwards upon this Business comes from himself: He speaks first concerning the Alteration that happen'd to the Coffee-Houses at *Constantinople* during the War of *Candia*, a very ticklish Juncture for the *Turks*.

The grand *Visir Kupruli* commands all the publick Coffee Houses at *Constantinople* to be shut up.

The Liberty of News-Mongers, who assembled at them, was so great, that the grand *Vizir Kupruli*, the Father of the two Brothers of the same Name, and famous for the same Dignity, suppress'd them all, under the Minority of *Mohamed* IV, with a Disinterestedness hereditary to that Family; without Regard to the Loss of the great Profits which he might have drawn from thence.

Before this happen'd, that Minister had gone *in Cognito* to the principal Coffee-Houses, where he understood by the grave Folks, that they sat very seriously upon the Affairs of the Empire, blaming the Ministry, and absolutely determining the most
important

important Affairs. His next Vifit was to
the Taverns, where he faw none but jolly
Fellows, who did nothing but fing and
talk of their Amours, or of their warlike
Exploits, being for the moft part Soldiers,
by which he judg'd it very proper to fup-
prefs that Amufement. M. *Galland* ga-
thers what we have intimated from M.
D'Hermitage, Phyfician to Monfieur the
Count of *Touloufe*, and who had been that
of the laft *Vizer Kuprult*, kill'd at the
Battle of *Salankamen*.

Since the Suppreffion of publick Coffee-Houfes, which ftill continues at *Conftantinople*, Coffee is not taken lefs in that
great City than before. There are thofe
that bring it into the Markets, and the
principal Streets, in great Coffee-pots, with
fome Fire under in a Chafing-Difh, and
diftribute it very handfomely to thofe that
call for it: The Paffengers ftop, and for
that end enter into the firft Shop they come
at, the Mafter of which very civily receives
them.

In the Time of M *Galland*'s being at
Conftantinople, there were in *Galata* but
two or three Coffee-Houfes tolerated,
in

in favour to the Sailors who came there
to fmoak with their Coffee.   However,
Coffee-Houfes are not prohibited in other
Cities of the *Turkifh* Empire ; I have
found it every where, even in the leaft
Boroughs, in my Voyage to the *Levant*,
but particularly at *Damafcus*, where the
publick Coffee-Houfes are better furnifh'd,
and more frequented by Men of Learning and Diftinction, than any where elfe.

It may be faid notwithftanding, that
their Suppreffion at *Conftantinople* has but
made the Ufing Coffee more common,
there being neither Houfe, nor Family, rich
or poor, *Turk* or *Greek*, *Armenian* or *Jew*,
all Nations very numerous in this Town,
where it is not taken at leaft twice a Day :
·Many take it almoft every Hour, becaufe it is
a Fafhion to treat all Vifitors with it, come
upon what Account they will, and that it
would be a Piece of ill Manners, either not
to offer Coffee, or to refufe it.   Whence
it happens that there are an innumerable
Deal of People, that drink above 20 or
40 Cups a Day, and without being the
leaft out of order, a Quality in which
Coffee has the Advantage of other Drinks.

Another

Another Property of Coffee, according to M. *Galland*, is, that it qualifies Men for entring into the Bonds of Society, and ſtrict Engagements, more than any Thing elſe that can be thought on ; and for making their Proteſtations ſo much the more ſincere, as they proceed from a Mind not overcaſt with Fumes, and are not eaſily forgot, which too often hap pens, when they are made by Men in their Wine.

Let us return to the Conſumption of Coffee at *Conſtantinople*, which muſt be allow'd to be very great, ſeeing, all Things conſidered, there are very few Families where there is not at leaſt as much ex- pended in Coffee, as is ſpent at *Paris* in Wine.   In the ſame Manner as we are uſe to give thoſe, that have done us a Piece of Service, Money to drink, ſo alſo at *Conſtantinople*, and elſewhere in the *Levant*, they give Coffee-Money, *Cahveh-Akcheſi.*

After having obſerv'd that Coffee comes by Sea from *Egypt* to *Conſtantinople*, and hat it comes to *Egypt* by the *Red-Sea*, our Author gives a particular Account of what relates to the Purchaſing of Cof. fee

fee for the Provision of Families; of the Artisans, who burn it and bruise it, who are oblig'd to follow the Army; of the Obligation of the Husbands to furnish their Wives *; of the Manner of Keeping it good, especially in long Voyages; and lastly, concerning the Coffee-Equipage.

He also gives a particular Account of the Manner of Preparing Coffee, especially in great Houses, where there is a particular Officer who has no other Business but to boil the Coffee, which is the Term the *Turks* use to signify its Preparation. They say also in their Language, to drink Coffee, and not to take Coffee, as we commonly phrase it. For which the Authority of the said *Turkish* Poet is cited; he brings in thereupon other Verses after his Way, which seem to be levell'd at some Physician, who blam'd the daily Use of Coffee †.

We may add here one or two Remarks to those of M. *Galland*; first, that this Officer,

* The Refusal or Want of Coffee, with regard to the Wife, is one of the lawful Causes of Divorce.
† These Verses are in the *French*, but we thought it needless to insert them here, as well as others, which are brought in afterwards.

Officer who prepares the Coffee in great
Houſes, who has the Overſeeing of all that
concerns it, and who, for that Purpoſe,
has a particular Chamber near the Hall,
where he receives Company, is call'd by
the *Turks Kahvehgi*, that is to ſay, the
Intendant or Officer of Coffee. Moreover in the *Haram*, or Appartment of the
Ladies of the Seraglio, there are for the
ſame Purpoſe many *Kahvehgi Bachi*,
who preſide over 20 or 30 *Baltagis*, employ'd in ſeveral Chambers or Offices
of Coffee; and when theſe Coffee-Makers
go from thence, Employs or good Pieces
of Land are given to them, and they
ſometimes even come to be *Capigi Baſhi*,
[or head Porter.]

M. *Galland* forgets not to ſpeak of the
Ichoglans, that is, Pages or Grooms of
the Bed-Chamber to Men of Quality, who
go to take the Coffee from the Hand of
the Officer, and who at the leaſt Sign
of their Maſter, who never ſpeak to them,
ſerve it to the Company with a ſingular
Addreſs and Neatneſs, preſenting it to
the Maſter of the Houſe laſt of all, except
in the grand *Vizir*'s Court, where that
Miniſter receives it at the ſame Time

Y   that

that it is prefented the Embaffadours. With Refpect to which Ceremony, we fhall add yet one Remark, which is, that when the Grand *Vizir* does not order Coffee for an Embaffadour, which very feldom happens, it is a Sign of ill Will or Difpleafure, and like the Forerunner of fome Breach.

The Coffee is prefented upon Salvers without Feet, commonly of Wood painted and varnifh'd, and fometimes of Silver, each of which holds 15 or 20 Cups, which are ufually of China; and among the more rich or curious Folks, half fet in little Silver Veffels. They call thefe Cups *Finjans:* They are not above half as big as ours, and are never filled up; not only that one might not fpill the Coffee, but alfo to the End that, the Coffee being juft boiling, one may hold it, without burning himfelf, with the Thumb underneath, and the two Fore-Fingers on the Edge, the ordinary Way of holding them. It is not brought with Spoons, as among us, becaufe they put no Sugar in the Coffee. They always take it extreme hot and very ftrong, which the *Turks* call *Agir Cahveh,* heavy

or

or very deep Coffee.   In the Serail, and Houfes of the Grandees, they put fometimes into each Difh a fmall Drop of the Effence of Amber.   Some, according to the Quantity of Coffee, boil with it one or two Cloves broke in two; fome with a little *Anis des Indes,* which the *Turks* call *Badian Hindi*; and others with *Caculeh,* which is the Grain of *Cardamomum minus.*

This Treatife concludes with a confide‧rable Curiofity, which is, a Coffee-Tree itfelf, which a curious *Turk* had taken care to rear, and drefs at *Conftantinople* in the Quarter of *Coffum Pafha,* on the Side of the Arfenal, but which, having been frozen by a great Cold, was cut by the Ground; and, in that Condition, fhot forth young Sprigs, which M. *Galland* has feen and examin'd.   He tells us, that the Leaves, which are green all the Year round, refemble pretty much thofe of the Laurel, only they are not fo pointed, are thicker, and of a deeper Green.   That *Turk* affur'd him, that this Tree had born Fruit, and M. *Gallana* adds, that M. *de Nointel,* then Embaffadour from the King of *France* to the *Porte,* had the Picture of it drawn;

which

which should be at *Paris* in some Place or other, where it is not, it may be, known.

This is all that M. *Galland* has been able to tell us of the Original and Progress of Coffee in the *Levant*, from whence it has spread throughout the *Ottoman* Empire. It has not been receiv'd, adds he, in *France*, and at *Paris*, but very lately; and one will be glad one Day to know in what Manner it was introduc'd. I have been told by the late M. *de la Croix* *, Interpreter to the King, that M. *Thevenot*, the Traveller, was the first who brought it to *Paris* for his own Use; and that he often treated his Friends with it, among which Number he was; and that, for his own Particular, he had continu'd from that Time almost daily to take it. The *Armenians* at length brought it into the Kingdom, and by little and little into the Reputation which it bears at present.

It is not easy to determine at what Time, and upon what Account, Coffee pass'd from *Egypt*, or *Constantinople* into *Europe*: It is notwithstanding likely enough, that the *Venetians*, by Means of their Commerce, and

* The Father of him lately deceas'd.

and the Proximity of the Dominions of the
Republick to *Turky*, communicated the
firft Knowledge of it to the other *Europeans*. There is a *Venetian*, as we have feen,
who has written the firft about Coffee, in
which he has been follow'd by the reft of the
Italians, before the *French* Authors took
Notice of it. But if in that Refpect *Italy*
* has the Advantage of other *European*
Nations ; 'tis certain, that Coffee has no
where been better receiv'd, or made greater
Progrefs than in *France*, and particularly
at *Paris*.

We grant in the firft place to M. *Thevenot*, upon the faid Teftimony, the Honour of having firft introduc'd the Ufe of
Coffee; but M. *Thevenot* is not the firft
that gave *France* the Sight of Coffee. The
Return from his firft Voyage is remark'd,
in his Obfervations, to be in the Year
1657. Now, in the Year 1644, my Father who went to *Conftantinople* with
Y 3 M. *de*

When,
and by
whom,
Coffee
was feen
the firft
Time in
France.

* It is very probable that *Peter Dellavalle* was one
of the firft that made Coffee known in *Italy*. Quando
io faro diritorno, fays he, tom. i. p. 99. portero
meco; e faro conofcere all Italia quefto femplice, che
in fin' ad hora forfe le é nuovo. That is, at my Return
I fhall bring it with me; and make known in *Italy*
that Simple which, perhaps, 'till now, has been unknown to it. He writ from *Conftavt.* in 1615.

M. *de la Haye*, and who afterwards made
a Voyage to the *Levant*, brought, at his
Return to *Marſeille*, not only ſome Coffee, but alſo the little Moveables and E
quipage, which he kept for his own Uſe
in *Turky*.   That paſs'd then for a real
Curioſity in *France*, and there is ſeen at
this Day, at his Country-Houſe, a Cabinet tolerably well furniſh'd, eſpecially
with *Finjans*, or Cups of very beautiful
old China; not to mention the little
Muſlin-Napkins, edg'd with Gold, Silver,
and Silk Borders, deſign'd for the ſame Uſe.
I aver that the Curioſity of my Father,
with Reſpect to Coffee, no more affected
the Publick, than that of M. *Thevenot*,
and that this firſt Uſe of Coffee at *Marſeille*, did extend only to a certain Number of Friends, who, like himſelf, had
contracted the Habits of the *Levant*.

But in Proceſs of Time, and about the
Year 1660, ſeveral Merchants of *Marſeille*,
who had made a conſiderable Stay in
that Country, not being able to refrain
from Coffee, which they had got ſuch a
Habit of, brought of it with them at
their Return, and communicated it to a
                                          great

great many *, who were accuftom'd to
it like themfelves; infomuch that Coffee,
becoming by Degrees familiar to the principal Merchants of *Marfeille,* and the Sea-
faring Men, fome amongft them. and
efpecially the Merchant-Drugifts, who carry on a great Trade at *Marfeille,* propos'd to have fome Bales brought from
Egypt. The firft Voyage contributed
much to encreafe the private Ufe of it,
which was already begun at *Marfeille.*
The Citizens of *Lyons* came afterwards
into that Fafhion, which foon made a confiderable Progrefs.

In the mean Time, about the Year 1671,
fome private Perfons undertook to open
at *Marfeille,* for the firft Time, a Shop,
or Coffee-Houfe, near the Lodge *. There
People fmoak'd, and there they play'd;
nor did the Place want Company, efpecially from the *Levantines.* Befides the
Merchants, and all the Sea-faring Men,
found the fame convenient to confer a-
Y 4   bout

---

* A very ingenious Gentlemen of *Provence,* who
furnifh'd me with fome Remarks relating to Coffee,
affirms, that he had taken of it at *Riez,* at a Perfon
of Quality's Houfe, in the Year 1666. † *La Loge*
is the Place where the Merchants meet, [like the
Exchange.]

bout their Bufinefs, and difcourfe about
Trade, which foon encreas'd the Number
of thofe publick Houfes, without dimi-
nifhing the Ufe of it in private. It was
taken alfo in the King's Gallies, and they
were *Turks* that prepar'd it.

At laft the Ufe of Coffee became fo
univerfal, that it alarm'd the Phyficians,
judging that this Cuftom was not proper
for the Inhabitants of a Climate hot e-
nough, and extremely dry. Nor did the
Phyficians fail of having Parties of their
Opinion, which bred a kind of Difpute,
and Divifion in the Town, fomething like
thofe which happen'd at *Mecca, Cairo* and
Conftantinople; the Caufe of Religion
excepted, for the Conteft was merely about
Phyfick. The Admirers of Coffee abus'd
the Phyficians fadly in their Affembly, and
the Phyficians in their Turn threaten'd
them with all Manner of Difeafes.

Things being at this Pafs, the Phyficians
found it would be proper, in order to dif-
credit this Liquor, to make it the Subject
of a publick Difpute, and to pafs their
Verdict, as it were, according to Law upon Coffee. To this end they took the
Opportunity of the Admiffion of a young
Phy-

Phyſician, in the College of Phyſicians at
Marſeille, to debate in the ſolemn Act,
which he was oblig'd to maintain in Preſence of the Magiſtrates, in the Town-
Houſe, the famous Queſtion concerning
Coffee. The Diſputation was held *February* 27, 1679; and without doubt the
Reader will not be diſpleaſ'd to ſee here
a Tranſlation of ſo much of it as relates
to Coffee. It is done from a true Copy,
which happen'd very luckily to be in the
Hands of a very curious Friend of mine,
who ſent it me from *Marſeille.*

*Queſtions relating to Phyſick, propounded
by Meſſieurs* Caſtillon *and* Fougue,
Doctors of the Faculty of Aix, *to M.*
Colomb, *for his Aggregation in the
College of Phyſicians at* Marſeille, *on
which he was oblig'd to diſpute on* Fe-
bruary 27, 1679, *in the Hall of the
Town-Houſe.*
The Second Queſtion, viz. *Whether the
Uſe Coffee be hurtful to the Inhabitants
of* Marſeille?

‘ Among an infinite Number of Re-
‘ medies, with which the *Arabs* have, in
‘ ſome meaſure, overcharg'd Phyſick, there
‘ has

The The-
ſis con-
tain'd four
Queſti-
ons; the
1. About
the *Je-
ſuits*
Powder;
2. Coffee;
3. the Li-
ver; 4.
the *Ova-
ria* of
Women.

' has been none which has obtain'd with
' more eafe the Approbation of all Na-
' tions, than the Drink of Coffee; for
' not only with the *Turks* it is fold at a
' very moderate Price in publick Houfes,
' but alfo among us this Liquor has already
' fo obtain'd, that it is well if, by the extra-
' ordinary Qualities which are attributed
' to it, it does not entirely abolifh the
' Ufe of Wine; tho', to fay the Truth,
' neither the Tafte, Colour, Smell, nay,
' nor the Subftance itfelf, and all the Pro-
' perties of Coffee join'd together, do
' come near even the Lees of that excel-
' lent Liquor. Such is the Force of Opi-
' nion and Prejudice; infomuch that the
' Things which are familiar to us, tho'
' they may be of fome Account, become
' contemptible to us, at the fame time
' that which is but out-landifh, tho' of-
' ten defpicable and of no Value, is won-
' derfully extoll'd.

' For the reft, the moft Part of Phyfi-
' cians, little curious of the Nature and
' Qualities of Coffee, believe it to be very
' wholfome only for thefe two Reafons;
' that the *Arabs* call it *Bon* in their Lan-
' guage, and becaufe it is brought us from
the

' the happy Region of *Arabia :* As if the
' Nature of that Remedy depended on its
' Denomination, and that of the Country
' which produces it ; and as if it was not
' abfurd to determine the Nature of Things
' by their Names, as *Hippocrates* fpeaks
' in his Book of Art.

' In the mean Time the ignorant Vulgar
' is cheated at the Expence of his Health ;
' for he takes Coffee for a kind of Pulfe,
' when indeed it is the Fruit of a Tree,
' which refembles the Spindle-Tree, or
' Prickwood, according to *Avicenna*
' in his Book of Plants, and to *Profper*
' *Alpinus* in his Treatife of *Egyptian*
' Plants. Upon this falfe Notion, they
' efteem Coffee a Remedy fo much the
' more efficacious, becaufe Hiftorians at-
' tribute the firft Difcovery of it to Goats
' and Camels.

' Some affirm, that it is in its own Na-
' ture cold, wherefore they recommend
' the Drinking of it, or rather to fip by
' little and little the Decoction extremely
' hot ; but 'tis certain, on the contrary,
' that Coffee is naturally very hot and
' dry, not only from the Authority of
' the Authors we have nam'd, but alfo
' by

' by its chief and moft fenfible Effects.
' The aduft Parts, with which it abounds,
' are indeed fo fubtle, and of fuch fur-
' prizing Motion, that, being diffus'd thro'
' the Mafs of Blood, they forthwith draw
' along with them all the ferous or wa-
' terifh Matter into the other Parts of the
' Body. From thence attacking the Brain,
' and after having diffolv'd all the Moifture,
' and grofs Corpufcles, they keep open
' all the Pores, and prevent the animal
' Spirits, which caufe Sleep, from being
' carry'd to the middle of the Brain, when
' the Pores come to be fhut. From whence
' it happens, that thofe over-heated Parts
' often caufe by their Qualities fuch con-
' tinual Watchings, that the nervous
' Juice, a Store of which is neceffary to
' recruit the Spirits, coming to fail through-
' out, the Nerves relax, whence follows
' the Palfy and Impotency ; and, thro' the
' Sharpnefs and Drynefs of a Blood al-
' ready quite burnt up, all the Parts to-
' gether become fo exhaufted of Moifture,
' that the entire Body is at length re-
' duc'd to a horrible Leannefs. All thefe
' Evils happen ofteneft to thofe who are
' of a cholerick Difpofition, to melancho-
' ly

ly People, to thofe who have the Liver
' and Brain naturally hot, and to thofe,
' in fhort, whofe Spirits are very fubtle,
' and whofe Blood is enflam'd. From
' all which it neceffarily follows, that the
' Ufe of Coffee is hurtful to the much
' greater Part of the Inhabitants of *Mar-*
' *feille.*'

'Tis after this Manner, that the Doctors
of the Faculty of *Aix* explain'd themfelves,
and determin'd, at laft, with regard to
Coffee. 'Tis true, that many People perceiv'd the Matter a little to much ftrain'd
on their Side, and that the Phyficians themfelves in general, were not a little inte-
refted in this Difputation, which contain'd, befides, fome falfe Reafonings
and Errors in Fact. However 'tis certain,
that Decifion had no more Effect, than the
Declamations of the *Mohamedan* Preachers
had formerly; the publick Coffee Houfes
were as much frequented as ever; nor
was the Ufe of that Liquor the lefs in
private Houfes, not only at *Marfeille*, but
throughout *Provence*, and the neighbouring Provinces: Infomuch, that by little
and little Coffee became at *Marfeille*
and *Lyons* a very confiderable Article of
Trade.

Trade. To which it may be added, that the Confumption which began to be made of it in the capital City of the Kingdom, in the Manner hereafter obferv'd, gave occafion to the Merchants of thefe two Towns to have Ships freighted with it; not only from *Egypt*, but alfo from *Smyrna*, and all the Ports where they could find it; which, at laft, has put this Trade to the *Levant* upon the Foot which we fee it at prefent.

The true Epocha of the firft Introduction of Coffee at *Paris*. The Progrefs of its Ufe down to our Time.
Before the Year 1669, Coffee had not been feen at *Paris*, and it was fcarce ever heard fpoke of, except at M. *Thevenot*'s, and the Relation *of Travellers; but that Year, diftinguifh'd in our Hiftory for the folemn Embaffy of *Soltan Mohamed* IV, ought to pafs for the true Epocha of the firft Introduction of Coffee at *Paris*: For that Embaffadour, and his Retinue, brought a great

---

* The Author *du Bouclier de l'Europe*, who was in *Egypt* in 1638, fays, fpeaking of Coffee, that it is an *Indian* Grain, like a Kind of fmall Bean, which they roaft in an Oven, &c. And the Author *de la Syrie Sainte*, who was in the *Levant* in 1659, fays, that Coffee is a black boiling Water, more wholfome than palatable, unknown in *France*, where it pafs'd for a Drink of Goblins.

a great deal of Coffee there, and they
treated with it as many Perfons of the
Court and Town, as paid Vifits out of
Curiofity to the *Turkifh* Minifter, as is
actually done [now] at the *Perfian* Embaffadours ; that many accuftom'd themfelves
to it at laft, putting in Sügar ; and others
who found benefit by Coffee could fcarce
be without it.

The Embaffadour who arriv'd in *France*
in the Month of *July,* 1669, had not his
publick Audience of the King 'till the 5th
of *December* following ; and he did not
leave *Paris,* for his Return, before *May*
1670, which was time enough to bring
in Reputation, and fomewhat in Fafhion,
at *Paris,* the Coffee which he had introduc'd.

After the Departure of the Embaffadour
that Fafhion was continu'd by feveral Perfons, who found Means to get Coffee, by
having it brought from *Marfeille* or elfewhere.   At laft there came to that City
an *Armenian,* whofe Name was *Pafcal,*
who, in the Year 1672, took up to fell
Coffee publickly at the Fair of S. *Germain* ; after which he fet up a little Shop
upon

upon the *Quai de l'Ecole,* or School-Kay, where he gave Coffee for two Sols six Derniers, or about two Pence Half-penny, a Dish ; but he had little Company besides Knights of *Malta* and Strangers, insomuch this *Armenian* was oblig'd to leave off, and to go to *London.*

Three or four Years after, *Maliban,* another *Armenian,* who came also to *Paris* with the same Design, open'd his Coffee-House in the *Rue de Buſſy,* near the Tennis-Court of *Mets,* about the Abby of S. *Germain.* He permitted smoaking also, and sold his Coffee at the same Price. From thence he remov'd to the *Rue Ferou,* near S. *Sulpice,* whence he return'd to his first Habitation in the *Rue de Buſſy*; but he did not stay long there neither, because he was oblig'd to go to *Holland,* after having settled in the same Shop, *Gregory* his Journeyman, or Associate, who came from *Ispahan* with other *Armenians.*

This *Gregory* remov'd afterwards into the *Rue Mazarine,* for the Benefit of the Neighbourhood of the Play-House, which acted then in the same Street, over-against that of *Guenegaud,* and settled himself in

the

the fame Place where the Widow *Gantois* keeps at prefent ; nor did he continue long there neither, for, the Play-Houfe removing, he went to live in the Street, and on the fame Side, where it plays at this Time ; and from thence remov'd once more to the Houfe which he has fince purchas'd, and where at length he dy'd very old the laft Year.

When *Gregory* quitted the *Rue Mazarine,* he had to fucceed him one *Makara,* a *Perfian,* who, after having for fome Time carry'd on the fame Bufinefs, return'd into his native Country, leaving his Coffee-Houfe to one that come from *Liege* nam'd *le Gantois.*

In thefe firft Times, a little lame Man, nam'd *Candiot,* went thro' the Streets of *Paris* crying Coffee ; and thofe who had a Mind to take any, call'd him, to whom he fill'd out a Cup that belong'd to the Houfe, or one of his own for two Pence, giving alfo Sugar with it. He had a Napkin ty'd about him very neat, carrying in one Hand a Chafing-Difh made for the Purpofe, upon which was a Coffee-Pot, and in the other a Kind of Fountain full

Z

of Water, and before him a Tin-Basket, where he kept all his Utenſils.

This *Candiot* had for a Companion in the ſame Trade, to carry Coffee about the Town, one *Joſeph* who was alſo come from the *Levant* to ſeek his Fortune at *Paris*, by Means of Coffee. After having ſet up and ſold it in ſeveral Parts of the Town, he dy'd at laſt, very well to paſs, in his Houſe at the Foot of the *Pont Notre Dame*, where his Widow now lives.

In fine, *Stephen* originally from *Aleppo* came alſo to *Paris* with the ſame Deſign, and was the laſt of all thoſe Foreigners. After but indifferent Beginnings, he kept his Coffee-Houſe a long Time on the Change-Bridge, and at laſt ſettled in the Houſe he now keeps in the *Rue S. Andre*, the Shop of which, one of the Cazgeſt, and moſt convenient in the Town, faces the *Pont S. Michael*.

Theſe were the Introducers * of publick Coffee-Houſes at *Paris* [and *London*.]

They

* The *French* Editor obſerves, that he has follow'd the Example of the *Turkiſh* Hiſtorian cited above, who, in a general important Hiſtory, has not even omitted the Name of thoſe who open'd the firſt Coffee-Houſes at *Conſtantinople*. And we have thought

fi

They were imitated by feveral other *Le-vantines*, who, in Procefs of Time, have benefitted not a little by their Trade.   I fay in Procefs of Time, for the firft Beginnings of all thofe Men have been very inconfiderable.   The modefter Sort of People at firft were at fome Difficulty to refolve entering into thofe Kind of Taverns, where they fmoak'd and fold Beer, not to mention, that the Coffee was not extraordinary, and over neatly ferv'd.

But fince fome *French* [and *Englifh*] concerning themfelves in that Bufinefs, have had the Thought to furnifh their Shops with Tapeftry, large Glaffes, Pictures, Marble-Tables, Sconces to give Light at Night, and other Appurtenances *; fince, to their Coffee well prepar'd, they have added Tea and Chocolate, Liquors of all Kinds, Bifcuits, and Comfits.   Thefe Shops, I fay, transform'd into very handfome Rooms, ferv'd for a Pattern to all others, and were the Rendezvouz of Numbers of

Z 2

fober

fit to infert his Account of the Introduction of Coffee into *France*, fometimes inferting the Word *London*, to which Place the Account is for the moft Part as applicable as to *Paris.*

  * This Practice among the *French* at *Paris* began in the Fair of S. *Germain.*

sober Men, who came to recreate themselves by taking a Dish of Coffee in good Company, entertaining themselves upon agreeable Subjects. Men of Learning, and of the greatest Gravity, did not disdain these Assemblies, so convenient for conversing upon Points of Learning, without Reserve or Ceremony.

In short, this Fashion of taking Coffee in such Places, and among Company, is so well establish'd at *Paris*, [and *London*] and has been found so proper to the forming agreeable Societies, that by Degrees those Places, or Coffee-Houses have been encreas'd to the Number of about three Hundred ; by which I find that they are now very near their Stint, especially since the Masters, who from the Beginning form'd a Society of Merchants of Liquors, have been at length reunited to a Body of Master-Distillers of the City and Suburbs of *Paris*.

In the Fairs S. *Germain* and S. *Laurence*, there are still to be seen several Coffee-Halls, held for the most Part by the principal Masters, which nevertheless do not give over their Trade with the Town. It may be said, that these Halls make one

of

of the chief Ornaments of the Fair. It was there that the great Silver Coffee-Pots, Chocolate-Pots, and other Furniture of the fame Metal, were firft feen; which are now very common for the moft part in the Coffee Houfes of this Town. The Ladies make no fcruple, during the Fair, to go into thofe Places, where there are found, befides Coffee, all Sorts of Liquors, Comfits, and feveral Sorts of Refreshments.

We fhall not finifh what we have to fay about the Coffee-Houfes at *Paris*, without adding, that the different Characters of the People that frequent them, appear'd about 20 Years ago to have been a true Subject of Comedy to a certain Author; he handled then this Bufinefs, which was proper enough to furnifh a good Piece, but his did not pleafe the Tafte of the Town, or bear acting above once. 'Twas neverthelefs printed under this Title, *The Coffee Houfe, a Comedy,* by *Peter Aubovin,* in the Year 1694. We fhall alfo fay a Word of the *Portefenille-Galant, containing the Converfations of the Coffee-Houfes, and other Works in Profe and Verfe.* The firft of which came out the

Z 3   15th

15th of *June*, 1700, with a Promife of
publifhing the reft the 15th of each
Month, a Promife which was never perform'd.   There is Room enough to believe that the Town was not very well
Pleas'd with this Effay, in which indeed
there was nothing form'd either in Profe
or in Verfe, but what was very common.
Tis a two Sheet Bufinefs, printed by
Moreau, 1700, with Licence.

For what remains, tho' the Number
of publick Coffee-Houfes are confiderable
at *Paris*, [and *London*] and that there are
found in them all the Conveniences we
have fpoken of, yet is there not the lefs
taken of it in private Houfes, almoft all
having it from the Cits to the Folks of
greateft Quality, amongft whom it is the
eftablifh'd Fafhion to take it in the Morning, or, at leaft, immediately after Dinner;
and treat with it in the familiar Vifits
which they receive; not to mention an
infinite Number of Perfons accuftom'd to
Coffee, who live in Societies, or who
are not in a Condition to appear handfomely at the publick Coffee-Houfes. And
now I talk of Men of Quality, let me
obferve, that it was thro' their Encourage-
ment

ment that Coffee-Houses first came in Fashion, and that we see them at last able to viegh with the most sumptuous of the Kind in the East; insomuch that the Gold and Silver, which are there in great Plenty, are not equivalent to the Value of the China-Dishes, and other Curiosities of that Ware, with which these Houses are fur-nish'd.

In the mean Time this Fashion, esta-blish'd in the Metropolis of the Kingdom, has been follow'd successively by all the Provinces, the chief Towns of which actually have their Coffee-Houses *; with-out mentioning all the Coffee that is con-sum'd in the Country, in all the great Houses and elsewhere, and what is also expended in the King's Armies both by Sea and Land.

'Tis without doubt this great Consump-tion, which about 25 Years ago stirr'd up some Politicians, who, upon the Occasion of the War, made an Offer to the King's Council, to bring a Profit to his Majesty

Z 4   by

* In *France,* at *Lyons, Toulouse, Bourdeaux, Rennes, Rouen, Dijon,* &c. and especially in the considerable Towns of *French Flanders.* As to *Great Britain* and *Ireland,* there is scarce a Town of any Note, but what has one or more Coffee-Houses.

by farming Coffee ; but thefe Propofals
had no Succefs, for the King, contenting
himfelf with a moderate Cuftom, has
been gracioufly pleas'd, for the Advantage
of Commerce, and the particular Benefit of his Subjects, to leave Things as they
were at firft.

The Commerce of Coffee, the Foundation of which is the great Confumption
we have fpoken of, is become indeed very confiderable in *France*. But that Trade
has had, like all others, its Changes : Efpecially at certain Times when the *Bafha's,*
and other Potentates of *Egypt*, became
more difficult in letting that Commodity
be tranfported, which has caus'd the
Scarcity of it, and rais'd the Price to fix
and feven *Haucks*, or about eighteen Pence
the Pound, as we have feen within this little while.   'Tis that alfo which gave Occafion to the two firft Voyages to *Arabia
Fœlix* by Sea ; Voyages which have made
great Plenty, and have put Things upon
a fure Foot more advantageous to the
Publick.   'Tis true, that the Merchants of
Marfeille have pretended to oppofe this
new Commerce, believing themfelves only to have a Right to bring it into *France,*
and

and that by the Way of *Egypt* and the *Mediterranean-Sea,* by Virtue of the Privilege of the Port of *Marſeille*, and for other Conſiderations. The Merchants of S. *Malo* have thereupon publiſh'd their Defence, and I know not yet what has been done in this Affair in the King's Council.

This is the only Diſpute, at leaſt the moſt ſerious, which has happen'd in *France* with regard to Coffee, excepting that of the Phyſicians of *Aix* already cited ; the other *French* Pyſicians in general, very far from running down Coffee, have prais'd and recommended it on ſeveral Occaſions.

I know very well that two Phyſicians of ſome Reputation in our Time, have ſpoken much againſt Coffee; the firſt is M. *Duncan* of the Family of *Montpelier* in his *wholſome Advice to all People aɡainſt the Abuſe of hot Things, and particularly of Coffee, Tea and Chocolate,* printed at *Roterdam* in 1705. , The Things contain'd in it are ſo extravagant, that the reſt of the Phyſicians, that are aɡainſt Coffee, have look'd upon the Zeal
of

Approbation of Coffee by the principal Phyſicians of France.

of M. *Duncan* as Paſſion and Fury *.
Tantopere invehitur, & debacchatur Duncanus. The Journaliſts of *Trevoux* gave
an Extract of this Book in the Month,
of *September*, 1706, and it may be ſaid
that thoſe Extracts gave more Pleaſure to
the Readers, than the Book itſelf, by the
ingenious Reflections and juſt Opinion
which is found upon that Work. The
other Phyſician againſt Coffee is M.
Hecquet,

---

* In the Theſis held in the Schools of *Paris*, the
21ſt of *March*, 1715. That Theſis was not favourable to Coffee, and, among ſome good Things, it contains Paſſages that look like Railery. For Inſtance,
Hæc pignitiæ merces & otii luſus intra clauſtrorum repagula jam penetravit. Garriendi tempuſve terendi gratia, ut hodie conſuevit, ſorbilletior. Cafe appetitus morbus eſt mulieribus & otioſis endemius ; and ſeveral others.
The Concluſion is, that the great Uſe of Coffee
ſhortens Life; but it happen'd to Coffee, as it did to
Tobacco, which has had alſo the greateſt Adverſaries.
James I. King of *England*, writ a Treatiſe upon the
Abuſe of Tobacco; the Jeſuit *Balde* a Satyr, and the
Abbot *Niſſeno* has maintain'd, that it has been brought
into *Europe* by the Artifices of the Devil. We ſhall
ſay nothing about another medicinal Theſis, held in
the ſame Schools of *Paris*, the 15th of *September*, 1695,
where it was determin'd upon a mechanical Propoſition odd enough, and after extravagant Arguments,
that the daily Uſe of Coffee made Men and Women
uncapable of Generation.

Hecquet, a Doctor of *Paris,* who, in his
Treatife *des Difpenfes de Carême,* printed
at *Paris* by *Leonard,* 1709, who reproaches the *French* 'with Drinking like
' the *Arabs,* and that they indulge a
' barbarous Tafte, which is, fays he, much
' to be dreaded,' *&c.* There appear'd on
the contrary, much about the fame Time,
a * *Latin* Differtation upon the Art of
Preferving the Health; the Author of
which is a Phyfician of Reputation, who,
fpeaking of Drinks, affirms in exprefs
Terms, and maintains upon good Argu-
ments, that Coffee is very wholfome. To
conclude, M. *Andry,* in his curious and
learned Treatife of *Lent*-Food, printed
by *Coignard* in 1713, not only allows
Coffee, but propofes a new Method of
Preparing it, which he believes to be more
wholfome than that in Ufe. We fhall
infert it here for the Sake of thofe who
may not have feen M. *Andry*'s Book.

' Hitherto there has been known but
' one Method of Preparing Coffee, and
' that is to roaft it. There is neverthelefs

NewMe-
thod of
making
Coffee,
propos'd
by M.
Andry.

* *Differtatio de Hygieine tuendæ fanitatis, & præ-
cavendorum imminentium morborum præcepta tradens,
&c.* 1 vol. 12. 1710. At *Valence* in *Dauphine.*

' lefs another, which it is ftrange that no
' body has yet thought on. It is to draw
' the Tincture of Coffee, as that of Tea is
' drawn, and to make by that fimple Me-
' thod only a Drink, which is fo much the
' better as there is nothing overheating in
' it, and it contains only a natural Extract
' of what is in Coffee, lefs fixt and more
' fublimated, that is to fay, the moft mer-
' curial, light, and at the fame Time more
' harmlefs, Part of that Fruit. Whereas
' the boiling of it waftes much of that mer-
' curial Principle, of that fweet and fub-
' tle Spirit. 'Tis certain that, by the com-
' mon Preparation, the Coffee lofes con-
' fiderably of its Weight; and any one,
' that makes the Experiment, will find
' that it waftes 120 Grains in the Ounce,
' that is to fay, a Quarter; fo great a
' Diminution muft needs caufe a large
' Diffipation of the volatile Spirits, which
' are the firft that evaporate. Be that as
' it will, the Drink ought to be prepar'd
' after this Manner : Take a Grofs of
' Coffee-Beans, well clean'd from the
' Husk, let them boil for the Space of half
' a Quarter of an Hour in a Pot of Wa-
' ter; after that draw the Liquor from
' the

' the Fire, which will be of a fine Citron-
' Colour, and after having let it settle
' some Time close cover'd, drink it hot
' with Sugar. This Drink sends forth a
' sweet Fume, which easily disperses, and
' has an agreeable Flavour: It fortifies the
' Stomach, corrects Crudities, and sensi-
' bly clears the Head. But one particu-
' lar Quality it has is, that it assuages the
' Sharpness of the Urine, and allays the
' most stubborn Cough, having myself
' made the Experiment upon several Pa-
' tients: The same Coffee, which has been
' once us'd, retains still Vertue enough to
' serve a second, and even a third Time;
' which proceeds from hence, that this
' Fruit, which is scarce soften'd at all in
' boiling, is of a Contexture perfectly
' compact, which prevnts the more sub-
' tle Parts of it fron evaporating all at
' once. If the Coffee be let to boil a
' long Time on a swift Fire, the Co-
' lour changes, and the Liquor becomes
' green like the Juice of an Herb: Tis
' then not so good, because it abounds
' too much with the earthy Parts; it also
' leaves at the Bottom of the Vessel a lit-
' tle green Slime, which sufficiently e-
' vince

' vince the Groffnefs of thofe Parts. Care
' then muft be taken not to boil it too
' much, with this Precaution, one may be
' fure to have an admirable Liquor for
' producing the wholfome Effects which
' we have obferv'd. There is alfo room to
' believe, that if this Fafhion was intro-
' duc'd, thefe would not be the only Ad-
' vantages which might be drawn from it.'

I fhall not fpeak here but *en paffant*
of a Manufcript-Memoir, which fell into
my Hands, writ by M. *Helvetius* the Father, at the Requeft of fome Men of Figure; a Memoir which is altogether in
the Behalf of Coffee, of which he defcribes the Nature and Qualities, as well
as regulates the Ufe and Preparation of
it, in a Manner fuitable to his Ingenuity.

Thofe who mind lefs their Health, than
to pleafe their Pallats, have found the
Way metamorphofe Coffee in feveral different Manners, to make it the more a-
greeable. The moft common of thefe
Changes are practis'd every Day by an infinite Number of People, who load it ex-
ceffively with Sugar, though the Coffee,
which they take, can never diffolve but a
proportionable Quantity; by this Means
they

they make a Kind of thick Syrup, often
hurtful, inftead of a temperate and wholfome Drink.   To pleafe the more dainty
mouth'd Sort, they have made of late at
Paris· Coffee Sugar-Plumbs, and at length
one has invented at *Montpelier* Coffee-
Water, which is a Kind of *Rofa folis,*
whofe Smell is very agreeable, and excels
that of boil'd Coffee.

Of two Poems, which the Author of
this Treatife has felected out of a great
Number, which have been made by the
French upon Coffee, we fhall only infert
here, that of *F. Vaniere* the Jefuit, in his
Prædium Rufticum, which is, fays our Author, one of the moft complete and perfect Poems that has been made in that
Kind.   The Poet, after having given in
the 8th Book the Character of divers
French Wines, and the Preference to the
Natural before the Artificial, fpeaks of
the admirable Effects of this Drink, and
particularly in Drunkennefs, which he explains phyfically.   Amongft the Remedies,
moft proper for clearing the Head diforder'd with Wine, he gives the Preference
to Coffee ; the other good Effects of which
the Poet occafionally defcribes, with the
fame Spirit.   *Ut*

Ut medeare malo, non est præsentius ullum
Auxilium, quam si terris faba missa pelas-
        gis
Intumuit; nitidos sartagine tosta per ignes,
Tritaque mox validis intra mortaria pilis,
Diluitur lympha, facilique parabilis arte
Vulcano coquitur, donec vas pulvis ad
        imum
Venerit, & posito mansueverit ollulæ motu.
Fictilibus rufos pateris defunde liquores,
Adde peregrina dulces ab arundine succos,
Ora sapore calix ne tristia lædat amaro.
Seu longas opus est studiis traducere noctes,
Sive graves caput tenebras induxerit Au-
        ster,
Seu nocuere dapes, illo medicamine vates
Ingenium emendet, lætusq; infecta resumat
Carmina, nec fontes alios, quibus ora Poetæ
Proluerint, fluxisse solo male credat achivo.

A young Coffee-Tree brought to the King's Gardens Observation and Description of that Tree.

We cannot finish this Treatise more agreeably, and in a properer Manner than with the Coffee-Tree itself, by speaking of that which we have said something of in the preceding Memoir, and which is at last come from *Holland* to the King's Garden.

Sunday 29th of *July*, 1714, M. *de Jus-sien*, Doctor of Physick, of the Academy of Science,

Sciences, and royal Botany-Profeſſour, was
pleas'd to bring there M. *Galland*, Profeſ-
four of *Arabick* in the Royal College; M.
Parent of the Academy of Sciences, and Pro-
feſſour of the Mathematicks, M. *Ouange*,
a learned and very curious *Chineſe*, and my
ſelf. We only went to ſee that firſt Coffee-
Plant mention'd in the ſame Memoir, but
we underſtood when we came there, that
Monſieur, the chief Phyſician, had, the
Night before, ſent the Tree which was
newly come from *Holland*, as a Preſent to
his Majeſty from the Magiſtrates of *Amſter-*
dam, from *Marly* to the Royal Garden.
We went thither to ſee it, and obſerv'd
it a good while with Pleaſure; it was yet
in its Caſe, and placed in the Glaſs-Ma-
chine, where is the Taper of *Peru* be-
ſide this Plant ; this Shurb may be about
5 Foot in height, and full an Inch thick:
It ſhoots forth ſeveral little Boughs which
raiſe themſelves along its Stem, and form
a Figure almoſt piramidical. Its Leaves are
almoſt all rang'd by two and two along
the Branches ; they are not ſo large as
thoſe which were ſent me and came from
Arabia, which I had brought along with
me. M. *Galland* found no Difference
A a   between

between this which he faw, and the young
Sprigs of a great Coffee-Tree which he had
feen at *Conftantinople*. We obferv'd upon this Shurb fome green Fruit, of the
Bignefs of a fmall green Plumb, fome red,
refembling very near a Cherry, and much
of the fame Fruit of a deeper Colour, and
almoft black with Ripenefs. It grows on
a very fhort Stalk between the two Leaves
and the Branch.

The *Hollander*, who had that Tree under his Care, and was come from *Marly*
to the Garden-Royal, with the Servants
of Monfieur, the chief Phyfician, told us,
that there was in the Plant-Garden of *Amfterdam* a great Tree of this Species, whofe
Height, to ufe his Terms, was equal to the
fecond Story of a Houfe, and proportiona-
bly large. That great Tree came originally from *Arabia*, brought from thence
very young, and tranfported to *Java*; from
whence, after fome ftay, it came at laft
to *Holland*, where it has throve to Perfection : The Fruit of this fame Tree,
planted in the Garden of *Amfterdam*, have
produc'd divers young Plants, fome of
which have born Fruit from the Age of
three Years. The Shurb fent to the King
was

was of that Number, according to the Account of the *Dutchman*.

M. *de Juſſien* brought us afterwards to ſee the other Coffee-Plant, that came before from *Holland*, which was ſtill a little Thing without Fruit, and not over a Foot and half long, but very freſh and in good Condition.

But to return to our Tree loaden with Fruit, with regard to which there needed no more to ſatisfy my Curioſity, but to view its Flowers; this was ſtill a Satisfaction which M. *de Juſſien* procur'd me about five Weeks after. I ſaw then theſe Flowers at the Beginning of *September* following, ſome in bud, and others quite open and full blown; and the more I beheld them, the more I was convinc'd of the Exactneſs of my Memoirs, and of all that was ſent me about this Matter. The Shrub of Coffee with the Flowers, which we are ſpeaking of, had Fruit on it very near their Perfection.

Before we end, we ſhall add for the ſake of the Curious and Strangers, that M. *Juſſien* not only takes a Pleaſure in courteouſly receiving ſuch, but that he alſo informs them of Matters after a manner equally
ly

ly folid and agreeable. His Knowledge and
Enquiries are not confin'd to Botany ; one
fees at his Houfe a large Clofet of natural
Curiofities, which may be call'd a compleat
Abridgment of Nature; and, to return to
our Subjeft, nothing can be more rational than what we heard him fpeak with
regard to Coffee ; as much contrary to fuch
as make it a Kind of Poifon, as to thofe
who look upon it almoft as a univerfal Remedy ; he has made fo nice a Scrutiny
into it, that even in Practice he makes no
Difficulty to purge certain Diforders in a
Draught of this Liquor.

To conclude, M. *de Juffien* is the firft,
in the Royal Academy of Sciences, who has
fpoken of the Tree and Fruit of Coffee;
and one may perceive in the Hiftory of
the Academy, that he has fpoken more
to the Purpofe than all the Botanifts that
have been before him.

F I N I S.

ANNALES

DES VOYAGES,

DE LA GÉOGRAPHIE ET DE L'HISTOIRE;

ou COLLECTION

Des Voyages Nouveaux les plus estimés, traduits de
toutes les Langues Européennes;

Des Relations Originales, inédites, communiquées par des
Voyageurs Français et Étrangers ;

Et des Mémoires Historiques sur l'Origine, la Langue, les Mœurs
et les Arts des Peuples, ainsi que sur le Climat, les Productions
et le Commerce des Pays jusqu'ici peu ou mal connus :

ACCOMPAGNÉES

*D'un Bulletin où l'on annonce toutes les Découvertes, Recherches et
Entreprises qui tendent à accélérer les Progrès des Sciences Historiques,
spécialement de la Géographie, et où l'on donne des Nouvelles des
Voyageurs et des Extraits de leur Correspondance.*

Avec des Cartes et Planches, gravées en taille-douce.

PUBLIÉES PAR M. MALTE-BRUN.

Correspondant de l'Académie Italienne, de la Société d'Emulation de l'Ile-de-France, et de plusieurs autres Sociétés
Savantes et Littéraires.

---

*Tome IIe de la IIIe Souscription,
et Xe de la Collection.*

Cahier V (XXIXe de la Collection).

La Traduction d'une foule de Voyages (dit le Rédacteur) a,
depuis trente ans environ, vivement excité le goût du Public, pour
les Connoissances si utiles et si intéressantes dont les Voyageurs
fournissent les matériaux et dont les Géographes élèvent et con-

TABLE

Des Articles contenus dans ce IIe Cahier du T. X^e.

NEW TRAVELS

IN

ARABIA FELIX

Or,

Notes on Trade in the Red Sea and Some
Remarks on the Customs, Habits, Laws, Armies,
Public Revenues and Population of Yemen in
Arabia Felix, compiled there, in 1788

M. Cloupet

Now for the first time translated by
Dominique de Moulins and Carl Phillips

THE OLEANDER PRESS

Arab coffee house (*Coll.* Philip Ward)

INTRODUCTION
Carl Phillips

In the second half of the eighteenth century, Carsten Niebuhr visited several ports on the Red Sea and, while in the Yemen, the Royal Danish Expedition of which he was a member resided for much of their time on the Tihama and in particular in the town of Bayt al-Faqih. Inevitably, Niebuhr's accounts include references to the coffee trade and the maps of Yemen and general information he gathered became a landmark in Arabian studies. However, although the Danish expedition is considered by many to represent the first scientific exploration of Arabia, there are others whose employment in commerce or other matters caused them to spend a limited time in towns such as Mocha and Bayt al-Faqih. The latter include Prutky, who provides a useful description of Mocha from around the middle of the century. Another was Louis Marie Joseph O'Hier de Grandpré (1761–1846). Born in Saint-Malo of Irish descent, he studied at Rennes before joining the mercantile navy. Between 1786 and 1789 he visited the coasts of East Africa, Arabia and India. His description of Mocha is one of the more detailed and interesting accounts from the late eighteenth century. A further short description of Yemen dating from the end of the eighteenth century is provided by Cloupet.

Biographical details about Cloupet have proved impossible to find. In her book *À la découverte de l'Arabie*, Jacqueline Pirenne lists Cloupet's *Nouveau Voyage dans l'Arabie Heureuse* in the bibliography to the chapter entitled 'L'Arabie du café', which is part of the section referring to 'Explorateurs d'Occasion'. This is the only reference given apart from La Roque's *Voyage de l'Arabie Heureuse*. In his introduction, Cloupet refers to the Abbé Raynal and states that the article is intended to provide some additional details to supplement the general picture provided by Raynal. Cloupet also admits that these details are perhaps not the most essential for historical purposes, whereas the objective of Raynal had most certainly been to present Arabia, alongside other regions, in a broad historical context to support his thesis concerning the European colonies in the Americas and the Indies. Abbé Raynal (1713–1796) was indeed a radical in his time and a supporter of the Revolution. In his book on the European colonies, about which he was most critical, he sided with the exploited native inhabitants. When it was first published, Raynal was forced into exile. Two years later he was allowed to return to France, but not to Paris. Cloupet's short text seems to have no political intent. However, it does provide some details about the procedures followed in the purchase of coffee. A certain lack of clarity about some of the weights and measures which were used emphasises the complexity of the situation faced by the merchants, as weights and measures often had different values in places located not far from each other. To some extent, Cloupet's comments about some of the people he encountered in places like Bayt al-Faqih highlight the naïveté of the European conception of the Arabs. However, the main value of Cloupet's description is to illustrate the demand for Yemeni coffee at the end of the eighteenth century despite the fact that it had been grown for more than fifty years in the colonies. The transplanting of Yemeni coffee in the colonies of the European powers was no doubt detrimental to the wealth of Yemen, but in no way did it bring to an end the Red Sea trade of the eighteenth century.

The second voyage to Mocha was followed by further enterprising voyages from Saint-Malo. As with the earlier voyages, these were sometimes accompanied by events that proved of wider significance than would first appear. In March 1714 the 'Chasseur', under the command of Guillaume Dufresne d'Arsel (1668–1738), and the 'Paix', commanded by Gravé de la Moncelière, departed from Saint-Malo. Shortly thereafter the French India Company sent to Mocha the 'Auguste', under the command of Léon Leblanc, who carried on board a letter from the minister Pontchartrain ordering d'Arsel to proceed to the Île Maurice (Mauritius) and take it for the French. This order was followed and on 20 September the Île Maurice became the Île de France. Meanwhile the 'Auguste' departed from Mocha with a cargo of coffee and, in addition to this, six coffee plants.

These coffee plants were subsequently planted on the Île Bourbon (Réunion) and within ten years the cultivators there were producing a large part of the coffee consumed in France. Coffee was similarly transplanted in the Antilles (1719) and Brazil (1721). Meanwhile, voyages to Mocha continued. In 1717 the French India Company's ship, the 'Comtesse de Pontchartrain' was sent to Mocha under the command of François de la Bouexière, and there were annual voyages in most of the years that followed. However, by 1734 the amount of coffee purchased from Mocha had dropped considerably and so the French India Company, which in 1723 had established a monopoly on the sale of coffee in France, decided to reorganise its trade, with a larger amount of goods being transited via Pondicherry, the French possession on the east coast of India. In 1734 there was also an attempt in Mocha to increase the amount of duty paid on exported coffee. Consequently the governor of Pondicherry sent a fleet of four ships to Mocha, under the command of Nicolas Jazier de la Garde, a nephew of the celebrated Duguay-Trouin. Mocha's bombardment persuaded the authorities there to agree a new treaty and revert to the earlier tariffs.

Around the same time as the French bombardment of Mocha, in the archives of Saint-Malo comes the first indication of a new quarter of the town being called Moka. This quarter developed outside the old city in the area of the reclaimed marshlands of Routhouan. However, it is probably a coincidence that the name first appears on documents around the same time as the reaffirmation of the treaty with Yemen. It is more likely that the quarter of Saint-Malo adopted this name at the time when the draining of the marshlands was first instigated in 1714, when a need arose for expansion resulting in part from the increased wealth generated by the merchants of Saint-Malo as a result of their role in the import of coffee.

A result of the availability of coffee from the Île Bourbon and the Antilles was that the amount purchased from Mocha declined considerably from the 1730s onwards. However, some was still sought from Mocha as it was considered to be of sufficiently higher quality. In Europe, alongside the thirst for coffee, there began an increasing thirst for knowledge, perhaps epitomised by an image of the great eighteenth-century French encyclopaedists engaged in conversation in Paris' Café Procope. In addition to bringing back to Europe the desired luxury goods, commercial activities also acted as a conduit for increased knowledge about places such as Arabia. In particular the coffee trade resulted in an increased awareness of Yemen and the Red Sea.

The Café Procope in Paris with some of its 18th century clientèle

BIBLIOGRAPHY

Cloupet. 1810. Nouveau voyage dans l'Arabie Heureuse; ou Remarques sur le commerce de la mer Rouge et quelques idées des Moeurs, Usages, Lois, Forces militaires, Revenus publics, Population du pays de l'Yémen de l'Arabie-Heureuse, puisées sur les lieux, en 1788. *Annales des Voyages*

(Paris) X, 1810 : 154–180.

Grandpré, L. de. 1803. *A Voyage in the Indian Ocean, and to Bengal ... To which is added a Voyage in the Red Sea, including a description of Mocha, and of the trade of the Arabs of Yemen.* 2 vols. G. and J. Robinson, London.

Niebuhr, Carsten. 1773. *Description de l'Arabie.* Nicolas Möller, Copenhagen.

Niebuhr, Carsten. 1792. *Travels through Arabia and other countries in the East.* 2 vols. Translated by R. Heron. Edinburgh. There have been several reprints.

Prutky, Remedius. 1991. *Travels in Ethiopia and other countries.* Translated and edited by J. H. Arrowsmith-Brown and annotated by Richard Pankhurst. Hakluyt Society, London.

Raynal, G.T.R. 1770. *Histoire philosophique et politique des établissemens & du commerce des Européens dans les deux Indes.* Amsterdam (6 vols.)

See also entries in the Bibliography appended to the Introduction to La Roque.

NEW TRAVELS IN ARABIA FELIX

Or, Notes on Trade in the Red Sea and Some
Remarks on the Customs, Habits, Laws, Armies,
Public Revenues and Population of Yemen in
Arabia Felix, compiled there, in 1788, by *M.*
Cloupet of the Île-de-France.

I. Trade

The Red Sea trade has greatly increased since Abbé Raynal
described the region. I have observed during my travels that
this celebrated writer is not always accurate about the conditions of the peoples and countries he has described, doubtless
due to the lack of careful observation or accurate information.
In all justice, however, I must say that the little he has written
about Arabia Felix is true enough and he has omitted only a few
details which, though not entirely essential for historical purposes, nevertheless seem to be of some interest concerning the
trade and customs of the Arabs who live near the Indian Ocean.
I have culled the following details from my notes of my own
researches.

Mocha receives today thirty ships from Surat and Bandar
Abbas, of varying tonnage, and laden with a wide variety of
merchandise. Jiddah receives some 50 ships, of which 5 or 6 are
from Bengal, all carrying rich cargoes. The total value of these
goods can be estimated at 40 million in French money, of
which 25 million represents the cost of the goods and their
freight, and 15 million the profit, once exchanged for silver and
gold, which passes to the treasury of Asia and is never seen
again.

European trade with Mocha is limited to only 2 or 3 vessels
a year. America, which now ranks among the trading nations, is
beginning to influence the purchase of coffee by Europeans
from Bayt al-Faqih.

Goods exchanged in this trade include iron used for ploughs;
steel; copper for pots and cauldrons; materials for tinning; pig-

iron and scrap iron; and textiles of both first and second quality.

A transaction on goods destined for Mocha must include only a quarter of the money to be used for their return, on which a profit of 35% to 40% can be expected. A larger amount would sell badly if it were not accompanied by three times the amount in Spanish piastres.

The English and the Armenians in the various trading stations of India are those who benefit most from the trade with Arabia. The French account for very little. That is to say, we do not make an impact in this important trade region due to the fact that we are confined to trading at Mocha, where we appear with a single European vessel, for which a cargo of coffee, our only reason for being there, can be acquired only if enough money is brought to pay for three quarters of the load. The English, on the other hand, whose connections spread all over the mercantile globe, can exchange coffee, when they want it, with the proceeds from goods made in their Indian territoies.

The Parsis from Surat and the Banians from Gujarat import a great quantity of ordinary goods into the markets of Mocha and Jiddah. The English and Armenians, by contrast, import the most expensive goods of the finest quality. This arrangement is connected with the price of the freight and the equipping of the ship. If the ship belongs to them, the expensive goods that they customarily send to Jiddah are sold for a profit equal to that of all the goods of ordinary quality, and yet entail much lower freight and other costs. Arab ships heading for the Red Sea make sure to obtain an English passport enabling them to fly the British flag and thus save 5% of the customs dues both at Mocha and at Jiddah.

Pilgrims heading for Makkah from such regions as Malabar, Gujarat, and the Indus Valley are only petty traders who combine their religious duties with their economic interests. They travel either to Surat or Bandar Abbas to catch the first ships plying to Jiddah. They pay a moderate fare because they take their food with them, but they have to pay freight charges of 8% on the sale goods. After the pilgrims have sold their cheap wares and prostrated themselves according to custom to absolve themselves of their sins, they re-embark on the first ship returning home, with the silver or gold they have acquired, and undertake the same voyage the following year.

Apart from the textiles coming from India each year, Arabia also imports silks, many kinds of spice such as cardamom, ginger and saffron; sugar; eagle wood from the Maldives, Sumatra and Borneo, as that from Cochin China is too expensive. Bengal provides a great quantity of cloth, muslin and sugar to the market at Jiddah. Jiddah, the nearest port to the Holy City of Makkah, attracts the largest number of people from distant parts. Here they find everything to satisfy their needs and expensive tastes. Caravans protected by their own guards guarantee safe transit to their destination, and the vessels from Surat do likewise by dealing with merchandise distributed to the neighbouring Red Sea ports.

A practice established by the Yemeni government requires that the price of merchandise to be sold, and the price of coffee to be bought, must be fixed by common agreement among the town merchants who as a rule gather at the commercial agent's. This is known as the first contract. This first contract is highly damaging to European interests, though the foreigner may withdraw his merchandise if the price is not right, and has the right to refuse to purchase coffee if, by mutual agreement, it is considered too expensive. Yet he nevertheless finds himself in a dependent situation to which, after much argument, he is forced to submit himself. The merchant body realises that a transaction arranged from far away, dependent on the monsoon which prevents sailing for five or six months, cannot be changed if a better result is not guaranteed. This lack of certainty and the inevitable delays force the foreigner to accept a higher or lower reduction on the sale of his goods, and an equivalent loss on the coffee to be bought at Bayt al-Faqih.

The knowledge of the commercial agent is of great help to minimise the effect of the secret agreement, however easy to discover, between the merchants. The latter, on the strength of their privileged position, try to price the coffee above its normal value. The commercial agent has to be firm and patient in his decisions, but always fair when offering the current price, which he must try to penetrate despite the secrecy. Patience in particular is needed because the Arabs, who recognise the impatient nature of Europeans, try to take advantage by prolonging the transaction to obtain a higher price.

The last session of the meetings, which completes the transaction, is held at the governor's house. Though secretly keen to sell coffee to the Europeans at the highest possible price, he seems to be chiding the merchant for his high valuation. The governor's final decision usually sets a rate one or two piastres below that demanded by the merchant, thus appearing to manage a compromise. The governor concludes the transaction by a sprinkling of rosewater and by offering coffee and a smoke from a pipe to each participant.

In this first contract, the buyer limits the quantity to a certain number of camels, a practice in that country, which equates two bags, per camel, weighing about one *bar*. He is then free to buy as he wishes, and chooses the best quality. The quality obtained on the first contract as a forced purchase is not usually very good.

Bayt al-Faqih is the depot for coffee grown in inland areas and, as such, the most famous market in all Arabia Felix. It lies some forty leagues from Mocha, eight leagues from the ports of Luhayya and Hudayda, and twelve leagues from the beginning of the coffee-growing area. This town, situated on an arid plain of burning hot sands, is the most unbearable town for Europeans that I know of.

Traders from Turkey and Persia go there to buy coffee, seeking out the inferior quality because it costs less. Whilst coffee is bought at Bayt al-Faqih, resins and other medicinal products are bought in Mocha through brokers under the supervision of an inspector assigned to this transaction. As these lastnamed goods are not the main ones attracting ships from Europe to Arabia, they are not subject to the formal arrangements of the first contract.

May is the month when the best quality coffees come down from the interior. The Europeans in charge of the transactions leave Mocha in small caravans accompanied by brokers from their country. Five days later they arrive in Bayt al-Faqih, travelling on donkeys or camels after the main heat of the day and during part of the night, a practice observed throughout the whole of Arabia.

Weights in Yemen are in *bar*, *saracella* and *man*, and measurements are in *toman*. The *bar* in Mocha weighs 450 pounds, the *saracella* weighs 30 pounds, and the *man* weighs 10 pounds. At Bayt al-Faqih, however, the *bar* weighs 740 pounds, the *saracella* weighs 18½ pounds, and the *man* weighs one-tenth of a *saracella*.

The *toman* is a measure for grains which gives a weight relative to quality. A *toman* of rice, for example, has a net weight of 190 pounds. Entry and exit taxes are set at 2¼%. One per cent goes to the taxman. For the *sarraf*, or money-changer, several other small taxes or presents are customary, the great majority of these being relative to the kinds of coffee, and may be estimated at 2%. In order to assess more precisely the expenses one is faced with when transacting at Mocha, I shall use as an example the one I had charge of in 1788. It will demonstrate how the price of coffee is arrived at in Europe.

The *bar* of coffee cost 89 piastres at three quarters of the first contract, and the taxes, commission fees, transport and daily expenses come to 12 piastres per *bar*. In addition to these sums, you calculate 8% for insurance and 70 piastres per barrel for freight, two *bars* of coffee being equivalent to one barrel. The coffee in Europe costs 21 sous 1 denier per pound; the piastre is at 5 pounds 8 sous.

For the last fifty years, the price of Arabian coffee has fluctuated only at times of bad harvests, and the price increase then has never been more than 2 or 3 piastres per *bar*.

Before the Franco-Yemeni Treaty of 1737, signed after the Company had taken over Mocha, the finances of the Company had been badly damaged, and countless dishonest actions had been perpetrated by the governors of Mocha and Bayt al-Faqih. This treaty, supported by force and a fair claim, put matters back where they should have been. The affairs of the nation have suffered no changes other than those relating to the first contract, the abolition of which could have been demanded by M. Nicolas, the man in charge of the expedition.

In Arabia Felix, the trade is entirely in the hands of the Banians from Gujarat who have lived in the country for generations. The government protects these cosmopolitan people who, like Jews, spend their lives trying to ruin people who trust them without taking precautions. These Banians calmly and stoically listen to well-deserved reproaches addressed to them about their misconduct. The government of the towns where they live levy taxes on them in proportion to the extent of their trade or according to their estimated wealth. As far as commercial transactions are concerned, the security of European traders rests with their brokers. These brokers ensure that entry and exit taxes are duly paid to the tax office, and they are responsible for the behaviour of individuals engaged in transactions.

In a normal year, the export of coffee from the country can reach as high as 70 million by weight. This amount may seem exaggerated if compared to previous times, when we are told it fell short of 13 million. But, to support this estimate, I should add that according to the customs office at Bayt al-Faqih, the amount sent to Jiddah the previous year reached 203,000 bales costing 300 pounds each. If 8 million by weight sent to Persia are added to this, the remaining 2 million or so must be the figure exported to Africa, India and Europe.

It must be understood that coffee has become more and more indispensable, and consequently the growth in its consumption has naturally extended its areas of production in Arabia as well as in the colonies. In order to obey a law from the religious authorities, Jiddah is the first to receive coffee intended for the Ottoman states, goods coming from India on Arab ships sailing in the same direction, and those coming from Europe, via Suez, on Turkish vessels bound for Arabia and the Gulf. In Jiddah, the 13% taxes levied are shared between the Grand Sharif of Makkah and the powerful ruler of Jiddah.

The reason for Jiddah's privilege is due to the prestige obtained through the policy of the Prophet Muhammad, who wanted not only to perpetuate his religious system by linking the sublime idea of God's unity to the religion founded before him by Abraham, but also to turn his homeland into the world's commercial hub and to give it, by combining economic interests with fanaticism, a prosperity worthy of his broad vision and of the spirit which led him.

European ships heading for Suez need not call at Jiddah to pay the tax required of Arabs and Muslims. They have to pay a tax of 8% if they trade there.

Resin, an interesting commodity, is considered only a secondary product in the Red Sea market. Its initial price is more or less equivalent to that of coffee, but its bulk is greater, its freight thus dearer, and there is less chance to sell it at a good profit in Europe, where sales are generally slower.

The currency in Yemen is the piastre, or Empire *écu*, and a small debased silver coin minted under the name of *kabir* or *khammasis*. These two are differentiated by weight and consequently by their value to the public, discussed below. Accounts are settled in local piastres, an excellent currency which differs by 21½% from the currency of Spain and the Empire *écu*. In Mocha, 80 *cabuts* are equivalent to the piastre of Yemen; and forty of a much heavier weight at Bayt al-Faqih equal one Spanish piastre. There, 120 *khammasis* are equal to the local piastre. Piastres are weighed just like the gold and silver in circulation. An Arab weight called *lokia* is used, being divided into ten parts called *kassalas*, and those are divided into a half, a quarter, an eighth and a sixteenth. To be valid, one piastre or Empire *écu* must weigh 8¾ *kassalas*. A hundred piastres must weigh 87 *lokias*, 5 *kassalas* making 11 marks, 2 ounces, 2 gros. Since the trade has increased in the Red Sea, the Spanish piastres brought to Mocha by the Europeans enjoy a profit of 4% to 5% against the Empire *écus* coming from Jiddah. These latter have lost value and consequently circulate at a loss in India, their final destination.

Our brokers, who keep the funds necessary for purchases, were the only ones enjoying the benefits of this exchange rate, to the detriment of the transactions, and had been very careful to prevent such information getting out. I was certainly the first person in charge of fitting out a ship to uncover this trickery through the checks I had made on every aspect of the trade. I reproached the brokers severely but, as I mentioned earlier, when describing their methods, they listened quietly without saying a word.

If European trade relations with India via the Red Sea can be established on a solid basis, given France's need to re-establish her maritime trade, Arabia Felix represents an interesting area which could prove very beneficial. Her products have contributed to the resurgence of that former splendour that communications between these two parts of the world had previously provided only to the republics of Greece and Italy. Unfortunately, the region separating the two seas is defended both by the native inhabitants and by our enemies, the English, as always anxious to defend their Indian territories and thus keen to prevent the development of French trade.

Yemen produces opium and a poor quality of indigo, both being consumed locally. The manufacture of ordinary textiles has become established. The Banians, who are as a rule industrious, have brought in workmen from the Malabar Coast with the agreement of the governors of the towns where they live, and colonials from Gujarat were employed there. If the Arabs, following the example of these intelligent and hardworking men, could emerge from their lethargy of the past centuries, they could dispense with goods imported from India, and could end their dependence on foreign industry.

The owners of the land where coffee is grown, called beduin, are on the whole quite rich because they love their work. Fields of fifty to sixty leagues in length and over twenty leagues in width are cultivated with very great care. Grains are abundant, as are some of our European fruits; it is true that the climate of this part of the country can be compared to that of the Île-de-France, a fact which encourages agriculture.

It is well known that sailing in the Red Sea can be done only by the aid of the monsoon. The winds blow nine months in the year from the south, between the end of August and mid-May;

then the wind changes direction from the north to north-west and continues until late August.

II. Habits, Customs, Laws, Armies, Public Income, and Population of Yemen

The people of these regions have habits and principles which differ from one town to the next. I have noticed that Arabs in Mocha are less jealous of their wives than are Arabs of the interior. In Mocha, women are willing to undertake rendezvous sought by Europeans, no matter what risk they run; in the interior they are shy.

Whether it is because of religious reasons, or whether women are attracted to the long beards sported by Arabs, they take little notice of Europeans who are clean-shaven. The following anecdote to illustrate the peculiarity of their taste deserves the telling.

A rich merchant of Bayt al-Faqih named Sarafi, whom I had befriended because we both spoke Portuguese fluently, had a sister reputed to be very pretty. I told him that I wished to see her secretly and in his presence. He made numerous objections based on the dangers of this situation. "If we are found out", he told me, "you will have to counter the effects of the fanaticism which can reach the greatest excesses. I should be punished by a heavy fine, unless you agree to convert to Islam." This made me ponder the pains I should feel during this operation. I have to confess that, by delivering myself into the hands of the Prophet's acolytes, I felt more fear of the circumciser's knife than of the daggers which threatened my life unless I abandoned a few small fragments of my skin to the fanatics. This sacrifice, which would have marked my conversion, would also have saved Sarafi's money.

In spite of the dangers which surrounded me, my curiosity led me to renew my efforts, so that my friend consented to my meeting his sister. Under the pressure I was exerting, he had the bizarre idea of marrying me to her. He invited me to grow my beard and adopt the religion of the country. He assured me that a dervish of his acquaintance was highly skilled at performing the operation, and that I should feel hardly any pain at all. I answered that, attached as every man should be to the religion of his ancestors, I should submit to his request only if I were lucky enough to be acceptable to his sister, and this was a necessary preliminary prerequisite for me to change my faith. "If that is the only thing that stops you", he assured me, "then you have nothing to worry about. I shall take all necessary measures to remove all dangers and tonight I shall introduce you to my sister."

This decision, as sudden as it was unexpected, caused me one of those sensations that make a man abruptly take stock of his life and show him, too late, how imprudent he has been. However, I did not want to show this and, at eleven o'clock that evening, dressed like an Arab, I was taken by Sarafi to his sister's quarters. She was made up and perfumed as by custom and was awaiting us, surrounded by her maidservants.

As soon as she saw me, she told her brother that she did not like me because I did not have a long beard. I said that I would let it grow. "No, no," she excaimed, while passing her hand beneath my chin, "he will never be able to grow his beard long. I don't want him for a husband." I had to withdraw in humiliation, having failed to please this charming prisoner, but very happy to reach home again safe and sound. This young lady was really beautiful, but her odd outfit, her long painted nails, and her breast covered in convoluted drawings of love symbols in the Arab taste, were unattractive to my European feelings.

A feature of Arab women I find very attractive is the way they colour their eyelids with a black substance called *kohl* which, by drawing it on both sides of their temples, make their eyes appear long and vivid, adding to their natural beauty.

In Mocha, Europeans are allowed to walk on the terrace of the house they live in. Inland, this custom is forbidden to them, and the inhabitamts have tried to overcome the situation prevailing in Mocha, where the Europeans' houses tend to be very tall, and overlook many others, so allowing infidel Christians to cast their curious eyes on Arabs who may be lying down with one of their wives in the morning on an open veranda.

Unlike European women, the young Arab women of marrying age here do not enjoy the pleasure of seeing their betrothed before the ceremony. In a reversal of ideas which shows the deficiency of their culture, and in particular how the men despise women, a woman is engaged to a man she has never seen; whose home may lie a hundred leagues from hers; and a man whom she is forced to go and live with. If, as is quite common with the weaker sex, she happens to have lost her virginity, she is sent back without pity to her family, who will deliver her to the penance of locks and stern eunuchs, to ensure her future abstinence.

A church bell calls the Christian faithful to attend divine service. Here, a dervish climbs up a minaret in the mosque at noon and calls loudly that all who have taken of food and drink, and washed themselves, and so on, should come to worship God and chant prayers.

Europeans are allowed to ride horses in Mocha, but if they go riding out of town (the only pastime permitted to them) they must enter and return by the Sandal Gate. The Mandal Gate, like the Governor's house, may be crossed only on foot. The Shadli Gate is a holy place, and no European may pass through it without being manhandled by the mob.

Bayt al-Faqih has no surrounding walls, and the governor resides in a fort nearby. Europeans may walk and ride anywhere, but commercial agents must remove their shoes before entering his reception hall. M. de Moncrif, the representative of both King and Company, following the example set by his predecessors, had agreed to perform this humiliating act. As a private individual, I refused to do so, and said that I should go back without buying anything if forced to comply. The governor told me I could do whatever I wanted. As a consequence, I gave orders to prepare my departure in a couple of days. When the governor realised my serious intention to go would deprive him of taxes accruing from my trading activities, he allowed me to present myself as I wished, providing I said nothing about it to M. de Moncrif who was due to arrive within the next few days. I was ready for him at this point, and had guessed that he would make such a demand. So I assumed the temporary role of my nation's representative and remained firm, to obtain the cancellation of this degrading act. It had been resented by all those who had traded before me, and especially by the King's and Company's representative. French pride had been subjugated for a long time by those who had traded at Bayt al-Faqih. So, as the royal representative had not done so, I took it upon myself to remind the governor of the Treaty of 1737, the terms of which did not require the French to submit to any humiliating custom. The custom must, therefore, be abolished before we traded further in Arabia. After two days of discussions through negotiators, it was agreed that the French would no longer have to suffer this degrading practice.

M. de Moncrif, surprised by my success, which could have been his own if he had fulfilled his duty, thanked me in public but later filed a complaint against me at the administrative office in Pondicherry because I had refused to hand over an exact account of my initiative at the Mocha embassy.

Everyone knows the Prophet Muhammad's interdiction regarding wine, but I have seldom resided in a country where strong alcohol is as sought after as it is in Arabia Felix. I observed this taste for alcohol among ordinary Arabs, and wondered whether the same propensity could be seen among those higher up the social ladder. Several important sayyids used to come and see me every day, and accepted a drink of sherbet according to custom. I ordered that alcohol should be added without warning them. They drank it with evident pleasure, and some of them liked it so much that they asked me for several dozen bottles, which I sent them as a gift. They thanked me profusely. These details may seem boring but, when customs and habits of people whose religious practices are related to the taste of something forbidden to them, it seems helpful to narrate the means secretly used, and I would say, like Abbé Raynal when he talked of royalty, "If you want people to obey your laws, these must not flout Nature."

San'a, the capital of Arabia Felix, is beautifully situated sixty

leagues from Bayt al-Faqih in lush and well cultivated surroundings. The Imam, or prince of Yemen, is so mistrustful of
the leading countries that all the chief governmental offices are
awarded to former slaves who have been freed by him or by his
predecessors.

The code ruling the people of this area is the Qur'an. Every
activity of life is subject to the ruler's judicial court. The prince
and his representatives are the ones who dispense all favours.
Properties are safeguarded after payment of a sum of money.
Revenues from taxes are not, as in Europe, taken from long-
suffering people who provide for the excesses of the rulers and
their courtiers; the income of the rulers derives from customs
duties and taxes levied on the movement of goods.

If the country finds itself in the unusual situation of being
threatened by an invasion, every male citizen becomes a soldier,
and has to provide his own arms and food. The transportation
of the army's equipment is managed by requisition. If the
Imam undertakes a war of conquest, he has to pay soldiers out
of his own treasury. In the prevailing atmosphere of respect for
ownership and independence, the ruler cannot afford to press
the inhabitants by force, which would be rejected and his
power overthrown.

The permanent army comprises 60,000 infantry and cavalry,
ill-equipped. There is no military discipline or strategy.
Fortifications are made up of very high walls defended by cannon of various sizes placed on scaffolding made of poor-quali-
ty timber and protected by mortar. The soldiers live underneath.

The Arabs trust their cavalry to protect them. But one incident at least has shown them that cavalry cannot protect them
from military action by Europeans. I have already mentioned
how the French captured Mocha in 1737 and the company's
motives to participate in this expedition, but I have so far not
described the details of the siege, and the curious incident
which hastened the town's capitulation.

The Arabs had been given advance warning of the hostile
intentions of the French, who had come in great numbers to

attack them, and so they summoned help. Twenty thousand cavalry and infantry defended the town, while a mere 1800 or so Europeans and sepoys prepared to attack. The French managed to position siege artillery and mortars in spite of some ill-directed fire from the defenders, who shut themselves in the town instead of coming out on to the attack. The French appeared at the ramparts just as the town commander was preparing to come out to ensure that no Frenchman could escape.

At that moment the French launched a bomb into the European customs yard which exploded at once, killing forty Arabs. A crowd gathered round to see what disaster had occurred, and were terrified, saying among themselves that if one single Frenchman, as far away as he was, had enough strength to hurl with one hand a ball so powerful containing some infernal devil in his service, who could kill to such effect before their very eyes, then they should fall back. And in fact they fled. The town, thus delivered to the French by such an astonishing and almost funny event, surrendered and the ruler of Arabia Felix was compelled to sign the treaty.

The tax revenues, limited to customs levies and income from the transfer of private properties in Yemen, are estimated at between six and seven million piastres. This figure covers the ruler's expenditure. Every soldier is paid four piastres monthly for his food and maintenance. Officers receive twenty piastres monthly. Governors, civil servants and religious leaders receive customs duties and a private income more or less connected with their functions. Countless petty problems arising from the conduct of their duties merely serve to keep them in their positions and perpetuate abuses.

Civil and criminal laws are the responsibility of the *Sharif* of each town, who delivers summary justice. A convicted criminal is released if he can pay a sum proportionate to his crime; if poor, he pays with his life at once. Civil matters are also settled by financial methods, which is why discussions about money matters are almost invariably resolved by arbitrators. If, as often happens, the two parties cannot agree, the sword decides. The first to be wounded is found to have lost his case.

The population of the country is estimated at about ten million; as diligence and hard work are not really their forte, most of them are very poor. Luckily for the poor, food is abundant and cheap, and the continuous use of coffee, of which the poorest can afford only the husk in hot water, readily provides them with a drink which is pleasant, and even rather nourishing.

From the seashore to the mountain range of the interior, the plains are arid and exceedingly hot. Some cereals, nevertheless, are grown for animal feed. Rainfall is scarce for most of the year, but relatively abundant in the hinterland from November to March. During the rest of the year, dew forms every morning which freshens the air and helps to preserve the vegeation. Rainfall is too abundant in certain coffee-growing districts, and varieties known as *cairia* and *godon* are grown there. The variety called *ouden* is better; it costs two piastres more per *bar*.

SOUTH ARABIA:
THE 'PALINURUS' JOURNALS
Jessop Hulton

A reprint of the rare diaries of a doctor and antiquarian visiting Muscat, Mukalla, Aden, Mocha and Socotra between 1832 and 1836, with a new scholarly introduction and bibliography by Carl Phillips.

RED WOLVES OF YEMEN
V.V. Naumkin

The four-year armed struggle against the British in Aden turned Yemen into a radical leftist independent Arab state inspired by Nasser's Egypt and other revolutionary models. Vitaly Naumkin has spoken with most of the participants and mastered the Arabic documents.

ARABIAN GULF INTELLIGENCE (1856)
R.H. Thomas

Being *Selections from the Records of the Bombay Government*, N.S. no. XXIV, covering all the Gulf islands and both shores, with primary sources on Kuwait, Bahrain, Muscat and Oman, Saudi Arabia, Qatar, and the U.A.E. With a new introduction by Robin Bidwell. 728 pp. + foldout maps.

TRAVELS IN OMAN
Philip Ward

The classic compendium of travel writings on Oman, with a detailed commentary on the same routes and places today. 584 pp., including 182 illustrations.

HISTORY OF SEYD SAID (1819)
Vincenzo Maurizi

Reissue of the first printed book devoted solely to Oman, by an Italian writing under the pseudonym 'Shaikh Mansur'.

KING HUSAIN AND THE KINGDOM OF HEJAZ
Randall Baker

A comprehensive analysis of the Hashemite dynasty of Hejaz, before the creation of the Saudi Kingdom. With portraits, photographs and maps.

SUDAN TALES
Rosemary Kendrick

Insights into the lives of British wives with husbands in the Sudan Political Service, 1926–1956. Profusely illustrated.

ARABIAN PERSONALITIES OF THE EARLY TWENTIETH CENTURY

The first authorised publication of the confidential British Government *Personalities: Arabia* (1917) prepared by the Arab Bureau of Cairo under D.G. Hogarth. With a new introduction by Robin Bidwell.

HA'IL: OASIS CITY OF SAUDI ARABIA
Philip Ward

The author's essay on modern Ha'il follows a compendium of classic accounts, with his translations from Euting and Huber.

OMANI PROVERBS
A.S.G. Jayakar

Traditional Omani sayings in Arabic, with English translations, and English equivalents. Introduced by Philip Ward.

A DOCTOR IN SAUDI ARABIA
G.E. Moloney

The personal and medical experiences of a doctor based at Riyadh University from 1977 to 1982. 365 pp, with 150 illustrations.

RAJASTHAN, AGRA, DELHI:
A TRAVEL GUIDE
Philip Ward

"There is no travel writer who comes within hailing distance of him. He is the first among unequals" — Premen Addy, in *India Weekly*.

ANNALS OF OMAN
Sirhan ibn Sirhan

A translation by E.C. Ross, with his own 'History of Oman from 1728 to 1883' and 'Ibadhiyah of Oman' and S.B. Miles' 'Note on the Tribes of Oman'.

NORTH FROM GRANADA
Roy Nash

Byways of southern Spain, taking in Baeza and Iznalloz, on the road north to Toledo and Madrid, tramping all the way on foot in the 1970s. Colour maps and photos.

TRAVELS IN ARABIA (1845 & 1848)
Yrjö Aukusti Wallin

A Fenno-Swede explorer in the lands of Northern Arabia, reprinted from the *JRGS* with a new introduction by M.E. Trautz.

BAHRAIN: A TRAVEL GUIDE
Philip Ward

The doyen of British travel writers on the model Gulf State. *The Middle East* wrote: "The true strength of this book lies with the author's fascination for his subject and his obvious delight in sharing that knowledge". Many photographs.

NATIONAL SERVICE 1950s
John Kelly

Libya during the 1950s, in the early years of independence. The author was a British serviceman in Tripoli and Homs. Maps and plates.

MOTORING TO NALUT
Philip Ward

A motorist's route across Western Libya on the road from Tripoli towards Ghadames. Photographs by Angelo Pesce.

BULGARIA: A TRAVEL GUIDE
Philip Ward

A comprehensive description of contemporary Bulgaria, with many maps and photos. Winner of the Grand Prize, International Travel Writers' Awards.

TRIPOLI: PORTRAIT OF A CITY
Philip Ward

An account of life in the Libyan capital during the monarchy of Idris I, with maps and photographs.

WESTERN INDIA
Philip Ward

Mumbai, Maharashtra and Karnataka are covered in depth, with numerous maps and photographs.

SOJOURN WITH THE GRAND SHARIF OF MAKKAH (1854)
Charles Didier

The first translation of a French travel classic on Sinai, the Red Sea, Jiddah and Ta'if.

MINISTER IN OMAN
Neil McLeod Innes

Memoirs of the Briton serving as Minister of Foreign Affairs to the Sultan, 1953 to 1958. Well illustrated.

ALBANIA: A TRAVEL GUIDE
Philip Ward

Tales of Enver Hoxha's troubled land, before the dictator's fall. Numerous maps and photos.

THE GOLD-MINES OF MIDIAN
Sir Richard Burton

Newly transcribed by Philip Ward from the author's annotated copy following the corrupt first edition.

BULGARIAN VOICES
Philip Ward

85 monologues from post-Communist Bulgaria in "a courageous attempt to break through Bulgarian muteness and isolation" — Ivan Kristev, *Times Literary Supplement*.

LIBYAN MAMMALS
Ernst Hufnagl

Fully-illustrated field guide to the mammals found throughout the Libyan mountains and deserts.

INDIAN MANSIONS
Sarah Tillotson

A social history of the *haveli* of Northern India, with numerous photographs and drawings modern and ancient.

GUJARAT, DAMAN, DIU
Philip Ward

The cities, deserts and national parks of north-west India as far as the border with Pakistan, with copious maps and plates.

ARABIC KEY WORDS
David Quitregard

Uniform with Latin, Greek, French, German, Italian and Spanish volumes, this compilation prints in order of frequency the commonest 2,000 words in Arabic, with indexes in English and the target language.

SOFIA: PORTRAIT OF A CITY
Philip Ward

Completing the Bulgarian trilogy, *Sofia* explores the strange and often bizarre life of the capital, called 'Wisdom', with many pictures and plans.

THE LIBYAN REVOLUTION
I.M. Arif & M.O. Ansell

A transcript of the Libyan Intellectual Seminar, following the overthrow of the monarchy by a group of army officers, with many of the early laws.

APULEIUS ON TRIAL AT SABRATHA
Philip Ward

The author of *Sabratha* narrates the trial of the Roman author of *The Golden Ass* on a charge of witchcraft.

THE EMPEROR'S GUEST
Donald Peacock

The notes and pictures preserved by a British prisoner-of-war of the Japanese in Indonesia, after eluding the Censor and the fierce prison guards, evoke the horrors and pathos of World War II.

POLISH CITIES
Philip Ward

Travels in Kraków, Auschwitz, Zakopane, Warsaw, Gdańsk and Malbork by a poet (*His Enamel Mug*, 2003) and novelist (*The Comfort of Women*, 2002) who has lived among the people of Poland.

RETHINKING ROMAN HISTORY
Jerry Toner

A new interpretation of Roman history, setting it in the mainstream of historical theory and practice.

HEJAZ BEFORE WORLD WAR I
David G. Hogarth

The first reprint of the Arab Bureau of Cairo's *Handbook of Hejaz*, to which T.E. Lawrence contributed.

HOME IN ANDALUSIA
Roy Nash

Before the present Spanish boom, Roy Nash lived for nearly forty years on the Andalusian coast: these are his anecdotes of that halcyon age.

DIARY OF A JOURNEY ACROSS ARABIA (1819)
George F. Sadleir

A detailed account of travels from al-Qatif on the Gulf to Yanbu' on the Red Sea via Dira'iya, 'Unaizah and Madinah. With an introduction by F.M. Edwards.

REPORT ON A JOURNEY TO RIYADH (1865)
Lewis Pelly

Travels from Kuwait to the Wahhabi capital one and a half centuries ago, by a British political agent. With an introduction by Robin Bidwell.